Jason O'Toole was born in Dublin in 1973. He has a BA in Humanities and an MA in Political Communication from Dublin City University. His journalism has appeared in many publications, including the *Sunday Times*, the *Mail on Sunday*, the *Evening Herald* and *Empire*. He is currently senior editor with *Hot Press* magazine.

D0756286

www.transworldireland.ie

BRIAN COWEN
The Path to Power

Jason O'Toole

TRANSWORLD IRELAND

TRANSWORLD IRELAND
an imprint of The Random House Group Limited
20 Vauxhall Bridge Road, London SW1V 2SA
www.rbooks.co.uk

First published in 2008 by Transworld Ireland

A CIP catalogue record for this book
is available from the British Library.

ISBN 9781848270299

Addresses for Random House Group Ltd companies outside the UK
can be found at: www.randomhouse.co.uk
The Random House Group Ltd Reg. No. 954009

The Random House Group Limited supports The Forest Stewardship
Council (FSC), the leading international forest-certification organization. All our
titles that are printed on Greenpeace-approved FSC-certified paper carry the FSC logo.
Our paper procurement policy can be found at www.rbooks.co.uk/environment

Typeset in 12.5/15pt Ehrhardt by
Falcon Oast Graphic Art Ltd.
Printed and bound in Great Britain by
CPI Mackays, Chatham, ME5 8TD

2 4 6 8 10 9 7 5 3 1

Mixed Sources
Product group from well-managed
forests and other controlled sources
www.fsc.org Cert no. TT-COC-2139
© 1996 Forest Stewardship Council
FSC

Contents

Acknowledgements   vii

Prologue: The Homecoming   1

1   The Early Years   7
2   The Roscrea Connection   14
3   Following in Ber Cowen's Footsteps   28
4   Into the Cabinet   41
5   Cementing a Political Reputation   57
6   'Angola'   79
7   Minister for Foreign Affairs   100
8   Finance   145
9   The 2007 General Election   173
10   Taoiseach   198
11   The First Hundred Days   218

Sources   245
Picture Acknowledgements   255
Index   257

Acknowledgements

I would like to my express my gratitude to An Taoiseach Brian Cowen for agreeing to carry out several in-depth interviews with me for this book.

I'm particularly appreciative of the help Albert Reynolds gave me with his unique insight into Brian Cowen's early political career. I am also tremendously grateful to Niall Stokes, my editor at *Hot Press* magazine, for his indispensable support and advice. I want to offer my heartfelt appreciation to my publisher Eoin McHugh at Transworld Ireland. My thanks also to my copy-editor Gillian Somerscales for her valuable support.

This book could not have been written without the help and encouragement of many people, including Mary Cowen, Michael Cleary, Michael Chester, Dick Roche, Sean O'Connor, Liam Kelly, Gerry Steadman, Darren Kinsella, Declan Cassidy, Sinead Dooley, Eoghan Harris, Paul Drury, Bernard Brady, Liam McGuinness, Tom Prendeville, Gosia and Rysiek Jaszowski, Anne Sinthunont, Tom Tuite, Martin Holland, Gary Walsh, T. S. O'Rourke, Brian Beharrell, George Fitzgerald, John Herdman, Jimmy and Fleur Forbes, Paddy and Rose

Gowran, Stephen and Emma Raeside, Frank Bambrick, Alfie Sage, Neville Thompson and Lee Dunne. Also thanks to all my colleagues at *Hot Press*, including Jackie Hayden, Mairin Sheedy, Stuart Clark, Roisin Dwyer, Duan Stokes, Graham Keogh, Mark Hogan, Cathal Dawson, Gavin Feeney and Brett Walker.

Finally, I would like to take the opportunity to thank Lidia and Jan Dacknowski for allowing me the use of their home in Poland to write a substantial portion of this book. I am eternally indebted to my family – particularly my wife Agnieszka, my daughter Marianne, my brother Keith, my sisters Lorraine and Amy, my mother Rosaleen and my father Gerald – all of whom made countless sacrifices to enable me to finish it.

PROLOGUE

The Homecoming

May 2008

'Our memory is about loss, grievance and exile and lost opportunities. Now we've a totally transformed country. Not one that will be guaranteed success in the future but one that should be facing the challenges that confront it now with a far greater degree of confidence, a far greater degree of self-belief than some would have us believe.'

So spoke Brian Cowen in his homecoming speech as Taoiscach in Tullamore, County Offaly.

As he stood on the platform in O'Connor Square on that warm spring day, he looked out over several thousand well-wishers who had come to celebrate the historic homecoming of Offaly's first ever Taoiseach and felt honoured that so many people had turned out to share his day in the sun. It was an emotionally charged moment for Cowen: the last time he had stood in this very spot to give a speech was back in the 1984 by-election prompted by the untimely demise of his father Ber Cowen. Cowen told the crowd how back then, in the mid-1980s, when he was starting out on his path to power, there was a sense of defeatism in the country. 'A sense that we'd never achieve the possibilities that the founders of our state had set for ourselves, a sense we'd gone in the wrong direction and that we might not be able to retrieve things. Politicians put themselves in front of the people to do two things. First, to tell the people as they see it how it is, and secondly to believe in the people, because it is the Irish people over the last twenty-five years who have transformed this country.'

Cowen spoke, without notes, for almost twenty minutes. He told the crowd that the only reason he was standing in front of them as Taoiseach was because of the confidence the electorate in Laois–Offaly had placed in him over the past twenty-four years. 'As I make that journey further, as a leader of a government that will forge a new future for our people, I ask you to stick with me. I ask you to believe in me. You will get from me everything I can do to make this a better country, not only at home but abroad as well. And I ask our own people to take up our responsibilities as citizens and not to look to government to solve every problem,' he declared.

'I will work with you day and night, hour and day, to make sure this is a better country for all. A country for my children and your children. A country that will be environmentally sustainable. A country that pursues excellence in providing public services. A country that will put the citizens at the centre of our concerns. Be part of what we can build now. And let's make sure that everything we've achieved is not dissipated and wasted on a "me generation" or a selfishness or a materialism that takes away what has made us what we are in the first place – decent, honourable and hard-working people who have a love of their country. That's what I'm about.'

Cheered on by the crowd, Cowen sang a bit of Frank Sinatra's 'My Way' before launching into 'The Offaly Rover', telling his audience: 'One of the requirements when you get into politics is that you have to be able to sing!' The audience loved seeing the Taoiseach sing; and Cowen was giving his supporters a clear signal that his rise to high office would not change him.

Recalling the event later, Cowen reflected: 'I've always enjoyed public speaking and I liked that part of the home-coming because I liked the idea of going back to that natural level of communication, which isn't through a PR company or a press statement or a soundbite or a clever phrase. It's a natural empathy – an empathy that one should have between the public representative and the public.'

Cowen's day had begun with the press on his doorstep. He knew that the media scrutiny would intensify dramatically now that he was Taoiseach, but even so he was surprised when a Garda knocked on his door to explain that a journalist and photographer from a national newspaper were sitting in a car outside the family home in the hope of carrying out an impromptu interview. 'Mr Cowen politely turned down the request. We were also informed that he did not take kindly to his home being photographed, but, well, the people like to know where their Taoiseach lives,' wrote Jody Corcoran in the next day's *Sunday Independent*.

The homecoming proper began at midday in Edenderry, where five hundred people – a sizeable crowd in this small town – had turned up to celebrate the occasion. From there Cowen moved on to Tullamore, where over five thousand people had gathered in the square to greet the local hero. The atmosphere was electric, almost carnival-like, the town saturated with bunting, tricolours and the white and gold flags of Offaly waving from many of the shops and pubs. People wandered around in 'Cowenista' T-shirts on which Cowen's face was superimposed on the iconic image of Che Guevara. The T-shirts were being sold at € 10 a go in aid of charity. 'I'm not suggesting that their policies are the same,' explained Tim Quinlan, who designed the T-shirt, to an *Irish Independent* journalist. Here Barry Cowen gave a moving speech to the crowd about how Brian had wept when his father died and promised never to let him down. The Taoiseach and his younger brother then embraced on the stage, both siblings shedding a few tears. It was a poignant moment.

Finally, at six o'clock that Saturday evening, Cowen drove into his home town of Clara. 'Welcome to Cowen Country' read a sign hanging among the vast amount of bunting; 'The Cowen We Love So Well' ran another, in a pun on a well-known traditional song.

The homecoming event was filled with emotion, but also with gaiety and songs. The following day in Ferbane, when Cowen was addressing the audience, a barman ran out of Hiney's public house and across the road with a pint of Guinness on a tray and offered it to the Taoiseach, who duly took a swig of the creamy pint before handing it back. Later, a very noisy gyrocopter buzzed over when he was giving a speech outside a community centre. Quickly the Taoiseach declared: 'Noel Dempsey's going to be checking that out on Monday. He's my Minister for Transport—' he paused: '—so far.'

The crowd roared with laughter.

But perhaps the most memorable moment was in Clara, when Cowen sang a song that had been written about his father. Taking three attempts to hit the right note to launch the song, he explained his hesitation by saying he wanted to make sure he sang it properly as he feared it might end up on television. How right he was. The performance was captured by mobile phone and was later to be found on the YouTube website. Eventually he launched into his passionate rendition – and, as he must have done all weekend, no doubt wished his father was standing beside him on the stage as he belted out the lyrics:

It was in the year of sixty-nine, Ber Cowen he did get in.
He was always fond of politics and the seat we knew he'd win.
And the neighbours from the country round, the farmers, big and
    small,
All voted for Ber Cowen, now he's a member of the Dáil.

Oh, Ber Cowen, he is a TD me boys, Ber Cowen, he is a TD.
And he got Clara a swimming pool 'cause it wasn't near the sea.
And he built a brand new pub, me boys, and let the old one fall
'Cause it wasn't up-to-date enough for a member of the Dáil.

Now, on one night in Mullingar, the greyhound won a race,
And you'd know it was a butcher's dog, the way he showed his pace.
And he wrapped around the tracks so fast and never once did stall;
Sure the people get the best of meat and the greyhound gets the fall.

Now, the wife, May, charms the people when she's serving in the bar,
And she listens to all their troubles no matter what they are,
And they ask her about her politics, she can answer one and all.
Sometimes we don't know which of them is a member of the Dáil!

Oh, Ber Cowen, he is a TD, me boys, an undertaker too,
With the biggest bloody hearse in town, when you're dead you'll
    know it's true.
And he'll fit you for a coffin, whether you are big or small.
Isn't it nice to know you'll be buried by a member of the Dáil?

1

The Early Years

Brian Cowen's return to his native Clara for his rapturous homecoming celebration as Taoiseach was a particularly remarkable occasion for his mother May, who knew more than anybody else in the square that day how much this moment really meant to him. As she stood in the crowd watching her son up on the podium, speaking fervently about his bond with his home town, May nostalgically reflected that her late husband would have been the proudest man in Clara to have witnessed this momentous achievement.

Growing up, May Weir had very little interest in politics. When she was a teenager, she left Clara and went to stay with relatives in America, where she stayed to work for seven years; but she never settled over there – her heart was still back in her home town and, more particularly, with Bernard Cowen, with whom she kept up a correspondence during this period abroad. Interestingly, May's own mother had made the very same journey some decades earlier and, just as she had done, May eventually returned to marry her local sweetheart, and settle down and raise a family in the town of her birth.

In January 1960 the second of May and Bernard's three

boys, Brian, was born in Tullamore hospital. He spent his formative years in the family's modest home in Clara, next door to his father's public house on River Street, Cowen's Bar. Here a portrait of Bernard, known affectionately as Ber, hung at the exit door as a reminder of the Cowen clan's political legacy and as a proud acknowledgement of the first Cowen to win a seat in Dáil Éireann.

Brian grew up in a strongly nationalist environment, his political ideology moulded by his father and grandfather. His grandfather, Christopher, known locally as Christy, a cattle dealer by trade, had been a founding member of the Fianna Fáil party and a staunch republican; he served as a local councillor from 1945 until his death in 1967, after which his son Ber took up his seat on the council. Those in Clara who can remember Christy say Brian is a throwback to his grandfather, both men being described as fiery and passionate about their politics. 'My father was calmer,' acknowledges Brian Cowen. 'He had very good judgement – of character and of situations. I had a fiery temperament, just like my grandfather, when I was growing up, but I have mellowed a bit since then.'

The Cowens were prominent, respected members of the community in Clara. They had originally got involved in the publican trade when Christy Cowen married Rosanna Dowling, whose family had a public house which dated back to the eighteenth century. In 1966 they had the pub knocked down and replaced it with Cowen's Bar. Ber Cowen started out working in his father's butcher's shop before going on to operate the family's undertaking business and even start up a small auction establishment. Even when he got involved in full-time politics, Ber continued to work in the family businesses. 'Ber Cowen never stopped working,' says Andrew

Dignam, the secretary of the local Fianna Fáil organization. But despite a seemingly impressive business portfolio – one Brian describes as nothing more than 'the usual stuff in a small town' – the family background was more comfortable than privileged. 'You had to have your finger in every pie to make a living at that time,' explains Cowen. 'There was no such thing as twopence looking down on a penny-ha'penny. There was no reason to be elitist; everyone went to the same school, the Franciscans, the school of hard knocks . . .'

In 1969, when Brian was just nine years old, Ber won a seat in the Dáil. It was a remarkable achievement in the fourth most marginal seat in the country. Ger Connolly, another Offaly man elected as a TD in the same poll, recalls Ber as a 'relaxed, courteous man, easy to get on with'. The Cowens, says Connolly, were a 'highly respected family, true to Fianna Fáil and easy to work with'. Ber himself was a popular man with a very simple and straightforward approach to politics. He had a deep respect for the Fianna Fáil party – and more importantly, as his son points out, for the people who worked within the organization.

It was during this period that the future Taoiseach recalls becoming acutely aware of politics, talk of which was, he says, 'as natural around our table as the dinner we were eating. It was the natural topic of conversation.' During Brian Cowen's formative years, the family household was a constant hub of activity for the local Fianna Fáil organization, and Brian was the most politically active and interested of the three boys. He would enjoy sitting in front of the fire and listening intently to his father discussing current affairs and local issues with constituents or the party supporters who would regularly drop by. Brian was fascinated by the 'whole interaction of the public and constituents in our household', but particularly by the organization of political activism in the constituency.

'There's no doubt that the way he was as a politician has influenced me a lot,' says Brian of his father. 'You are born into a tradition – for me that was the case, though it is not the case for everyone, obviously, certainly not nowadays.' But even though Brian was born into a strongly party political background, he maintains that it didn't take away his independence of thought.

Politics to the Cowen clan was always about public service. It was about representing the people and doing a job for them. So the family were bitterly disappointed when Ber lost his Dáil seat in the 1973 general election, despite increasing his first preference vote – he had been beaten by just twenty-three votes, a narrow margin resulting from a pre-election transfer of votes pact made between Fine Gael and Labour. 'But, at the end of the day,' as Cowen remarks, 'there was always an understanding that the people decide who their representatives are. This is not in your own gift.'

During his absence from the Dáil, Ber spent almost four years in the Seanad after being elected to the Agricultural panel. Then in 1977 he won back his Dáil seat, and never lost it again; in fact, he always managed thereafter to increase his personal vote, regardless of what the national trends were at the time. Today, Cowen is proud of the fact that he has managed to continue his father's work by helping to make the Laois–Offaly Fianna Fáil organization arguably one of the strongest political units in the party's setup. Offaly was traditionally known as the 'faithful' or 'loyal' county, which is a reference to the locals' passion for the GAA. Today the epithet underlies the ethos that was ingrained into the local Fianna Fáil organization by the likes of TDs such as Ber Cowen, Kieran Egan, Nicholas Egan, Peadar Meagher, Gerald

Connolly, Paddy Lalor, Patrick Boland (the first ever Fianna Fáil TD in the Laois–Offaly constituency) and Liam Hyland – and ultimately into Brian Cowen's own mindset. 'There are no factions. There's no disunity. There's no organization within an organization here. There's none of that messing. It wouldn't be tolerated. It's not a question that it wouldn't be tolerated by me – it wouldn't be tolerated by the local party full stop,' says Cowen. But Cowen does not take his party's popularity for granted; he is known for his dedication to constituency work, which he sees as a team effort with him leading from the front as the local TD. He was taught by his father that the grassroots members of the organization work as a 'buffer' between a public representative and the people. 'What I mean by that,' he says, 'is that I would regard the membership of the party organization as being there to serve the party's interests – not to be manipulated by strong individuals within the organization, who sometimes fashion it to their own particular electoral purposes.'

'He found the local party in a good state and is anxious that when he departs it be in as good if not a better state,' says his brother Barry.

Clara, which had a strong Quaker influence, was a settled and quietly prosperous town. Unusually for rural Ireland, it was an industrial town in the middle of an agricultural area, and enjoyed full employment in the 1960s and 1970s – largely thanks to the Goodbody family, whose jute factory, set up in the nineteenth century, still employed around eight hundred people. 'The social history of the place is unique because it was a factory town. It was a town where everyone knew everyone,' Cowen recalls. From the 1930s to the 1960s, many of the boys and girls would leave school at the age of fourteen and start working at the factory; but eventually its output was reduced and operations scaled down, and the majority of Brian's generation managed to finish their secondary school education. For Brian himself, there was never a question that he would work there – he was always destined for other things. Ber and May Cowen were determined that their three sons would have the best possible education.

Up to the age of eleven, Brian attended the Clara National School. Neighbours recall the young Brian having good manners; he would never fail to greet the locals with a cheery but respectful 'hello' as he walked to school each morning. 'Brian was a very courteous, very nice country boy. He was a typical Offaly lad, very mannerly, very helpful,' recalls Ger Connelly. After primary school, Brian spent a year at the local secondary school, Ard Scoil Naomh Chiaráin. From here he would go to the Cistercian College of Mount St Joseph in Roscrea, County Tipperary, where Ber's brother, Father Andrew, was a monk and a teacher.

Brian and his brothers enjoyed a happy childhood. After school had finished for the day – from the age of ten upwards – Brian and his brothers would have chores to carry out in the family businesses. 'We were never bored,' recalls Barry Cowen. 'Whenever there was an election on there was a new fever and we grasped that. Growing up in a pub you meet all sorts and that helped form us into what we are.' Brian was an avid reader (by his late teens he had a passion for historical and political biographies) and had a great interest in music; he loved listening to traditional Irish and folk music and learned songs from his father, having inherited Ber's love of singing. He remembers that 'there was a strong tradition of music, and some amateur dramatics and musical societies in Clara and Tullamore at that time. Clara also had a strong showband scene. So, there were a lot of guys who could play music, and there were even some rock bands.'

But it was sport, particularly Gaelic sport, that was Cowen's first love in these years. As a young boy, he loved swimming and would spend the warm summer days splashing about in the pond at the back of the factory or around the mill – this was before the local swimming pool was built in the town in the early 1970s as part of a voluntary effort by locals, including Ber Cowen, who raised funds to get it built. At school, he developed a passion for sports, giving much of the credit to the Franciscan Brothers who ran the primary school: 'They were very much involved in our education and our development as footballers, hurlers and sportspeople generally,' he recalls. 'You mucked around and you played football and hurling with all these guys.'

Soccer was also popular in the town, and Cowen would occasionally join in a kickabout with the local factory team. In fact, he was offered the chance to play competitive matches with the team, but turned down the offer because he felt it was not his sport. For, as far as he was concerned, no other sport could match Gaelic football or hurling. The Cowens were fervent GAA supporters and a young Brian went to many of the big games in Croke Park, irrespective of whether Offaly were playing or not. He was determined to follow in the footsteps of his uncle Father Andrew, who had been a goalkeeper with the first Offaly team to win a Leinster championship back in 1947. From the age of seventeen, Cowen played eight consecutive seasons for the Clara Senior football side. He is remembered as having been a formidable club player and was selected for the Offaly Minor Under 21 teams. Former teammates describe Cowen as a 'committed, wholehearted player'.

2

The Roscrea Connection

In 1972, at twelve years of age, Cowen was sent to boarding school and quickly came to realize that Clara, the focus of his life up to this point, was not the centre of the world. He was to spend the next five years studying at the Cistercian College of Mount St Joseph in Roscrea – formative years that, he acknowledges, played an important part in his development and, ultimately, helped to groom him for a life in politics.

Cowen was not the only future politician of prominence to enter the cloistered precincts of Mount St Joseph around this time; indeed, the school's alumni from this period are almost a *Who's Who* of Irish political life. Former pupils include two of Cowen's predecessors as foreign minister – Labour Party leader Dick Spring and David Andrews – along with a number of members of influential political families, including the Reynoldses, Nolans, Mulcahys, Crottys, Springs, Gibbons and Enrights.

Ber and May Cowen had decided to send all three of their boys to Roscrea because Ber's brother, Father Andrew, taught there. This connection made it less painful for young Brian to leave his family behind as he set out for boarding school.

Father Andrew had attended Cistercian College himself and had been elected house captain by his fellow students. Now, as a monk in the adjoining monastery, in the early 1960s he served as dean of games and as a teacher, primarily of Irish and English; later, he became the master of novices in the abbey. He was a forceful personality. 'He radiated energy and restlessness and he would have been something of a beacon for the young Brian,' recalls former *Irish Times* editor Conor Brady, once a student at the college and now a member of its board of governors. Cowen himself remembers his uncle as a larger-than-life character who had a great influence on him as a boy.

The Cistercians are traditionally not a teaching but rather a contemplative order; in fact, after the closure of Mount Melleray in the mid-1970s, the monastery in Roscrea became the only Cistercian house in the world that had a school attached to it. The school at Mount St Joseph was opened in 1905, the land having been acquired some twenty-five years earlier by Count Arthur Moore, MP for Tipperary, who invited the Cistercians to build a monastery there in memory of his son, who had died tragically in his teens. 'The abbey is built in the classic tradition, set down at Cîteaux and Clairvaux in France in the eleventh century. It is said that a monk who knew the plan of Cîteaux could find his way today, blindfolded, with perfect certainty, through the cloisters and principal rooms of Mount St Joseph,' explains Conor Brady.

The Cistercian philosophy is spiritual yet down-to-earth, and Cowen recalls the students having a 'respectful observance', influenced by the routine and simplicity of monastery life. The boys would be aware, for example, of the monks rising each morning at precisely three forty-five for the first of the seven daily prayer gatherings. 'The presence of the monks has always had a very stabilizing influence on the boys,' says the dean of students, Seamus Hennessy. 'It's a very calm place to be, but we also have a coordinated regime 24/7. It's lights out at ten-thirty every night in dorms. Even though the boys can hear the first bell of the morning and go straight back to sleep, they are living in a spiritual, contemplative place which helps to form who they are as adults.'

Here the students were being prepared for the modern world, as well as having a strong Christian philosophy and adherence to a certain moral code instilled into them by the monks. The current President of Cistercian College, Dan Smyth, a brother of the former Fianna Fáil minister Michael Smyth, remembers teaching all three of the Cowen brothers. He particularly recalls Brian, whom he describes as having 'a wonderful heart. He was bright, bright, bright – a very able fella who was a pleasure to teach,' with a great aptitude for learning and for debating. Cowen relished the broad, holistic educational ethos at Roscrea, which was distinctly different from the narrower and more exam-focused approach pursued at that time in other schools. Acknowledging that the Cistercians sought and got outstanding results from the 'excellent teaching staff', Cowen felt there was a genuine commitment to a wider approach to education. 'It wasn't all about academic achievement. There had to be a certain rigour to the way you think, and also to the way you act. And, I suppose, basically trying to instil the Christian ethic,' he recalls.

Also, participation in sports was strongly encouraged, with athletics featuring prominently. Cowen played in the school teams at rugby and hurling, in which half-back was his best position. At a Leinster Schools rugby trial at Donnybrook he played full-back opposite Hugo McNeill, who was already school's captain from the previous year. 'Obviously, Hugo got the job!' recalls Cowen of the boy who went on to become a member of Ireland's Triple Crown-winning team.

Each morning on his way to prayers, the young Cowen would pass by the school's motto, inscribed in Latin on the mosaic floor at the front entrance to the College: *Insideat coelis animo sed corpore terris.* In English, this translates as: 'While conscious of earthly needs, we seek the things of heaven' – or, to turn it around: 'While our minds soar to the heavens, we keep our feet firmly planted on the ground.' Those who know Cowen say this is a motto which informs his personal and political outlook. 'It's the first thing that greets students every morning. If you reflect back on past political students like Dick Spring, David Andrews and Brian Cowen, you get that sense of level-headedness from them. They all had a great sense of humour and a high value system. They were happy young men but they kept their feet on the ground,' says Seamus Hennessy. 'The goal here is the pursuit of excellence; for each boy to be the best he can be, not only to take their place in the Ireland of today but to make a difference and help to transform the country. That has been the philosophy of the school since it was founded in 1905.'

But while the school imbued the boys with a sense of discipline and a sense of the need for balance between the practical and the ideal, the Cistercians could also be flexible and open in many ways, and encouraged the expression of individuality. 'You have to remember [Cowen] was part of a very questioning generation in the sixties and seventies, who were not prepared to blindly accept what they were told by the adult world,' recalled Dom Kevin Daly, the current Abbot of Mount St Joseph and dean of discipline at the College during Cowen's school years. 'Even their long hairstyles, as evidenced by the class photos back then, became more challenging to parents and school authorities at the time. On the whole we are pretty casual in school on dress. We encourage our boys to get muck on their boots. As a boy, he was very principled, and continues to be so today. He doesn't buy into the "anything goes" philosophy and has always stuck to what he believes in. He could take off all the staff but never in front of them or in a way that was hurtful. But he was by far the best mimic in the school. Boys here have always been allowed that freedom to be themselves. They are given the space to do that.'

In political circles today, Cowen is widely renowned for his public speaking skills. Many commentators have remarked on his ability to present complex and very detailed arguments without the usual support of notes clutched in hand. For this Roscrea must take a good deal of credit. The school has a long tradition of fostering public speaking and has tended to do exceptionally well in inter-school debating competitions, in both Irish and English. Former Taoiseach Albert Reynolds believes that part of Cowen's brilliance as a politician is the direct result of skills honed in the cut and thrust of competitive school debates while at Roscrea. 'He probably didn't think it at the time, but debating prepared him well for his introduction into national politics with the sudden death of his father,' he points out.

Not long after arriving at Roscrea, Cowen discovered that he had a gift for public speaking – both in English and in Irish – and within a couple of years was captain of the school debating team. Through debating, he was able to overcome a natural shyness and gain the confidence to become more assertive. He also found it taught him a great deal about how to structure arguments, focus his mind on listening to the other point of view, and counter a point made by an opponent. 'I think it's good in your formative years to apply that sort of rigour to your thinking. It disciplines your approach to analysis of a problem or how you approach persuading people on a certain point of view. If you take the more difficult side of the argument, it tests you. It adds to your vocabulary and your articulation of ideas. I would like to see more and more of it throughout the curriculum, throughout schools,' he explains.

Cowen won many awards for debating, most notably – some years after leaving Roscrea – the prestigious Eamon de Valera Centenary Debate in 1982, held at the Burlington Hotel in Dublin in honour of Ireland's first Taoiseach. That night, he was crowned one of the main public speaking winners in English, alongside future fellow TD Mary Hanafin, who won in the Irish category. Dom Daly remembers being impressed with how Cowen could 'whip out a killer line to demolish his opponent just at the exact moment it was needed'. Expanding on this point, he recalled one particular evening when the government of the day was put on trial and its fitness for office was being challenged: 'Brian excelled that night but the poor chairman was frightened that things were getting so hot, he thought he would have to call security. He had a terrible time trying to call order. Brian always had his facts ready but he spoke from the heart. Usually one of the team would be the researcher, but he always went off and did his own research.'

After five years at Roscrea, Cowen decided to read for a law degree at University College Dublin (UCD) – his choice of subject influenced, according to a later humorous recollection, by the fact that he would have to attend only a mere eight hours of lectures a week during the first year of study, which he found attractive because it 'did not over-exercise' his mind. Although Cowen's Roscrea years were now behind him, he regularly returned to visit his uncle and to walk the grounds – as he still does today, though Father Andrew is no longer alive. According to Conor Brady, Cowen considers himself part of Roscrea's 'extended family' and retains close emotional ties with the College and the monastery. Soon after becoming Taoiseach, Cowen made a very personal journey back to Roscrea, taking the time to reflect on his life's journey. Tragically, Father Andrew had passed away only days before Cowen was appointed Taoiseach. As he strolled through the grounds, he recalled how his uncle had predicted that he would one day become, as Cowen likes to describe the Taoiseach's job, first among equals. Speaking at the time, Cowen told Ger Scully, editor of the *Tullamore Tribune*, that his return to Mount St Joseph Abbey had given him 'a feeling of quietness and solace. I had forgotten how refreshing it can be.'

There is a very strong past pupils' network at Roscrea, and Cowen always does his best to attend any reunions organized, relishing the opportunity to catch up with former classmates – even though now the gatherings are sometimes tinged with sadness. 'It is only in recent years that we've lost some guys that I went to school with – who have died – and that brings people back together as well, when you start meeting up. So, having had the good times as we went through college we are into a phase now, unfortunately, where some of our people are going and that makes you reflective too,' says Cowen.

But the memories of his schooldays themselves are good ones. 'I had a very enjoyable time there. I often say that I got two great things in Roscrea – I got a great education and a great appetite. That's because you'd eat anything when you came out of it. You know yourself, it's not your mother's home bacon, but . . . and that's good too, because you develop a sort of independence. It hardens you up a bit, you know? It's part of growing up. I enjoyed it there and it gave me the opportunity to meet guys from other backgrounds and parts of the country.'

Outside the school regimen, Cowen delighted in the new freedom which student life in Dublin offered him. When he wasn't studying, he played rugby and Gaelic football; he was also frequently to be found enjoying the banter in the UCD bar. But family ties remained strong. While Cowen had always been close to his father, his bond with Ber strengthened considerably during his student years in Dublin. 'There was a natural inclination to call into the Dáil pretty regularly, anyway, if only to get a decent bit of grub! The food in the flat wouldn't have been great. One had other uses for disposable income at that time as a young fellow – more liquid lunches than anything else!' he recalls, light-heartedly.

Perhaps surprisingly, given his enthusiasm and flair for public speaking at Roscrea, Cowen didn't take part in the UCD debates. He puts this down largely to the other attractions on offer: 'I went through a phase at that time of concentrating on sport and life and having fun.' But he also points out that the student debates were held on Friday nights, which 'didn't really suit' him as he used to go home most weekends to help out his elder brother Christy, who was by now running the family pub. He did occasionally attend a debate in UCD, and once put his name down to speak on the issue of Northern Ireland. 'But they didn't reach me. Lucky enough they didn't, because I was so appalled at some of the stuff I was listening to – what some of the more established speakers of my time had to say on the subject. I thought they were quite naïve. Regarding Britain as an honest broker in the late seventies, I thought, showed an astonishing blindness to the reality of what was happening,' says Cowen.

Back in Clara at the weekends, Cowen would roll up his sleeves and settle down to work in the bar and lounge – work which, he feels, taught him more about human nature than he ever learned at school or university. Working in a pub environment, Cowen believes, can make you streetwise, give you a practical intelligence that a college education itself cannot guarantee. Many of the people he met while serving in the bar influenced his thinking about life. In particular, he got a sense from these people that contentment is far more important than mere success or material wealth.

Cowen took real pleasure in serving the 'great characters' who frequented the bar and listening to their stories, particularly the older men, one or two of whom had served in the British army and fought in the First World War. 'I got very interested in their times,' Cowen recalls. 'I think this might be down to the fact that my mother's father, Tommy Weir, had served in the war and was actually injured. He died in 1964 and I have very few memories of him.' He became fascinated with Clara's connection with the war and would happily sit and chat with the customers as they reminisced about their great adventures and also about some locals who tragically died on the battlefields of France and further afield. The few veterans of the First World War would tell him about their experiences of fighting on the continent. Others would talk to him about working in aviation factories in Coventry during the Second World War. 'He loves a good yarn. A real life story. He's not into jokes as such. He loves characters,' points out Michael Duignan, a sports panellist on RTÉ's *The Sunday Game*.

Cowen believes that the insight into the human condition and human character he gained working in the family businesses has stood him in good stead in political life. 'What I regard as one of my best advantages as a politician is that I'm a good judge of character. I'm a good judge of what makes people tick. That is an important part of my repertoire because it's important to be able to understand how a person is thinking, why they're thinking it, where they are coming from. We might never end up bosom buddies but at least we should deal with things professionally and in a way that meets with the seriousness of the substantive issues.'

Like his father, Cowen enjoyed the *craic* in a bar environment – and he still does. For him, a bar is a place where he can unwind, escape the daily routine of politics and have light-hearted conversation, listening to the lads telling yarns. 'It is good to talk about other things and not to have your life dominated by politics. It takes up enough of our time as it is. I enjoy the *craic* and other things, local issues, local chat, sport,' he explains.

Cowen is known for having a dry sense of humour and a sharp mind that is always quick with a retort, both attributes developed during his time working in the family bar – as was his skill as a raconteur, one of the traits that has made him popular among constituents and fellow politicians alike. Cowen is an accomplished mimic, a talent which he inherited from his father. When he was working behind the bar, Cowen would enjoy going home and retelling stories or describing encounters with the many characters he served. 'The real wit and humour I enjoy is recounting actual things that happened. You know, the innocence of people and the way they'd look at something,' he says.

Cowen recalls his family home during these years of his

growing up as one that was filled with 'wit and mimicry and a sense of humour, a sense of life and gaiety and an interest in music and games and sport – and mixing that with work and trying to get ahead'. This jovial but practical ethos in the family home, he believes, was an enriching one that shaped the type of person he is today.

After completing his second year of study at UCD in 1979, Cowen decided to travel to New York and stay with relatives on Long Island. As a child, he had a fascination with America, derived from the stories his mother and grandmother would tell him about their experiences of living and working there. So, while Cowen could never envisage himself emigrating, he decided to go over for a few months. To support himself, he picked up some of the 'usual student work' – occasional cleaning jobs, demolition work on apartment blocks: it was exhausting, but Cowen relished it. 'It toughened me up,' he says. It also gave him more insight into human experience. He was working with a hard bunch of men, and he found them fascinating. He struck up a friendship with a Vietnam veteran named Al who had come back home intending to study, but instead – finding himself plagued by a depression derived from his hellish combat experiences – was spending his days doing manual work; Cowen observed that the experience of war had transformed some of the vets he met into 'disturbed people'. He also worked on the demolition sites with some Italian Americans who were living in Little Italy and didn't know much English even after twenty years in New York.

As far as Cowen was concerned, working on the sites was a good lead-up to pre-season training, getting him into physical shape for when he returned to Ireland to play football the next spring. On his days off, he would head out on the subway into Manhattan or catch a ride from his relatives to Gaelic Park in the Bronx, where he could play football with the other expats; in the evenings, he would socialize back on Long Island. Gaelic Park had been bought by the GAA in 1926; by 1979, when Cowen was playing there, the sports facilities were experiencing a slump in popularity, dispelled a few years later when a new influx of Irish migrants hit the city. Cowen still likes to revisit Gaelic Park when he is in New York but, as he points out, 'it is a totally different place' today: taken over by Manhattan College in 1991, it now puts on soccer, lacrosse and softball as well as Gaelic sports, all played now on artificial turf that recently replaced the natural pitch on which Cowen was used to running around during that summer of '79.

Throughout his student years Cowen remained very much involved in local politics. On his visits to the Dáil to pick up a few bob from his father, he would often sit and chat with Ber about constituency issues. 'I had a great interest in politics and a great interest in my father's career,' says Cowen. 'I was always very supportive and very much involved in the organization [in Offaly] in terms of assisting him and the work that he was doing.' But he would not participate in a 'front line way' because he didn't want accusations of nepotism from within the local party structure. 'I was very conscious that I didn't want it to be suggested that you were too prominent ahead of your time. There were other senior organizational people here that I worked with, for whom I had the highest respect and from whom I learnt a lot as well,' he explains.

During this period, Cowen wasn't publicly articulating his views on issues; instead he was quietly working away in the background. 'I was learning. I was watching. I was interested in how the whole thing worked.' He had quickly become a highly respected figure in the party's youth wing, Ógra Fianna Fáil. 'He displayed political skill and insight way beyond his tender years,' recalled Pádraig Boland, party chairman in Offaly, writing in the *Offaly Express*.

Cowen started his political career by attending so-called 'after-church gate meetings' during election campaigns to canvass for his father. He liked the way people in rural areas would actually come out and listen to polemical speeches. 'There was that natural interest. It was an avenue for people to show their interest,' he recalls. He used to love standing outside the polling booths, handing out leaflets to urge voters to give Ber Cowen their number one vote. With a certain nostalgia, Cowen regrets some of the changes that have come about in the style of grassroots politics.

'Now you can't put up a poster near a polling booth; you can't stand outside the poll as loads of people are going in the door, or when they come out, to see if they voted for you or not! It's all got to the point now where it's a case of, "Oh, no! This is all very unfair." OK, there were too many hanging around polling booths, and people were inundated with leaflets going in and there was a lot of annoyance and inconvenience. It's like everything – if it's overdone it gets a bad name,' he says. 'But I do hark back to some of those practices that served us well in the past simply because we should never underestimate the value of participation.

'People felt a part of something. Now, we are told that it's all done through television and it's all about the amount of make-up you have on you and what colour is your tie. We are starting to live in superficial times, and there's a lot of pseudo-scientific analysis going on about what politics is about. I just find it amusing. I know there are whole degree courses built up in universities on this – and it's interesting research and there may even be grains of truth in it – but, at the end of the day, in my opinion, to be a good politician you have to have a passion for it. You have to have a belief in something – even if you're all wrong, at least you have a belief in something that you are articulating – you are not putting a gun to anybody's head. The people will let you know very quickly whether you are talking *ráiméis* or not because if they think you are they'll give you very few votes. But at least you're out there. I think, at the end of the day, that's what the democratic life is about. That there are people who have ideas, who have a passion for what they are doing, and I respect political opponents who have that passion. I enjoy listening to them and I enjoy the competition of ideas. But what we have to make sure is that what we say is articulate, that it's relevant, and that it is honest.'

3

Following in Ber Cowen's Footsteps

While on a parliamentary trip to the Middle East in 1975 Ber Cowen contracted malaria, a misfortune which precipitated a marked decline in his health. As a result of this illness, Ber was forced to alter his lifestyle. 'He didn't drink for the rest of his life, I would say. He'd have a glass of wine or something on a social occasion,' remembers Cowen.

In January 1984, Ber Cowen was attending a local agricultural convention in Tullamore when he complained of severe headaches, which had first started earlier that same morning. Suddenly, he collapsed. Tragically, just a week short of his fifty-second birthday, he had suffered a brain haemorrhage.

The previous night, he'd been trapped by the bad weather in Dublin and his good friend Albert Reynolds had offered him a bed for the night. Back at Reynolds' apartment in Ballsbridge, the two men passed most of the night discussing their favourite subject: politics. They took single beds in the same room so that they could continue talking, reflecting together on the history of Fianna Fáil. 'We didn't get to sleep until five in the morning,' Reynolds recalls.

The next morning Reynolds had to dash off to an appointment. He remembers leaving the bedroom, telling Ber: 'You
take your time getting ready – and I'll see you next week.'

But they were the last words Reynolds ever spoke to his
good friend.

At six thirty that evening Reynolds was emerging from a
function in Cavan when he heard on the news that Ber had
collapsed at a meeting in Tullamore and been taken to St
Vincent's Hospital. Reynolds rushed straight to the hospital,
where Ber was on a life-support machine. 'It wasn't switched
off at the time, but he was unconscious; they kept him going
until the rest of the family could arrive, I suppose,' says
Reynolds.

It was at this point that Reynolds met Ber's three sons for
the first time. All three young men were distraught; though
they clung to the hope that their father might survive,
Reynolds sensed that they had known 'from the minute they
arrived' that Ber was gone. He spoke to them briefly and
they told him they were glad to hear that Ber had spent his
final night in Dublin with a good friend like Reynolds.

There is a general misconception that Brian Cowen had
vowed never to enter politics because he simply didn't want to
undergo the same type of stress that his father endured. It has
been suggested on more than one occasion that he was thrust
reluctantly into political life when he was prevailed upon to
contest the by-election which arose from his father's sudden
death. But in fact Brian Cowen was always planning to 'have a
shot at politics', as he puts it. Not long before his death, Ber
Cowen had told Brian that he was considering retiring from
politics and suggested that Brian might consider running
in the local council election due in 1984. 'As it so happens,
my dad wasn't going to stay in politics that long. A month

29

before he died, in fact, we discussed it one Christmas night,' remembered Cowen when he was interviewed on *The Late Late Show* in September 2008. 'He suggested to me that maybe I should consider putting my name forward, that he was going to get out of politics.' He is adamant that the decision to contest his father's Dáil seat wasn't a difficult one to make. However, he acknowledges that events faced him with that decision sooner than he had envisaged. 'Our dad died very suddenly and it was a shock to us all,' says his brother Barry. 'Brian was quite young and just qualified as a solicitor with his whole life ahead of him. I've no doubt that over time he would have gone into politics but maybe at a time of his choosing.'

The mid-1980s were not an ideal time to enter politics in Ireland. The economy was stagnating and the prevailing mood was one of gloom. Many of Cowen's generation – including many friends and acquaintances he had been in school and university with – were leaving the country in a desperate search for work. With the optimism and energy of youth, Cowen sought to 'get in there and see if we could do something'. But he remembers having a more realistic thought in his head too: 'You're not going to change the world here, mate, but you can do something that will really impact positively on the community you live in.' Nor were his horizons exclusively local. This was also a period when Cowen, interested in current affairs more widely, was – like many of his generation – becoming aware of and fascinated by global politics, in particular the East–West tensions of the Cold War: he still finds it difficult to believe that it could have been possible for the Soviet Union to collapse 'in front of our eyes on television without a major catastrophic conflict'. Equally surprising to Cowen has been the fact that within just fifteen years of that extraordinary event, several of the former Eastern bloc countries joined the European Union, proving themselves 'progressive and committed to democratic ideals' – in stark contrast to the turn of events in Yugoslavia, where the 'local strongman politics' of the pre-Communist era re-emerged, 'with terrible, catastrophic consequences'.

In October 1980, Cowen had started working with the Tullamore-based law firm Brian P. Adams & Co. It was here that he served his three years' legal apprenticeship as a solicitor, graduating from the Law Society in October 1983. After his father's untimely demise, Cowen decided in 1984 to start up his own law firm at premises Ber Cowen had mortgaged on William Street in Tullamore, which he had been using for business meetings and occasional constituency matters. Cowen felt compelled to 'take on the responsibility' of maintaining the building, and opted to start a law practice there with a Dublin man named Tom O'Donovan, who was working with a rival law firm in Tullamore at the time. The firm of O'Donovan and Cowen is still operating in the town today, with the Taoiseach's name proudly displayed on its sign. With no family background in the profession, it was not easy for Cowen to get his legal career off the ground. In retrospect, he reflects that he might have been wiser to have taken the bar exams and become a barrister instead of a solicitor. He had a love of advocacy and the idea of making robust arguments in court very much appealed to him.

'I liked court work when I was a solicitor, but I wouldn't be that gone on the office part of the work,' he reflects. 'I'm not a great administrator in that sense. Some people are very good at all the paperwork, but I was more of the guy who could get business. We all have our talents. Office management wouldn't be my forte, but thankfully I had a great partner in Tom O'Donovan and he was very strong in all those areas.'

Shortly after his father's death, in March 1984, Cowen was coopted onto Offaly County Council, and he spent a few months working as a councillor before contesting the by-election for his father's Dáil seat in June of the same year. Cowen was not confident of winning the seat – in fact, he was not even confident of securing the party's nomination – and dreaded the thought of letting his father down by actually losing the by-election. He recalls being 'relieved' and 'very proud' when he was selected by Fianna Fáil ahead of two other potential – and more experienced – candidates. 'Some members of the party asked me to show my interest in running for my father's seat. But, at the end of the day, when the election was called three people put their names forward – myself; Gerry Lodge, who had run as the fourth candidate in previous general elections, alongside my father; and the late Seamus Loughnane, who was a good friend as well. We contested the convention held that May at the Bridge House in Tullamore, which was chaired by Brian Lenihan Senior. Charlie Haughey, the party leader at the time, attended the event. I can remember there was a huge crowd at it. I was very honoured to be selected but, based on the canvass we had done, I was confident of making it. But saying that, the other candidates did well – there was a good split in the votes.'

Barry recalls his brother being very anxious throughout the by-election campaign, with the date of the poll scheduled for the same day as the European parliamentary elections in June 1984 – five months after Ber's death. But his confidence in campaigning soon grew. 'It became apparent from a relatively early stage that he was quite good at it.' Albert Reynolds came out to Tullamore to canvass with Brian: it was the first time the two men had met since that emotionally charged moment at Ber Cowen's bedside, but now, on the campaign trail, a genuine friendship developed. Reynolds was impressed with Cowen and would later say that he felt even then that this novice politician would some day become Taoiseach.

When that eventually happened, Cowen's neighbours jokingly told several newspaper reporters how they remembered seeing him set out for the Dáil for the first time as a TD in his battered second-hand car, and doubted whether he would even manage to get out of the county!

That first arrival at the Dáil was a bittersweet occasion for Cowen. As he walked past the security checkpoint and into the courtyard, Cowen had a reflective moment of both pride and sadness. On every other occasion, in his student days, Cowen had come here to visit his father, but on this day he was following in the dead man's footsteps. 'Yes, he would have been very proud,' Cowen told himself as he walked up the steps and through the revolving door of Government Buildings.

For the next eight years, Cowen worked both as a TD and in his Tullamore legal practice. Determined that he would not lose his father's seat, he put huge energy into the constituency work. With professional demands on all sides, Cowen was rarely at home; but the pressure didn't trouble him. 'Surprisingly, when you're younger you don't see the problems. You just go at it,' he says now.

Nevertheless, somehow he did contrive to make time for a personal life. Shortly after winning his Dáil seat, Cowen began seeing his future wife Mary Molloy, whose father had been a close friend of Ber Cowen. They had much in common – both came from political and publican backgrounds – and were married in September 1990. Today, Mary Cowen plays a vital role in constituency affairs. Her husband explains:

'We confide and talk things over. I get her view on things. She has a very commonsense point of view. She doesn't get involved in internal organizational matters in terms of how and who we select and all of that, but once an election is called she's very active and very well regarded by all the activists in the area, wherever she canvasses. She's got a very good knowledge of those parts of the constituency with which she is acquainted. She's a great canvasser and concentrates on that activity in her home area in South Offaly, as well as locally here in Tullamore. Her own family are well known in many of these locations. Her personality is very much suited towards that type of activity. She's very easy to talk to and to work with.'

Cowen feels it an unfortunate perception in contemporary politics that you can't have influence unless you hold a cabinet position. He believes that the role of a TD is constantly and unfairly disregarded. When he talks about his political philosophy, the first point he always makes is that, regardless of whatever office he may hold, he is 'first and foremost' a TD. 'Those responsibilities don't change whether you hold high office or not,' is his strongly held view. Today, despite being Taoiseach, Cowen feels that a significant part of his duty is still to represent the interests of his constituents. 'Of course, you have to put them into the context of what the national position is,' he says.

It angers Cowen when commentators too readily criticize TDs for taking on the many requests and representations which their constituents put to them. He detests the phrase 'clientelism' in relation to TDs' interaction with constituents. 'I know of no TD who goes out seeking this work – this work arrives at your doorstep because people, as citizens, wish that their elected representatives would represent them on these issues. And while they might be seen from the outside as mundane individual issues, they're huge issues for the individuals concerned,' he says. Cowen believes that much of his own work representing constituents as a TD was necessary because the system of public administration failed to accommodate what he describes as 'local discretion'.

Cowen is a firm believer that flexibility is needed 'to accommodate the fact that no application form, however comprehensive, fully encapsulates a particular circumstance or a constituent's dilemma in respect of some particular area'. He believes that contemporary politics in Ireland needs to find a way to 'fashion the bureaucracy' so that it will be properly responsive to local needs. He says he understands and respects the need for a framework of rules and regulations within which public administration operates, so that it is, and is seen to be, transparent and objectively based; but this, he argues, is not enough.

'I do feel sometimes that the failure of all of us to find that discretion,' he explains, 'to find that ability to cover the grey area in the "black and white" situation, is sometimes felt by the citizen to be the result of an uncaring system, which is not the case, of course – it's about the fact that there are principles of accountability on the spending of public money, which we all understand. But that is a constant challenge and one that I think is crucial to how we perform in the public sector in the future. We need to try and look at ways of addressing that so people can see that, in fact, what we do have, thankfully, in this country is a public administration system that is built on the principles of integrity and honesty and accountability, but also that has the ability to respond in a compassionate way where genuine special circumstances arise.' Cowen also believes that 'devising schemes of support that put the citizen's needs at the centre – rather than in-flexibly requiring the citizen's needs to fit existing schemes if they're to get any help at all – is the challenge we face'.

During those first eight years of his political career, when he wasn't helping constituents or responding to their complaints, Cowen's other main priority was to build up the local party apparatus, his political base, in Offaly, and to work co-operatively with party colleagues throughout the Laois–Offaly constituency. So successful has he been in this endeavour that the party organization in his constituency is now regarded by many as the most integrated and best-run political machine in the country at local level.

Because the dual mandate was still in force at the time, Cowen had the opportunity for a time to hold seats both on the local council and in the Dáil. He felt this allowed politicians to 'close the gap' between the local and the national perspectives 'on what the implication of policy in any area would be'. Cowen learned a great deal during his time on Offaly County Council about the real practical importance for his constituents of fundamental day-to-day issues such as housing, water schemes, and the provision of infrastructure and services. 'You're talking about the development of town and city planning: a very practical day-to-day appli-cation of how laws are impacting on the daily lives of citizens,' he says. Today, he is in two minds about whether the ending of the dual mandate in 2003 was a good idea. Under the previous arrangement, he believes, TDs could bring the leadership, knowledge and experience they gained in the Dáil back into the local political arena, most particularly and most beneficially when formulating wider council policies, and could bring the national perspective into the local council chamber in a way that was helpful to local councillors. 'It gave people an understanding of what the rationale behind the policy proposal was. That's lost a bit now, as we've now divided that area with the local representative and once you become a national representative you can no longer serve on the local council. I always felt that there were pluses and minuses to that argument. I could understand why the decision was ultimately taken, but I felt there was an important plus in having TDs on councils as well.' He recognizes, however, that the decision to end the dual mandate is unlikely to be reversed.

Cowen found his years on the back benches highly enjoyable and educational. He grasped the opportunity to participate in debates when matters arose on which he felt he could make a useful contribution, and his ability to speak well and effectively on such occasions brought him to the attention of the then leader of Fianna Fáil, the notorious Charlie Haughey, who admired Cowen's pugnacious style and his incisive – and often decisive – retorts in debate. Cowen also enjoyed going to the weekly meetings of the parliamentary party, which gave him direct input into policy; he relished being in a position to argue his case and bring motions forward for the party's consideration. He also listened intently, and sought to learn as much as he possibly could at this time from ministers and other senior colleagues as they explained policy approaches and upcoming legislative measures. 'You hear what the background and rationale are for any measure, and why certain laws were to be amended, and so on; so you get a very good feel of how policies are developed – and you get to learn from the great experience of your colleague TDs on how they would interpret the pros and cons, the adaptations and amendments that need to be considered in respect of government proposals, based on what they were hearing at that stage of the process. I regard all of that period as a very instructive and positive experience and, in my opinion, a necessary experience,' he says.

However, Cowen also believes that certain of his local council colleagues had a greater influence on his future political style than some of the high-profile cabinet ministers he encountered in those years. Cowen observed closely how these councillors operated, and today pays tribute to the honest motives, the 'good and genuine' ambitions, of these individuals who worked tirelessly to improve the quality of life and general circumstances of their constituents. He mentions Eddie Joe Dooley, a former chairman of Offaly County Council and director of election for the party during election time, as making 'a big impression' on him 'in terms of one's demeanour in politics', as well as party member Justin Graham, who served with Ber Cowen in the Tullamore electoral area, Seamus Loughnane, Paddy Scully and Paddy Gorman. 'Those were the type of guys I looked up to – quiet but authoritative people who knew what the party was about. Team players, as they say,' he recalls.

Cowen was also heavily influenced by several backbench TDs from that time, learning from them how to derive the best results for his constituents from the many offices of government. 'You pick up good tips and you improve your working method by watching more experienced people at work in close proximity to what you're doing yourself in your office in Dublin,' he says. At one stage or another, Cowen shared offices with the likes of David Andrews, Charlie McCreevy (who had once shared an office with Ber Cowen), Jimmy Leonard and Gene Fitzgerald. 'They were all very different but very effective public representatives in their own way. They really were hardworking and very conscientious TDs. I learned a lot from them, particularly about how to solve constituency problems,' he says.

But it wasn't all hard work during that period. There is one famous yarn about how Cowen and McCreevy dashed off to the Punchestown racecourse one evening, prior to a vote in the Dáil scheduled for eight thirty that night. 'McCreevy was pretty adamant that this horse we went off to back was going to win but, unfortunately, it was beaten by a nose,' remembers Cowen.

Quickly, the two men jumped back into the car and headed back to the Dáil.

'What's wrong with you?' McCreevy asked an obviously disappointed-looking Cowen.

'I spent too much money on that horse – more than I should have. I lost a good few bob there,' Cowen moaned.

'You didn't lose it! We know where it is,' replied McCreevy, with perfect comic timing.

Cowen didn't mind spending eight years on the back benches before being promoted to cabinet. He was content as a TD and recalls having no expectation of anything more during his first two terms. He was realistic and knew that there were many other TDs in the party who might well be seen as having a stronger case for promotion on the grounds of length of service, experience or recognized potential. But Cowen did build up an impressive political curriculum vitae during those first two terms in the Dáil: he was a member of the Offaly Vocational Education Committee from 1989 to 1992; at the same time (1991–2) he served on the British–Irish Inter-Parliamentary Body and as a member of its sub-committee on political and security matters. Also during this period he was a member of the Fianna Fáil commission to review the aims and structures of the party.

For something like two years after he was first elected to the Dáil, Cowen still continued to turn out to play Gaelic football in Offaly – and he was a formidable player. Back in 1981, while still preparing for a legal career, he had been picked to train with the Offaly Senior football team that winter and the following spring. Unfortunately, he was dropped from the squad after the League campaign in 1982 – only to see Offaly subsequently go on to win the All-Ireland championship that year. But he was philosophical. 'I had no problem with the decision. Probably at around that time I was a bit light. I was probably eleven-and-a-half stone, probably less – I hadn't as broad a girth as I have now!'

By 1986, though, Cowen was immersing himself in local politics to such an extent that he found he could no longer give so much time to sport; in fact, he began to realize that he would have to hang up his boots in order to focus completely on his new career. Fitness had always been a high priority for Cowen: he was a firm believer in putting in the effort during training to justify selection on match day. Unfortunately, he was now finding that the training sessions were conflicting with his attendance in the Dáil and constituency meetings. Cowen did not want to be one of those players who skipped training but would still turn up expecting a game on the weekends; so, at the age of twenty-six, he played his last competitive game for Clara. 'I gave up a bit sooner than I should have,' he says. 'I sort of started to fall away from participation as a player. I regret that now. People told me at the time that I would regret it and that I should keep it up. And I didn't – and *que sera sera*, that's the way it went.'

4

Into the Cabinet

After nearly eight years on the back benches, in 1992 Cowen was eventually rewarded with a ministerial post in Albert Reynolds' first cabinet. On his appointment as Minister for Labour, Cowen could no longer practise law and had to step back from the legal practice he had helped build up in Tullamore. 'When you become a minister it's cabinet procedure that you can't do any other work,' explains Cowen, 'but I remained a non-practising partner.' It was not a difficult decision, even though Cowen realized that from a financial point of view the legal profession offered a far more secure career. 'Well, the truth be told, my passion is in politics, really,' he explains. 'My profession is a profession – it's a way of making a living. I didn't hesitate about making the move. I have no regrets about pursuing a full-time political career since I became a minister in 1992.'

Reynolds became the country's eighth Taoiseach – its ninth leader since Cosgrave – after his predecessor Charles Haughey stepped down on 11 February 1992. Haughey's hold on political power had been progressively slipping over the course of the previous year, as a result of a sequence of political crises. The first in a series of events that gradually undermined Haughey's authority concerned Brian Lenihan's candidacy for the presidency. Back in 1982 Lenihan, a long-time friend and loyal lieutenant of Haughey, was widely alleged to have attempted to put pressure on President Hillery – at Haughey's behest – to reject the then Taoiseach Garrett Fitzgerald's request to dissolve his government. If Hillery had done so, Fitzgerald would have been forced to resign, allowing Haughey to attempt to form an alternative government without having to go before the electorate. However, during the presidential campaign of 1990, Lenihan insisted on television that he had made no such attempt. Unfortunately for him, Lenihan had given an interview to a UCD student, Jim Duffy, in which he had admitted to telephoning the President back in January 1982. As the story slowly unfolded – forcing Lenihan repeatedly to change his recollection of events – his credibility was undermined, calling into question his suitability for the highest office in the land. Support for his candidacy ebbed and his opponent, the Labour Party candidate Mary Robinson, won the election to become Ireland's first female President.

But that was only the beginning. Haughey's coalition partners, the Progressive Democrats, then put pressure on the Taoiseach to force Lenihan's resignation from government as Tánaiste and Minister for Defence. With Lenihan refusing to fall on his sword, Haughey made the difficult political decision to dismiss his long-standing political ally and friend.

Many within Fianna Fáil were angered by Haughey's handling of the situation, and these feelings were only exacerbated by the ensuing controversy over Lenihan's replacement at Defence. Haughey's choice had fallen on the

Donegal TD Jim McDaid, who on the morning of his appointment had been captured on camera smiling broadly as he emerged from the Four Courts in Dublin following a ruling that Maze prison escapee James Pius Clarke should not be extradited to the UK. McDaid insisted that he had been present at the hearing solely because Clarke's mother was one of his constituents, but the incident prompted Fine Gael to object to his appointment. Raising the stakes, the PDs declared their intention to bring the government down if the contentious appointment went ahead; as a result, McDaid effectively had to resign from the cabinet before even being officially installed in post.

Cowen, like many of his party colleagues, was incensed by the PDs' blackmail tactics. 'They can't choose our ministers,' he was heard fuming at the time. He felt that the interference in the cabinet selection of McDaid showed a lack of 'mutual respect'. During the March 1991 Fianna Fáil Ard Fheis, Albert Reynolds, who was then Finance Minister, lashed out at the junior coalition partners over the McDaid and Lenihan episodes. 'Fianna Fáil does not need another party to keep it on the right track or to act as its conscience,' Reynolds stated to rapturous applause.

In his warm–up speech before the party leader's address the following year, Cowen was even brusquer. 'What about the PDs?' he asked rhetorically, before providing an answer which was greeted with loud and unequivocal enthusiasm: 'When in doubt, leave them out.' Interestingly, years later, when Cowen, now Taoiseach, was asked for his views on the Progressive Democrats, he quipped: 'When in doubt, leave them in.'

A short time after the 1991 Ard Fheis, at an event in Cork, Reynolds boldly challenged Haughey for the leadership of Fianna Fáil, openly announcing that he was willing to put forward his name as party leader if the position became vacant. An irate Haughey subsequently sacked his former friend, who had been a key supporter of his own challenge for the leadership, and went on to sack other disillusioned ministers who had spoken out against him. However, Reynolds' expulsion from the cabinet prompted a backbench TD named Sean Power to put a motion of no confidence in Haughey's leadership before the parliamentary party in the autumn of 1991 – a vote Haughey managed to win by fifty-five to twenty-two.

Cowen was one of the TDs who backed Reynolds in his failed leadership bid of 1991. 'I was in the minority in that proposal and that was fine. I accepted it, and we moved on,' he recalls. His support for Reynolds was rooted not in any factional allegiance but rather in a conviction that the party would be better served by a new regime at the top. Cowen is quick to point out that he was also friendly with people who didn't support Reynolds, and that he has never allowed differences of opinion on any particular issue to compromise friendships with other members of the party. 'If I liked the person I liked them. Part of my liking them is respecting that they have a point of view that is probably as sincerely held as mine. At the end of the day, what you try to do is to come to a collective decision that is sensible in the circumstances, and where a vote is required when a consensus can't be arrived at, then you vote on it and you get on with it.'

Immediately after the vote of autumn 1991 it appeared that Reynolds' political career – and those of his supporters – was all but finished. However, it soon became clear that it was Haughey's career that was doomed. Former Minister for Justice Sean Doherty, who had taken the blame for the scandal surrounding the tapping of journalists' phones in the early

1980s, surprised many when he proclaimed on RTÉ television that Haughey had not only known about this illegal activity but actually authorized the bugging. The PDs instantly announced they would pull out of the government if Haughey remained as Taoiseach. Reluctantly, Haughey announced his retirement at a parliamentary party meeting on 30 January 1992, and Reynolds won the leadership contest that followed with ease, defeating the challenges of Mary O'Rourke and Michael Woods. On 11 February 1992, the day Reynolds took over, the now defunct *Sunday Press* quoted an anonymous member of his campaign team as saying: 'The leadership race didn't begin when Haughey announced his resignation to the parliamentary party. It was all over by then because Reynolds had enough pledges in the bag at that stage.' Reynolds had been gathering support for his nomination for several months, many TDs having been approached the previous summer with discreet enquiries as to whether they would support his candidacy. Cowen rejects the suggestion that he had been 'working' on his colleagues to ensure that they voted for Reynolds as party leader. 'Prior to Charlie Haughey's decision to step down as Taoiseach I did not canvass my views with anybody else,' says Cowen. 'It was only afterwards that I sounded out some of my colleagues to see who they intended to vote for in the impending leadership contest. Your job is to call it as you see it. I served on the back benches for eight years under Charlie Haughey and, on a personal level, I got on well with him.

'Gerald Connolly on the Offaly side of the constituency was, if you like, the senior man. He was there longer than I was and he had been appointed as minister of state in all of Charlie Haughey's governments – so it was clear that there were never going to be two ministers of state from the one constituency. That was the political situation and I had no problem with that.'

But the political situation changed when Reynolds was elected Taoiseach. There was considerable controversy when the new cabinet was announced. At a stroke, the new Taoiseach summarily dismissed eight members of Haughey's frontbench team, including long-serving political heavy-weights such as Mary O'Rourke, Ray Burke and Gerard Collins. Reynolds also sacked nine out of the twelve junior ministers, the majority of whom had been loyal Haughey supporters in the no-confidence vote of the previous year. The only survivor was Haughey's protégé Bertie Ahern, who remained on in the position of Minister for Finance, after agreeing not to challenge Reynolds for the leadership. In place of those dismissed, Reynolds installed many of Haughey's most vocal critics, including David Andrews, Séamus Brennan and Charlie McCreevy; he also promoted a number of younger TDs from rural constituencies, such as Noel Dempsey and Cowen, who was then thirty-two years old.

The appointment was unusual, in that a backbench TD would normally be given a junior ministerial role before moving into the cabinet; but Reynolds had seen great promise in Cowen since canvassing with him in his 1984 by-election campaign, and decided to throw him in at the deep end. Thus he became Minister for Labour, a post he held from 1992 to 1993, at which point he was moved to energy, a ministry which was eventually expanded to cover transport and communication.

Reynolds, in fact, saw Cowen as a potential future Taoiseach even then – and believes he was not alone in doing so. 'I knew he had the potential to be a minister straight away rather than starting out with a junior ministerial post. Everyone saw him as a future Taoiseach. He has proved himself in various departments,' Reynolds recalls. 'I put him into Labour first and I knew I'd test him there.'

In Reynolds' view, Haughey would not have brought Cowen on: first, he says, because he would have considered him too bright; second, because Cowen was not one of Haughey's people; and third, because Cowen's courage in boldly stating his views on government policies and actions within the parliamentary party would not have endeared him to Haughey. 'Brian was a party man rather than a government man,' says Reynolds.

Cowen's elevation made him the first ever politician from Offaly to hold a senior ministerial position, and the appointment gave his constituency a welcome shot in the arm. At that time, morale was abysmally low in Offaly. Unemployment was high: the midlands were reeling from a range of economic setbacks – such as the closure of the Midland Butter and Bacon plant in 1989 – and there was also a growing uncertainty over the future of the most critical element in the local economy, the peat industry. At the time, local journalist Kevin Farrell suggested that if Edenderry were to be twinned with anywhere then Bosnia was perhaps the most appropriate choice. 'Against the background of low confidence, it is impossible to exaggerate the impact of the appointment of Brian Cowen to Cabinet,' argues Declan McSweeney in his memoir, *A Scribe in Cowen's Country*.

So Cowen's journey home to Clara after the announcement of his appointment was a jubilant event. He was welcomed in the town square by Senator Sean Fallon who, with remarkable foresight, told the gathered crowd: 'I believe it is only a matter of time – maybe fifteen or sixteen years – before Brian Cowen will be returning to Offaly for a much bigger occasion. This man will be coming back to us as Taoiseach.'

There were many emotional scenes that night: it seemed that all the constituents who crowded round to congratulate the new minister wanted to make a point of mentioning how tremendously proud his father Ber would have been to see his son appointed to the cabinet. 'Yes, he would have been very proud,' Cowen would reply.

Even the local political opposition, in the person of Fine Gael councillor Frank Feery, was there to greet him and spoke glowingly to Cowen about his father. Many present on that night can still vividly recall the cheers and the immense pride at seeing one of their own – a man, as the song goes, from 'The Little Town of Clara' – elevated to such an important political position.

Haughey had famously dismissed Reynolds and his supporters as the 'Country and Western wing' of Fianna Fáil. It was a nickname that stuck, particularly because of Reynolds' background in the showband scene. His appearance on Mike Murphy's TV show on RTÉ, *The Live Mike*, when he sang 'Put Your Sweet Lips Closer To The Phone' – while wearing a Stetson – was doubtless also a contributing factor. Reynolds would later recall the TV appearance as being an 'awful' experience. Even today, though, he is dismissive of the tag; he believes it was invented by the likes of Haughey and his people to create a division within the party.

'I never bought into this idea of camps,' says Cowen. He has always seen himself first and foremost as a Fianna Fáil party member, believing that unity and discipline in the party are vital to its future. 'That's necessary so the party can serve the people better – not for any other reason. Creating different factions is not good for the party because it distracts the party from its core mission, which is to serve the people,' says Cowen. 'So, I've never been party to any factions of any description.' Nor does he believe there is any conflict between loyalty to party and loyalty to country.

At the same time, Cowen has always felt that party members should be able to speak out while policy is being formulated rather than automatically toeing the party line. He believes in a competition of ideas, and in testing ideas in debate. But once decisions are taken, he believes, then it is incumbent on each TD to accept that democratic decision. 'You should proceed in a way that doesn't seek to undermine or prolong argument about a decision,' Cowen maintains. 'I'd recognize and respect colleagues with different opinions, but once the discussion is over and the vote is taken, then we close ranks behind that decision and move on. That's the only way in which I believe a political party can effectively operate.'

Cowen recalls that Reynolds – both as a cabinet minister and as Taoiseach – operated an open-door policy for ministers and TDs alike, encouraging backbenchers to go to him to discuss political issues of the day. 'He'd be as helpful as he possibly could,' says Cowen. But while it is a widely held perception that he was Reynolds' protégé, Cowen never saw himself as being taken under the Taoiseach's wing; and while he considered Reynolds a good friend, he certainly didn't expect any special favours. 'Albert had been good to me in many respects, at a personal level, as well as being supportive – as he was to all of his parliamentary colleagues in trying to assist in any way he could,' says Cowen. Reynolds expresses similar sentiments. He says Cowen came to his attention following the death of his father Ber, who was a close friend, but is adamant that there was no favouritism in his promotion to the cabinet. If Cowen had not been good enough, Reynolds says, he simply wouldn't have been appointed. But from the very first day Cowen stepped into the Dáil, Reynolds had kept a careful eye on his performance – both on the ground in Offaly and during debates in the chamber – and had been impressed by his ability to stand up and present an alternative point of view when he didn't agree with something. 'He was a great thinker. His father was a good thinker too, but – I hope I'm not being unfair – Brian was at a different level,' recalls Reynolds. 'His appointment was far from favouritism. It was his ability first and then his loyalty – that's the way I put them. I could see a great future in him.'

It has gone down in political folklore that on being appointed to his first ministerial role Cowen strolled into the Department of Labour unannounced and quietly observed the goings-on there, chatting with one of the members of the cleaning staff to get an inside track on the setup in the department. Cowen maintains that the story is not quite correct, but he does admit that there was a bit of wry humour involved on his part. When he arrived, Cowen was met by a number of assistant secretaries from the department – 'They knew I was coming, obviously' – but not by the most senior member of the staff, the departmental secretary Kevin Bonner. Cowen had been informed that Bonner would be absent owing to a previously scheduled commitment to senior recruitment interviews on that particular day; but he pretended to be surprised that his departmental secretary was not on hand to greet him. So when Bonner arrived back in the department the following morning, he was told: 'The Minister was wondering where you were yesterday.' Sheepishly, he immediately went to Cowen's office to apologize profusely for the breach in decorum. Cowen just smiled and said, 'Sure,

don't worry about it. I knew you couldn't be here anyway.'
Both men then laughed. Recalling the incident, Cowen says:
'It was just a nice icebreaker between us in terms of our
relationship and how we would get on.'

Cowen relished his brief eleven-month stint in the
Department of Labour. Interestingly, his immediate predecessor was the future Taoiseach Bertie Ahern, who had
gone on, as Cowen himself did in due course, to be Minister
for Finance. As labour minister, Cowen was required to focus
primarily on the area of employment – including regulation
and training – and on industrial relations. This involved
spending a great deal of time liaising with FÁS, the
government employment development agency, with leaders
from the trade unions, and with representatives from the business community. In Cowen's view it was a good first ministry
to get, 'because of its overarching responsibilities'. He felt,
too, that his training as a solicitor was a real benefit to him in
taking on the job because he had a comprehensive knowledge
of the law relating to unfair dismissal and other labour-related
matters. 'You get to know leading trade unionists, people
within business, and indeed within the government system
and the industrial relations machinery,' says Cowen. 'You get
to know the various players across the whole industrial field. I
established a lot of good relationships there and learned a lot
about the political system and how it operates.'

One vital relationship that developed during these months
was with Kevin Heffernan, then chairman of the Labour
Court, whose father came from Offaly. Heffernan used to visit
Cowen regularly to keep him 'abreast of things that were
going on down there'. These meetings could sometimes go on
for hours: Cowen recalls long evenings during which they'd
chat about GAA and greyhounds as well as industrial

relations. 'Of course, we'd spend the first hour talking about football! And then we'd get on to the business of the day,' he says.

While Cowen enjoyed this portfolio, it was a testing role in which he encountered a number of difficult situations. This was a time when the economy was in a parlous state, and as a result the volume of strike activity was high. Cowen had to deal with a Post Office strike and a bank strike, as well as a number of industrial relations problems at Waterford Crystal that 'required a lot of handling'.

Between 1988 and 1992 Waterford Crystal had returned losses totalling IR£80 million, and had suffered a serious setback in 1990 when its staff went on strike for fourteen weeks. When Cowen entered the frame, the mood in the company was still tense: staff were being offered a profit-sharing scheme as consolation for compulsory pay cuts of between 7 and 25 per cent. Cowen was on hand to guide the company's management and unions as they attempted to negotiate an industrial relations agreement to turn around the company's fortunes – a process which finally culminated in 1994 with an 'investment and competitiveness' agreement. This focused on modernization and committed the management to making sure that their workforce had access to further training to ensure the company never fell behind in cutting-edge technology; thus Waterford Crystal's survival was ensured.

The nationwide bank strike of 1992 was a particularly difficult dispute to resolve. Memories of the three-week stoppage, initiated by the staff of the four main banks and the Irish Bank Officials Association (IBOA), are still sharp. 'A lot of people would look back on 1992 and see that as having been a totally bitter experience, from the employers' point of view and from the unions' point of view,' says Larry Broderick, the current general secretary of the IBOA. The dispute even divided bank staff, some of whom crossed picket lines and were ejected from their union as a result. 'The original strategy was to expel them. We then decided to take a broader view and said that if the people they had passed in 1992 supported their re-entry then they could come back,' recalls Broderick.

The banks themselves were playing hardball with their staff. In contrast to the 1970s, they were able to continue functioning, albeit in a much reduced fashion, because of ATM machines. This put them in a much stronger position when it came to negotiating with the unions. Fiona Kelly, producer of the RTÉ radio series *Passing the Picket*, believes that the strikes damaged the unions most in the long term. She explains: 'This was around the time that the banks were trying to bring in the so-called yellow-pack workers, which the Irish Bank Officials Association was really against. During the 1992 strike, the banks managed on a skeleton staff. And there was a lot of fall-out from this. Afterwards they were saying, "Well, actually, we managed to run our branches fairly efficiently with less than half our normal numbers." That was quite bad news for the IBOA who lost a lot of members as a result.'

In order to secure a breakthrough in what had become an intractable dispute, Cowen insisted on both parties coming together at the Department of Labour on a bank holiday Monday with no refreshments other than water. 'That concentrated minds a bit,' Cowen later recalled. 'I had both sides there for the final negotiations, and obviously it was difficult but it had come to a point where conditions had been established and it could be solved. We brought them in that day as a reminder that it was time to get this sorted out.'

When he first took up the post, Cowen gave an interview to the *Tullamore Express* in which he emphasized that one of his main priorities would be to examine how best to assist Irish people in finding suitable employment abroad. Soon afterwards, he instructed FÁS to secure work placements in Europe for the growing numbers of economic emigrants. Cowen was frustrated by the fact that many Irish people faced little real choice but to go abroad to find work, and that they often had to take up positions for which they were vastly overqualified. He felt strongly that the government should open offices across Europe, working in collaboration with other training authorities and employment agencies in those countries, to ensure that Irish people were more likely to get jobs suitable to their talents and qualifications. 'I felt it was just a rational, sensible thing to do,' he says.

Speaking in the Dáil on 26 February 1992, Cowen outlined his proposal:

'Too often and for far too long the political system has kept its head stuck in the ground, ostrich-like, and has been afraid to look at the job opportunities available in the European Community. I believe that our young people in particular are as entitled as anyone else in the member states to be in a position to take on board the opportunities that exist in the European labour market. There is good reason to believe that there are prospects for getting European funding for our national placement authority, FÁS, becoming involved in the manpower agencies in Europe. Our young people should have the option to work in Europe. We are putting our heads in the sand if on the one hand we talk about an integrated Europe but are not prepared to look out for the job opportunities that may be available to our people in Europe. We are being inconsistent and illogical. When Monnet and the others set up the European Community their idea was to create the free movement of capital, services and labour.'

Cowen went on: 'We have demographic problems which mean that we are not providing the level of jobs required to deal with the unemployment problem. No government of any political colour could provide an immediate solution to that problem.' It was time, he said, that everybody in the Dáil faced up to that fact; and he pledged that 'as Minister for Labour, I will ensure that whatever alternatives or opportunities are available, either in this country or in Europe, the people who seek job opportunities will be given some options and that we will be fighting for those jobs in the same way as every other member state is fighting for jobs for their people'.

Cowen described his proposal as 'open, honest, politics', acknowledging that the government's obligations to its emigrating citizens did not end when they boarded the plane. He felt a very real sense of responsibility towards those who were leaving the country in search of work, and sought to find the most effective ways of introducing policies which could be of some practical assistance. He knew it would have been easier to abdicate responsibility by saying, 'Right, they're not here any more. We wish them well.' But he viewed this as a 'patronizing attitude' that was simply unacceptable.

As he had anticipated, the proposal was controversial. Cowen was accused by the opposition of promoting emigration and even of encouraging a defeatist attitude. 'There were elements of the opposition who shot it down,' he recalls.

Cowen knew that his proposal would be politically controversial, but – even though he has always enjoyed challenging what he describes as 'stale thinking' – he was surprised by the disingenuous outrage it generated. Nevertheless, he strongly believed his approach was the best one, and was convinced that it was best 'to take on the controversy and . . . ride out the storm' in the interest of those emigrating. Eventually, a system was put in place by FÁS, working with some of the placement agencies, to assist the Irish working in the EU to find work suited to their qualifications. For Cowen, this was the most significant contribution he made during his short tenure in charge of the labour portfolio.

5

Cementing a Political Reputation

The unstable relationship between Fianna Fáil and the Progressive Democrats resulted in the government's collapse in November 1992, a mere nine months after its formation. In retrospect, many would argue that it was a miracle that the two parties managed to maintain a working relationship for even this length of time, as there had been obvious tension from the moment the government was formed.

From his first day in office, Reynolds had faced two particularly contentious issues: first, the tribunal of inquiry into irregularities in the beef industry, set up – at the PDs' behest – to examine what they called the 'unhealthy' relationship between Charles Haughey and beef baron Larry Goodman; and the 'X Case', in which the Attorney-General, Harry Whelehan, refused to grant a fourteen-year-old girl, pregnant as a result of rape, permission to travel abroad for an abortion. Both issues strained relationships between the coalition partners. Reynolds had attempted to find a sensible middleground position on the X Case, but in doing so alienated both the media and the Church. A referendum on abortion was eventually called, but the wording of the proposed change to the constitution caused considerable tension between Fianna Fáil and the Progressive Democrats.

Given these fault-lines in the governing coalition, it seemed that it would be only a matter of time before the government suffered a fatal split. Its death knell eventually came in the shape of the beef tribunal. Reynolds was convinced that since Haughey's resignation he had become the PDs' target. He once told government press secretary Sean Duignan: 'The PDs set up the tribunal to get Charlie. He went down before it really got under way. So now they've decided that I'm the next best thing.' It appeared that Cowen shared this opinion, expressing similar sentiments – if somewhat more robustly – during another conversation with Duignan: 'The PDs have already seen off a Fianna Fáil Taoiseach, Tánaiste and Minister for Defence. They are now trying to bring down Albert. Well, they can shag off.'

At the tribunal, the PDs' leader Desmond O'Malley criticized Reynolds, in his former capacity as Minister for Industry and Commerce, for his action over an export credit scheme, describing it as 'wrong . . . grossly unwise, reckless and foolish'. This prompted an irate Reynolds to refer to O'Malley's testimony as 'reckless, irresponsible and dishonest'. On 4 November 1992 – one day after Reynolds celebrated his sixtieth birthday – an enraged PD leader called a news conference in the Montclare Hotel to announce his party's decision to pull out of government.

The ensuing general election was a disaster for Fianna Fáil. After a short campaign, which coincided with the abortion referendum, Fianna Fáil won just 67 seats out of a total of 166 – representing a loss of ten TDs. The party's manifesto was reasonably good, but the electorate lacked enthusiasm, as Reynolds realized when he made a visit to Kerry on the campaign trail and not a single person turned up to see him. Several of Fianna Fáil's cabinet ministers, fearing a backlash from the electorate, focused their attention on their own constituencies, rather than canvassing with the Taoiseach. Worse still, there was a profoundly defeatist mood in the Fianna Fáil camp, with cabinet ministers actually declining media interviews in order to avoid having to defend their party's record in government under Reynolds. Cowen was stunned when he discovered that some of his colleagues were shirking their responsibility to the party in this way, and immediately contacted the party press office about the situation. 'He offered to go on television and radio, anywhere, any time, to defend his leader and try to put the party's election manifesto across,' points out Stephen Collins in *The Power Game*.

In the event, Fianna Fáil could consider themselves lucky to have won enough seats to put them in a position to negotiate with Labour, who had won an unprecedented thirty-two seats, to form a government, thus banishing the PDs to the opposition benches. Reynolds decided to give Cowen the responsibility, along with Bertie Ahern and Noel Dempsey, for the negotiations; their counterparts on the Labour side were Ruairi Quinn, Brendan Howlin and Mervyn Taylor. Neither Reynolds nor the Labour leader Dick Spring was directly involved. From the outset Labour were impressed with Fianna Fáil's declaration that any coalition between them would be a 'partnership', a phrase used despite some internal unease and talk in some quarters of preferring opposition to working with Labour.

The government was finally formed on 12 January 1993 – but it was not long before tensions between the two parties emerged. While no one in particular could be blamed for this, there was a general feeling that there was a 'job for the boys' approach on Labour's part, with relatives and friends of politicians being appointed to key government positions. Commenting on this, Cowen was reported as saying: 'Jaze, lads, ye're giving us an awful bad name.'

Indeed, Cowen appeared disposed to remind Labour of his disapproval at every opportunity. Pat Rabbitte, who would eventually become leader of the Labour Party, recalls Cowen getting a good jab at them in the Dáil, on a day when Tánaiste Dick Spring – commonly referred to at that time as Labour's 'conscience' – was due to be flying back from the US in time to close the debate on behalf of the government. 'Labour deputy Sean Ryan was addressing the House and a far-from-happy-looking Brian Cowen, as a front-bench spokesman, was on the Fianna Fáil bench, and having great difficulty containing himself,' recalls Rabbitte in *Tales from the Bar Dáil* by Ted Nealon. 'He finally muttered something to Deputy Ryan to the effect that the Labour Party was once again struggling with its conscience, to which Ryan, wisely or unwisely, replied: "Well, at least we have a conscience."

'Cowen looked at his watch and said: "Oh yeah! What time is it landing?"'

Now, in the new administration with Labour, Reynolds expanded Cowen's brief by putting him in charge of the newly formed Department of Transport, Energy and Communications. Reynolds, who as Minister for Posts and Telegraphs had modernized the telephone communication network throughout Ireland, had decided to bring the three related sectors together because he felt they all needed a dramatic shake-up. This change brought together, under one department, all of the semi-state enterprises – most of them, in effect, monopolies – that had been established by de

Valera's government in key sectors of the national infra-structure, such as transport, energy and communication, as well as in larger-scale industries. As a result Cowen had to deal with a whole string of such bodies, including CIE, Aer Lingus, Aer Rianta, TEAM Aer Lingus, the Electricity Supply Board (ESB), Bord Gáis, Bord na Móna, Telecom Éireann and An Post. 'It was a huge department in that respect,' says Cowen. 'Much of that end of the economy was in the state sector, in what we called the semi-state sector. They had a sort of commercial mandate but they also had social objectives as well, initially when they were formed.'

Reynolds believes that Cowen's new job was a difficult but very enriching cabinet position – and that it helped form Cowen into the politician he is today. 'I had worked those three departments myself and I knew that there was a lot of experience to be got there. It needed a worker and a fella who wasn't afraid to make decisions to try and lift it from where it was, because it needed to be lifted. That's why I picked Brian,' states Reynolds. 'He had to be able to take on such different jobs. That's the way you get tested.'

Cowen came into his new department at a difficult moment of transition. Ireland was in the aftermath of a recession. Personal tax rates and unemployment were still high. EU directives were starting to come into play which required Ireland to open up the economy to competition – with far-reaching repercussions for the semi-state enterprises now in Cowen's ambit, for his first major task was to explore how to transform these entities into commercially competitive enter-prises operating within the context of EU law. For Cowen, it was all about striving for more efficient, more effective, more transparent pricing mechanisms. Coming from a constituency where the semi-state sector – particularly the ESB and Bord na Mona – had traditionally made a major contribution over the years, he had the advantage of understanding the ethos of these sectors from a grassroots perspective. But he also knew that living in the past was not an option: working practices had to change, and 'good, innovative managers' had to be appointed, in all these companies, in order to see through the necessary EU competition changes.

At the same time, Cowen was deeply involved in implementing the recommendations of the Culliton Report. The previous Fianna Fáil–Progressive Democrat administration had commissioned Jim Culliton, a prominent businessman, to draw up proposals for a new industrial policy for the country. Culliton's report set out a very ambitious plan for opening up all of the economy to competition, in the hope that this would lead to greater efficiency and increase economic activity in the country. A task force was established to begin implementing the Culliton Report, under the chairmanship of Dr P. J. Moriarty, a former chief executive of the ESB; Labour's Ruairi Quinn and Cowen met with top officials every week to discuss its progress. Cowen feels that many of the developments now taking place – such as the Telecom Éireann employee shareholding scheme – represent the benefits of putting the Culliton Report into practice: essentially, moving away from state monopoly to commercial business, resulting in a more competitive environment.

Cowen also spent a great deal of his time during this period dealing with aviation issues. The exorbitant pricing of tickets on the Dublin–London route, monopolized by Aer Lingus and British Airways, needed to be tackled; Ryanair was beginning to emerge as a serious player. But the first and most pressing issue demanding his attention as soon as he took up the post was the financial crisis at Aer Lingus. The

Department of Transport had been traditionally regarded as the downtown office of Aer Lingus. 'And that had to change because they were in deep trouble,' says Cowen. To help rectify the situation, he appointed the highly respected businessman Bernie Cahill, who had led the sugar group Greencore, as executive chairman with specific instructions to introduce new strategy with senior management colleagues. Soon afterwards, the Cahill Plan emerged. Cowen helped Cahill implement the report, with weekly meetings to discuss progress. These meetings between Cahill and Cowen took place early in the mornings, prior to cabinet meetings, so that Cowen had the up-to-date position on any relevant issue that might arise at Cabinet. After his tragic death in a boating accident in Cork in 2001, Cahill was described by the Aer Lingus group's chief executive John O'Donovan as a person of 'unparalleled business acumen' who had made an immense contribution to the restructuring and survival of the national airline. The then Taoiseach Bertie Ahern said that Cahill had made 'an important contribution to the Irish economy'.

Cowen felt it was vital to open Dublin airport up to private investment, rather than allowing Aer Rianta to have a monopoly in all types of commercial development there. He therefore introduced a policy on airport development that brought in more players, including private sector investment, to create more jobs and other aviation-related facilities. While the implementation of this policy faced a series of crises and difficulties, Cowen says he likes trying to solve problems and approaches them in as 'determined but rational a way as possible, to get the job done'.

Cowen's period in charge of transport also coincided with a looming crisis at Aer Lingus's aircraft maintenance subsidiary, TEAM Aer Lingus. He had a tough time negotiating a complex and far-reaching productivity agreement that had to be implemented in order to ensure the national airline's survival. Cowen spent months working on conciliation talks and bilateral discussions between management and unions. He was adamant that the issue could be resolved if all parties would agree to the settlement terms put forward by the Labour Relations Commission. Speaking in the Dáil on 23 June 1994, Cowen said that the government's motivation was to maintain employment in TEAM Aer Lingus and 'not to precipitate a crisis but to avert it'. He continued with an unflinching outline of the problem:

'Let me reiterate the facts and how they can be confronted to the mutual benefit of all parties to this dispute. The first is that TEAM Aer Lingus is grossly uncompetitive, which is accepted by all parties to the dispute. The company's unit costs are too high in relation to its competitors and that is why it has run out of work and money. Unit costs are a function of wage costs and output and must be tackled if TEAM is to survive, let alone prosper. Everybody involved who has commented on the TEAM crisis accepts this. As I already stated in this House, it is my wish and that of the Government that not alone should TEAM survive, it should also prosper. To do so it must tackle costs and boost output by increasing its market share through new business. The core of the present impasse is in what order these should be tackled. Here again, we must be guided by the facts.'

These facts were daunting. TEAM Aer Lingus had virtually run out of cash: its bills and wages were being subsidized by the national airline, Aer Lingus. It was losing over IR£1 million every month, a figure Cowen feared would rise even further as the market for aircraft maintenance went into its usual seasonal decline. 'The inescapable logic of this is that wage costs must be tackled now, if the company is to survive,' he argued strongly at the time. 'Another factor which must be addressed is the seasonality of the business . . . Its competitors have not just recognized that fact but geared their production and working schedules accordingly. TEAM must do so also if it is to survive.'

While Cowen had many astute ideas on how to develop the company, he stressed that 'no one person or group has a monopoly on good ideas' and that he wanted 'all ideas examined'; this included having those put forward by TEAM Aer Lingus workers 'thoroughly examined and professionally assessed'. Cowen believed that the workers themselves, who together held the majority of the company's shares, should take a substantial part in the dialogue about how the company could make itself commercially viable. 'This is, and always will be, my general approach,' Cowen pointed out at the time.

Cowen was also conscious that any resolution of the crisis would have to satisfy the European Commission. Thus it would be vital to demonstrate that all equity injections into the Aer Lingus group would 'not alone yield the cost savings specified but will also ensure the future viability of the group'.

According to Sean Duignan, Cowen was at loggerheads with his Labour colleague Ruairi Quinn over the Aer Lingus problems. 'It was a difficult time for the Labour Party on that issue. But, in fairness, we adopted the plan. It was my job to put it through,' admits Cowen. In fact, Cowen was invited by the Labour Party to attend one of their parliamentary meetings to explain the details of the Cahill Plan. So when Quinn apparently took it upon himself, without prior consultation with Cowen, to launch an initiative to start fresh talks between the TEAM parties, Cowen is alleged to have been 'absolutely livid'. 'Says he'll resign if Quinn is allowed to get away with it,' Duignan wrote in his diary. Again, when the giant multi-national Cable & Wireless attempted to buy a substantial percentage of Telecom Éireann, Duignan recalls Cowen not being able to 'hide his fury' at Labour's attempt to block the deal.

Cowen, however, dismisses the suggestion that there was any tension and maintains that there were simply the 'normal discussions' in cabinet over the Cable & Wireless situation. Reynolds agrees with Cowen's assessment of the situation: 'I'm not so sure that it was tension. In fact, it didn't come across to me as a tension. There was a bad relationship in the unions and Aer Lingus at the time. Brian was there and the negoti-ations weren't going that well and, of course, Quinn was taking the other side – the trade union movement's. There was a conflict there. I knew there were problems there that had to be sorted out and Brian took a tough line.' After the negoti-ations, Reynolds would occasionally be approached by some of the trade union officials, several of whom commented that Cowen was very tough during the talks. Reynolds would always respond, 'The guy is fair and he's honest and he's not out to do you or anybody else – he's out to do his job. If he finds people straight, he'll be straight with them. That's the way he wants it and I can't say anything against him for that.'

Cowen is not the type of individual to hold political grudges. There might be robust exchanges in the heat of the moment, but he takes a pragmatic perspective. 'I never had any ill feeling towards anyone in any of these operations. Quite the contrary, I saw my job as trying to work with them. I'm a great believer in established process, on the basis that everyone is coming to the table to solve the problem, not to use the process as a means of avoiding the problem. That's a dis-tinction I would continue to make in respect of all my approaches to any of these issues,' says Cowen. 'I believed in giving credit where it was due and backing those who had worked hard or had brought things to a point which was sufficient to save the company and, at the same time, recognized that more work would need to be done going forward from there. That's always the best type of approach to take. I was never ideological in that sense.'

The TEAM Aer Lingus saga reached crisis point when Cowen considered the possibility of employing an examiner, as he was beginning to feel that the best solution was to look at receivership or liquidation for the ailing company, rather than to see the whole enterprise go to the wall. He recalls with appreciation the input at this crucial moment of Philip Flynn – former vice-president of Sinn Féin, trade unionist, industrial relations consultant, government adviser and financier:

'That was in line to happen in TEAM Aer Lingus and we were waiting for the results of a ballot from the craft unions and there was no sign of it coming. And there was a cabinet sub-committee waiting to hear what it was saying. We had a few colourful conversations at that time with those who were withholding the information, but we finally got it and we made our decision. There was a bit of a battle with that, but, in fairness, everyone knew it was the only option we had. When they came to a conclusion through that process out in the Marino Institute under the chairmanship of Phil Flynn, I very much backed that outcome and then it was up to management to build on it for the future in terms of what further efficiencies they might want to grant. Having got that process completed, management were trying to pocket that and then say, "OK, we've got this far, now we want more." And I said, "Hold on a minute. Others have helped to broker this deal. You've got to live with it now and manage the thing going forward and achieve further efficiencies as you go along." So, I very much backed Phil Flynn's ultimate position on that,' recalls Cowen. 'It wouldn't have been solved without Phil Flynn's astute chairmanship of the talks on TEAM Aer Lingus. He was a very talented guy.'

The 'Shannon stopover' was another contentious issue for Cowen. At the time, the United States–Ireland bilateral air services agreement required that air carriers between the two countries provide capacity into Shannon. 'In other words,' explains Cowen, 'every transatlantic flight had to stop off at Shannon airport. They couldn't fly direct.' The rule – which stemmed from the days when aircraft had a shorter range and could not fly so far as Dublin from America – was draining Aer Lingus's coffers. The general view at the time was that the Irish government would not get US agreement to any change in this provision without great difficulty; but from the Irish viewpoint change was imperative. 'Modifying the Shannon stopover was part of the survival plan for Aer Lingus at the time,' says Cowen.

Reynolds rang Cowen out of the blue one day in 1993 and said, 'You better go over to Washington and meet the Transportation Secretary there and sort this out.'

Cowen accepted the instruction without demur and simply asked, 'When do I go?'

'You can go over there tomorrow or the next day. Ring Dermot Gallagher, our ambassador, and he'll get you in,' Reynolds said.

Cowen immediately rang Gallagher and was assured that he would get the visiting minister in to see the Transportation Secretary. 'He had an excellent network in there in terms of how well the Irish could access the US government. It was quite amazing. It was the envy of every other embassy in Washington, I would say,' says Cowen. This was the same year in which Reynolds had made his first St Patrick's Day visit to meet Bill Clinton, who stated: 'I'm not only a friend of Ireland for one day of the year – I'm a friend of Ireland for 365 days of the year.'

The Department of Transportation delegation had headed over some days earlier to try to negotiate a new bilateral air transport agreement. They were finding it very difficult to make headway with their US counterparts, who were insisting on operating an open skies policy regardless of Irish requirements. Cowen was becoming increasingly exasperated by how everybody seemed to be dismissing out of hand the possibility of a new agreement. It appeared to him that some thought changing the stopover would mean the end of everything at Shannon. He even remembers one person saying to him, 'There would be rabbits on the runways at Rynanna' – the area where Shannon airport is located.

When Cowen arrived in Washington he met with his American counterpart, the Transportation Secretary Federico Peña. A Mexican migrant, Peña had become the first Hispanic mayor of Denver, Colorado, where he had been involved in building a large airport, before becoming a member of President Clinton's cabinet. Cowen suspected that his American counterpart would be particularly understanding about the Shannon dilemma considering that he had an Irish-born wife; and he brought this fact up as an icebreaker before getting down to the business at hand.

'Federico, I think we should try and solve this problem ourselves,' Cowen stated.

'Well, we've a very difficult issue,' replied the American.

'I know it's a very difficult issue, but we have to solve it because I'm convinced that if we don't solve it, our bosses are going to solve it. And we won't look very well. This will be so important from all points of view that I can see the Taoiseach ringing the President of the United States on this issue. Shannon Airport mightn't be much on your radar, but it's very much on our radar. We want to come to an arrangement that doesn't mean that all the planes have to land there. Keep some of its business. If you were Mayor of Denver still and your Democratic Party had disaffiliated from you, you'd regard it as a serious issue to deal with.'

'Yes, that's true. I would,' Peña conceded.

Cowen replied, 'That's what's happened with us. The Fianna Fáil party executives down there are pretty riled up about this – and they are riled up for the reason that they are worried about Shannon being taking out of the equation altogether. We are not going to take Shannon out of the equation but they are worried that we would. That's the problem we have, so let's solve it.'

The two men eventually agreed on relaxing the regulations on a 'one-for-one' basis, with transatlantic flights split equally between the airports in Dublin and Shannon. 'For every direct flight to Dublin, there would be one flight landing in Shannon,' explains Cowen. Both he and Peña knew that this could be no more than a transitional arrangement, but at least it provided the Irish government with a solution for the immediate future that would help Aer Lingus financially. And, more importantly, it ensured that Shannon airport was not completely bypassed. Cowen was delighted that he'd persuaded Peña to come to this political agreement, which he knew would impress Reynolds.

The two men then both went back into the full negotiations, which were getting heated by this stage, and told the delegations what they had agreed as a basis for a resolution of the problem that could pave the way to an agreement. 'And we sorted it out. But it was just another indication of how the political dynamic can work,' recalls Cowen.

The agreement caused considerable controversy back home. Síle de Valera – the granddaughter of Fianna Fáil's founder Eamon de Valera – resigned from the parliamentary party in 1993 because of the change to the 'stopover' policy. However, she eventually came back into the fold the following year, only finally to step down in 2006.

Cowen also had to take a tough line with Telecom Éireann, which was IR£800 million in debt at the time. He brought in a former director of operations at British Telecom, Alfie Kane, to resuscitate the ailing company with new ideas and a fresh outlook. More innovation followed: 'Just before I left office, we were already in the process of being about to provide the first mobile telephone operator outside of Telecom Éireann itself. Ultimately, that happened in Michael Lowry's time. There've been a number of others since. So, in all the areas I was dealing with there were a lot of changes. I remember giving a fixed–line licence to a young man named Denis O'Brien at that time. The idea that someone else other than Telecom Éireann would have a licence was regarded by some as revolutionary – old thinking dies hard. Now you see all the mobile phone operators that we have. It shows you how much the country has changed in a short period of time,' says Cowen.

Similar structural changes were implemented at the ESB, where the company, the trade unions and Cowen's department together undertook a cost and competitiveness review to drive costs down in relation to energy. The reorganization of the ESB that is under way today was in the early stages of development in Cowen's time.

*

As Minister for Energy, Cowen was in charge of mining licences. In October 1994 it was discovered that he held shares in Arcon Resources, to which he was in the process of granting a licence for a lead and zinc mine at Galmoy, County Kilkenny. Apparently, Cowen only discovered this fact when he was approached by a reporter from the *Sunday Business Post*, who raised the potential conflict of interest and told him he had shares in the company. 'God! Have I?' was his response.

In 1990 Cowen had purchased one thousand shares in a company called Conroy Petroleum at a cost of IR£960; this company had since been taken over by Arcon. It was a potentially embarrassing situation for Cowen, who immediately sold off his shares at a loss, recouping only IR£430. Cowen then confessed his error to Reynolds, who accepted that he had done nothing untoward. Cowen had not technically violated cabinet guidelines and so could not have been sacked from the government in consequence – as was being wrongly suggested in some quarters, particularly in parts of the opposition and the media. A similar incident had occurred involving a TD of another party eleven years previously, and now the opposition, smelling blood in Cowen's case, attempted to censure the minister; but they failed to create a 'Cowengate' scandal. Some thought Cowen got off lightly when Reynolds suggested that an apology to the Dáil should suffice. 'I am genuinely sorry,' he said, 'that an oversight on my part in failing to link, however inadvertently, a nominal shareholding in the then Conroy Petroleum and Exploration Company, with a possible perception of a future conflict of interest in dealing with a mining application by Arcon, should be a source of some embarrassment to me or my colleagues.'

It was noted that Cowen's apology was a typical piece of political rhetoric, particularly in referring to his error as giving rise to a 'possible perception'. The opposition also noted that Cowen did not apologize directly for creating a conflict of interest, but only for causing his colleagues 'some embarrassment'. Later, in the Dáil bar, some opposition TDs could be heard muttering that it seemed implausible that Cowen could have simply forgotten that he owned shares worth almost IR£1,000.

At the time, Cowen was appalled by the suggestion that he would do anything untoward on the basis of a commercial shareholding. He was also annoyed that he had left himself open to an unnecessary political attack. In retrospect, he freely admits that he could have offloaded the shareholding when he assumed office. 'You could hold shares – under a certain amount – but the concern was that I hadn't indicated publicly that I had these shares. I think the point was there and a controversy arose over it. Obviously, if you are Minister for Energy it is not clever to have any shares because of the perception that it creates of you having an interest to protect. I was actually losing money on these shares,' he recalls.

The furore quickly died down. However, four months later, in February 1995, when Fine Gael's Phil Hogan – who had sought Cowen's political scalp over the Arcon shares question – found himself in the spotlight, it was noticeable that Cowen in turn pursued him with a vengeance. Hogan was at that point Minister of State for Finance, and found himself under fire when on budget day his press secretary inadvertently faxed an internal confidential briefing on the budget out to the national newspapers, mistakenly thinking that it was a press release. This error came at a time when several leaks of budget details had already been made by parties associated with the government (Fine Gael, Labour and the Democratic Left). 'It was a breathtaking exercise in irresponsibility, as each party jostled to claim credit for various parts of the impending budget,' wrote Gene Kerrigan and Pat Brennan in their book *This Great Little Nation*.

Already exasperated by the budget leaks, Fianna Fáil decided to attack Hogan by accusing him of creating them. After all, his internal memo – complete with his contact details on each page of the faxes sent out to the newsrooms – was the only proof of information actually being leaked. Hogan's defence that his secretary had simply sent out the wrong document to the press fell on deaf ears. After suffering Hogan's attack the previous year, it was now Cowen's turn to put the metaphorical boot in. 'He has to go,' stated Cowen. 'Wrongdoing has been established.'

The next day Hogan went into the Dáil and apologized profusely. He admitted that the error was his fault and not his press secretary's, because he had not made clear which document was a press release and which was the internal memo for his government colleagues. He was in a rush to get to the Dáil chamber, he explained. But plausible though this excuse sounded, the opposition had no intention of accepting it; apparently realizing this, Hogan dramatically – and somewhat unexpectedly – resigned his government position. There was complete silence in the chamber when Hogan announced his decision. Cowen himself felt genuinely sorry for him, and later that night some Fianna Fáil backbenchers could be heard in the Dáil bar muttering their admiration for the former minister. Even Bertie Ahern stated that Hogan was an honourable man who had, unfortunately, become the fall guy for colleagues who were leaking information.

*

Reynolds' government fell in cruel circumstances. Less than a year after his crowning achievement of signing the joint Downing Street Declaration with Prime Minister John Major in London on 15 December 1993, he resigned. Tension had been growing between Reynolds and Dick Spring, who had threatened to pull Labour out of the coalition if anything negative was printed about Reynolds in the report of the beef tribunal. When the report was published in July 1994 Reynolds was vindicated; but his wish that this should be immediately reported in the media caused more friction between him and Spring – friction that never eased. The previous month, disagreement between Fianna Fáil and Labour had erupted over certain financial matters, including an amnesty for tax evaders and a complex addition to a Finance Bill that was due to be published. Also in June, the results of two by-elections meant that a new government could be formed without Fianna Fáil's participation, which made it considerably easier for Labour to pull out of the coalition with a possible view to doing a deal with the opposition to form a new administration.

There was some consolation for Reynolds when the IRA called a complete ceasefire on 31 August 1994. It was a moment to rejoice for Reynolds, who had declared that Northern Ireland was to be his number one priority in government. Unfortunately, the rejoicing was not to last long. Reynolds had decided to appoint Attorney-General Harry Whelehan president of the High Court. When it later emerged that Whelehan had mishandled an attempt to extradite a paedophile priest, Father Brendan Smyth, Spring dramatically led his ministers out of a cabinet meeting to discuss their next step. Optimistically, Reynolds felt that a deal could be brokered; in the event, he was forced to go before the Dáil to submit a grovelling apology. 'He [Reynolds] finally delivered the speech in a robot-like monotone, apologizing to Dick, saying he would not have appointed Harry if he knew then what he knew now,' recalls Sean Duignan. 'Then he had to watch Dick with the air of a condemned man staring at the executioner's hand on the switch.'

It was not enough, and Spring pulled his party out of the coalition – ultimately forcing Reynolds, on 17 November, to resign as Taoiseach and leader of Fianna Fáil. Cowen went in to see Reynolds, who said, pointing to the Taoiseach's seat, 'I'm leaving this office – but I hope to return some day to this building to see you in this chair.' A Fianna Fáil press secretary then walked in to explain that somebody was urgently needed to appear on RTÉ television's *Prime Time* programme. 'I'll do it,' Cowen volunteered. He was the only member of the cabinet who agreed to take part. Afterwards, he cut a forlorn figure as he joined Sean Duignan in the latter's office for 'a couple of jars' over 'a few yarns' to help them drown their sorrows.

Cowen recalls the morning when Reynolds handed in his resignation. 'It was an emotional time for the family and I shared their upset about it, but I did not burst into tears, as has been reported in the past,' he points out. 'I empathized with the family.'

Duignan remembers the atmosphere afterwards being almost akin to that of an Irish wake. 'Tea and sympathy were dispensed in the Taoiseach's dining room, which took on the appearance of an executive funeral parlour as Kathleen Reynolds and her daughters, Cathy, Leone, Emer and Andrea, patiently listened to the condolences of a long line of friends of the famiglia,' he says.

Cowen might have felt genuinely sorry to see Reynolds, who had treated him almost like a son, end his tenure as

Taoiseach before it had even really begun. But mostly he was frustrated by being in opposition: he wanted Fianna Fáil to be in power. 'It was a pity that that government came to a conclusion the way it did, really. It was a government that was achieving a lot of things and, unfortunately, the whole affair that came out of the Attorney-General's office at that time brought it to an end.'

A committee chaired by Danny Wallace TD looked into the circumstances regarding the collapse of the Fianna Fáil–Labour coalition government. Interestingly, many of those called in to make statements to that committee were cross-examined, but Cowen never was. He says he stands by the statement he made to the committee 'to this day' as an accurate chronological account of that government's demise.

Fianna Fáil returned to the back benches with Bertie Ahern appointed as the party's new leader. During the next three years in opposition, as the 'rainbow coalition' headed by Fine Gael ran the country, Cowen was spokesperson first for agriculture and then for health, replacing the Galway-based TD Máire Geoghegan-Quinn, who had decided not to stand in the next general election. His reputation as a debater increased considerably during his time in opposition as he consistently and ruthlessly attacked the rainbow coalition's policies. It seemed that every time Fianna Fáil needed a champion in the Dáil they would call on Cowen. As Maol Muire Tynan stated in the *Irish Times* a couple of years later, 'His reputation as the paratrooper who takes no prisoners is fortified in every Dáil altercation that comes his way.'

Despite the fact that he was no longer a minister, Cowen decided against going back into legal practice – even though he would have been perfectly entitled to double up as a lawyer and TD now that his party was in opposition. 'I was determined to help the new leader Bertie Ahern, and that meant working full-time with my colleagues as we tried to rebuild the party and position ourselves for a return to power,' Cowen remembers.

For the first two and a half years of this period Cowen was Fianna Fáil's opposition spokesperson for agriculture. Cowen was happy to take the brief as another string to his bow; but also, more importantly, it was a role in which he could instantly feel at home, given his family background in farming – his grandfather was a cattle dealer and his father a butcher; and his father, moreover, had formerly been a minister of state in the Department of Agriculture, albeit for only eight months in a short-lived administration under Haughey.

In the mid-1990s, when Cowen held this portfolio, agriculture and consumer issues were coming to the forefront of many Dáil debates. This was a period when policy reform – such as the introduction of rural development programmes and rural environmental protection schemes – loomed large for the farming community. Today, Cowen feels that there are still huge challenges facing the Irish agricultural community, particularly in terms of the changes under way in world agriculture and the growing concerns over food security. He believes that it is vital to the future of Irish agriculture that it emphasizes its basis in the country's grasslands and continues to provide wholesome and high-quality food.

6

'Angola'

Fianna Fáil returned to power in 1997 after winning a general election in which Fine Gael failed to impress the voters with John Bruton's slogan, 'If it ain't broke, don't fix it.' The incoming Taoiseach, Bertie Ahern, offered Cowen the post of Minister for Health and Children. Cowen knew he was taking on a difficult task – particularly considering that all previous health ministers since Fine Gael's Michael Noonan had been deemed failures during their terms of office. However, Cowen's political ambitions made it impossible for him to turn down such a high-profile cabinet position, albeit perhaps the most challenging of all.

At this time, the health department faced pressure on a number of fronts, including a dramatic shortage of hospital beds, a looming nurses' strike and the controversy surrounding the report of the Finlay tribunal, appointed to investigate an episode in which over a thousand women had been infected with the hepatitis C virus during the late 1970s following use of a contaminated blood product. Prior to Fianna Fáil's return to power, the Fine Gael-led government had refused to publish the tribunal's report, claiming that it couldn't be done for legal reasons. While in opposition, Cowen had mounted a very strong argument during a Dáil debate as to why the report needed to be brought out into the public domain and vowed to publish it immediately if his party won the forthcoming general election. Now, on taking over the health portfolio, he straight away did so.

Cowen's time at Health was not without its own controversies – beginning with his idiosyncratic description of his department. The health portfolio has been described in many negative phrases, 'poisoned chalice' being the most popular. But Cowen came up with a new one that raised some eyebrows when he described it as being akin to Angola. 'The Angola reference is often misinterpreted,' says Cowen. He insists that he wasn't attempting to refer to the health system as being of a third world standard, which was how the comment was originally perceived. Instead, he was trying to convey his sense of how often a sudden urgent problem could blow up unforeseen at the end of a week grappling with complex problems. He would be heading for the lift to go home on a Friday night and suddenly some official would emerge and say, 'Minister, can we see you for a minute?' 'At that time the late Princess Diana was involved in the anti-landmine campaign – and it reminded me of Angola, where you could step on a landmine, very quickly; suddenly, out of nowhere, despite your best efforts, something would come from left field – and that was the nature of the department. It was really a reference to that kind of issue that can suddenly pop up like a landmine, and that requires a lot of political acumen to deal with,' he explains. 'It warned me in the future not to be humorous to journalists if they don't take your sense of humour!'

Cowen also came under attack for smoking cigarettes – apparently he is the only member of the cabinet to do so

– while holding the position of Minister for Health. Occasionally, when Cowen was having a puff on a cigarette and a passer-by would comment on the irony of seeing the health minister 'setting a bad example', he would good-humouredly retort: 'I didn't ask for this job! You get the jobs you get.' Besides, as Cowen later explained in an interview with *Hot Press*, he didn't smoke very much: he described himself as a casual smoker who would 'only smoke now and again when I have a drink or something'. He did not, he emphasized, get up in the morning with the need to get dressed quickly and dash out of the house to buy cigarettes in order to feed a nicotine craving. 'I might spend a month not smoking and then have a few – that sort of thing. So, I am not a heavy or a constant smoker at all. But certainly, when I was Minister for Health, I reduced my level of smoking to practically nil. So, I was conscious of that at the time. I probably should give them up completely, but there are some temptations that I just can't avoid – from time to time.'

Cowen felt that the criticism of his smoking was an example of a 'politically correct' culture that has become somewhat overbearing. He fears that this culture is threatening to take the sense of individuality and character from politics, a trend which he believes doesn't serve politics well. 'We need characters, we need people that have a bit of colour, a bit of difference. I am not saying that I am the best example of that – but I think that at the end of the day, our politicians have to reflect our people and I think our people are a diverse, colourful lot,' he argues.

Cowen had only just taken up the health portfolio when he faced his first major political controversy. He came under fire for his decision not to release the findings of a IR£100,000

study carried out by Trinity College's sociology department –
at the behest of, and with funding from, the government – on
how best to handle the contentious issue of Irishwomen
travelling across to the UK mainland to get abortions. The
then Democratic Left TD Liz McManus, who later became
deputy leader of the Labour Party when the two parties
merged, was foremost among Cowen's critics. 'Brian Cowen is
like one of those busybodies who go into libraries and tear
pages out of books which they think are unsuitable for the
public,' she told the press. McManus, a consistent campaigner
on feminist issues, argued that the report was public property
and should have been released. She reckoned that the government felt the details of the report were simply too hot to
handle. She argued further that – having passed a law giving
women the right to acquire information on abortion – the government, and Cowen in particular, was now preventing this
information from being published.

Various theories circulated about Cowen's reluctance to
publish the report. It was suggested in the *Irish Times* on 7
February 1998 that Cowen feared its contents would generate
a public outcry. Others suggested that acting on the report
would have required financial or social action that the government was not prepared to take for fear of a backlash from the
electorate. It was also argued that the government wanted to
put the contentious issue on the proverbial long finger –
preferably until after the next election – in an effort not
to alienate voters. Whatever the precise reasons were in
reality, it was clear that the report contained information
that the government didn't want out in the public domain.
So, instead of publishing the report, Cowen eventually re-
directed it to a cabinet sub-committee and to the all-party
committee on the constitution. In doing so, he ensured

that the abortion issue would drag on for some time to come.

Cowen had been at the helm of the health department for little more than a year when the opposition were seeking his resignation. In May 1999 the Labour Party's conference made the national news when its members called on Cowen to step down with immediate effect, arguing that 'despite the increased resources available to him, the health services under his watch are stretched to breaking point'. However, even Labour members acknowledged during the conference that Cowen was a highly intelligent man and 'in many ways' very compassionate, compliments not usually heard during calls for a minister's resignation.

Even though Cowen would later state that he 'enjoyed his time in health', it was widely perceived that he was simply putting on a brave face as he stoically dealt with crisis after crisis. It was reported – inaccurately, it must be stressed – that he even considered the prospect of leaving the high-pressure ministerial post (and thus, in all probability, losing the chance of any future senior government position) by letting it be known within party circles that he would be interested in becoming Ireland's next European Commissioner: a prestigious position, certainly, but one that has yet to advance a politician's career at cabinet level. 'It wouldn't be right to say that I didn't show any interest in the position, but I wasn't going around looking for the job. There were a number of people being mentioned in the media. There's no harm being mentioned in dispatches but it doesn't mean you are looking for the job,' Cowen recalls.

Ahern met individually with each of his cabinet ministers to gauge their thoughts on who should be nominated to this important post, and the general consensus appeared to be that Cowen and Máire Geoghegan-Quinn were the favourite candidates: the majority of ministers agreed that one or the other would be the most appropriate choice, despite the risk of losing a by-election in the process. Ahern even went as far as sounding out which candidate would be preferred by the incoming EU Commission President, Romano Prodi, who stated that either would be acceptable. But Ahern also suggested, unbeknown to his cabinet, a third option for the post: the Attorney-General, David Byrne SC. Again, Prodi agreed that he too would be an excellent choice; and, despite having little experience of working within the EU admin-istration, he was selected as the nominee, to widespread surprise and indeed disapproval from cabinet ministers who objected to having been kept in the dark.

In opting for Byrne, Ahern was perhaps wisely avoiding the risk of losing a by-election that would follow the nomination of a serving minister. His choice also brought the Progressive Democrats' Michael McDowell into the political spotlight as the new Attorney-General: an appointment widely explained in terms of cementing the commitment of the PDs to the governing coalition, ensuring that it would serve its full term.

The newspapers had speculated that Cowen was privately 'cheesed off' by losing out on the job – as too was Geoghegan-Quinn, who had become the favourite in the press reports. Reflecting on the episode today, Cowen is adamant that he never canvassed for the position and in fact would have politely turned it down had it been offered to him.

Shortly after this, Cowen came under fire again on the abortion question, accused of blatantly sidestepping the contentious issue. After two and a half years of consultation, Cowen was heavily criticized for opting simply to publish a green paper on abortion that would then go on to sub-committees for further discussion, rather than, as had been hoped, to go ahead with a referendum. Political commentators argued that such procrastination was designed to ensure that the government would not be in a position to go to the electorate in a referendum before the next general election, having learned from the experience of two previous difficult referendum campaigns that it was best to bury the abortion debate for the immediate future.

Cowen argued that the green paper – which he had even ordered to be rewritten without officially informing the cabinet sub-committee supervising the document, wishing to eliminate so-called 'civil service jargon' from it – would help to throw new light on the subject. He wanted 'to see all sides of the debate coming to a clear understanding of each other's point of view'. The paper commissioned by Cowen included the following options: an absolute constitutional ban on abortion; retention of the status quo, blocking information on how to get an abortion abroad; legislation to regulate abortion in circumstances defined in the X Case; permitting abortion on grounds beyond those specified in the X Case; and reversion to the position before the constitutional amendment of 1983 according equal right to life to unborn child and mother. Professor William Binchy of the Pro-Life Campaign dismissed the green paper, claiming that it 'did not contain new information or new analysis that has not been raised before'.

Confounding the critics who alleged that he was attempting to stall the issue until after the next general election, Cowen did attempt to make progress in September 1998. In the event, however, the possibility of the All-Party Oireachtas Committee on the Constitution reaching a consensus on the abortion green paper was scuppered when the two main opposition parties rejected a referendum. Fine Gael's health spokesperson Alan Shatter said his party remained committed to the view of the party's leader, John Bruton, that 'it would probably be unwise in practical terms to proceed with another referendum or with legislation'. The Labour Party leader Ruairi Quinn explained his reluctance by stating that the constitution was 'not the appropriate place' to try to deal with such a complex issue. Thankfully, Cowen was eventually relieved of further grappling with the question when he was appointed Minister for Foreign Affairs. The chairing of the government's sub-committee on the abortion green paper was left to the incoming Minister for Health, Micheál Martin, who at the time was being described by political pundits as the rising star of Fianna Fáil.

Cowen constantly turned down the frequent media requests for 'one-on-one' interviews during his first eighteen months in charge of the health department. It was an unusual stance for Cowen who, until taking up the 'poisoned chalice', had always been approachable to the media and rarely if ever turned down interview requests. Cowen would later explain that he was reluctant to talk to the press during this period because he felt the health department needed to 'retire from the limelight' after the constant negative press. He wanted simply to get on with the task of improving the service to the public. 'I think it takes twelve months to get into a job. From a media point of view the department was pulled and dragged all over the shop. I came in as minister and decided that I was just not going to do that. Health needed to catch its breath. If that involves taking it off the front page, well then, that's fine,' he said at the time.

Though Cowen did not give any interviews during this period, he did award a public relations contract for the sum of IR£100,000 to Drury Communications, thereby attracting fire from the opposition in the Dáil. He eventually gave his first major interview as health minister to the *Irish Times* in November 1999, apparently in order to dispel the rumours that he loathed being in charge of the health department. The resulting profile even started with the declaration that Cowen loved his brief. He declared robustly that it was 'crap, nonsense' that he was already literally praying for a cabinet reshuffle. 'I'm working hard. We're making decisions, getting things done. Maybe it's down to my demeanour or something. I'm very interested in the job. I love it,' he declared.

'I was glad to be in the cabinet. I'm a traditionalist on these matters. The Taoiseach is elected, he picks his cabinet and decides who he wants. The views of my colleagues in cabinet are as valued as mine, and all bring forward their views. Health is not run by me in isolation, same as education is not run in isolation by Micheál [Martin]. When there is trouble I have no problem being the one to deal with that, it's my job. The idea that we are skulking and sulking around about jobs is ridiculous. I'm not in the job to be the most popular man in Ireland. My job is to take decisions in the best long-term interest of the system regardless of whether they make me popular or not. Strategic decisions take longer but will make for a better health system. Over a four- to five-year period I think we will be able to say we have addressed many issues.'

At the Fianna Fáil Ard Fheis the weekend prior to the publication of this interview, Cowen gave a passionate speech. In it, he acknowledged that the public continued to be 'bemused' – perhaps 'annoyed' and 'frustrated' would have been more apt terms – by the health service, particularly by the fact that, despite more money than ever being thrown into health, the same problems seemed to be not only reappearing but dramatically increasing. In fact, the total budget for health had virtually doubled during Quinn's and Cowen's tenures, with day-to-day expenditures during Cowen's first year in office reaching IR£3 billion; and yet waiting lists for operations were at an all-time high of over 34,000 in total. People could not understand how a country at the height of an economic boom, the Celtic Tiger roaring at its loudest, could have a public health system that was justifiably being described as probably the worst of any EU member state. Cowen spoke of his genuine concern about the length of time people had to spend waiting for procedures – in almost half of all cases, longer than the time limits set out by the health department. A government report of 1999 had found that there were an estimated 150,000 patients 'inappropriately placed' in acute beds, and he talked about a need for a 'seamless system' that would allow patients who no longer needed acute care to be transferred from hospitals into alternative accommodation or moved back into their communities, in an effort to free up hospital places.

Cowen saw an urgent need for fundamental restructuring of public health. He refused to adopt a 'steady as you go' approach – he wanted a long-term plan. At the same time, he was aware that change needed careful planning: 'You have to structure your response, and see if you have to build up capacity. You don't want to turn around and increase capacity by 300 per cent and then find it's too much. That's waste.' He felt that the public needed to 'recognize what it is the system can deliver and what are the impediments. Some more resources would be a help, but these have to be planned.' He considered it vital to the creation of a modern health service that proper investment was channelled appropriately into the health board system – and that it was also carried out within budgetary limits. Cowen felt that strict budgetary regulation was essential because previous health ministers had allowed the health system to become a black hole into which they had continued to pump money blindly, allowing the health agencies to run dramatically over budget. This, in his view, was where his predecessors had failed: they had, he argued, tried to alleviate the problems of the day by pumping in extra money, but this wouldn't resolve the problem in the long term. Or, as Cowen put it, 'If your engine is old and in need of replacement, how many times do you take it to the mechanic?' In other words, he wanted the 'machinery replaced before it dies'.

On 10 February 1999 Cowen was the subject of a much-publicized attack by Fine Gael leader John Bruton at the party's Ard Fheis. It was probably in retaliation for a verbal exchange between the two men during a Dáil debate at the end of January, when Cowen described the Fine Gael leader as 'the Inspector Clouseau of Irish politics' and then barked across the chamber floor to Bruton: 'Fool! Fool! Clown!'

Michael Noonan kicked off proceedings at the Ard Fheis by describing Cowen as the 'Dr Strangelove of the Health Service', in reference to the bizarre Peter Sellers character in Stanley Kubrick's black comedy; he then likened Bertie Ahern to the fumbling, idiotic Spanish waiter Manuel in the British comedy series *Fawlty Towers*. Noonan also charged Ahern with 'selective amnesia' when it came to discussing the so-called sleaze factor associated with Fianna Fáil in the recent past. He went on: 'The Taoiseach's failure as a private investigator is only matched by his selective amnesia. There will shortly be a new disease recorded in the medical journals to be known as ASAS – Ahern Selective Amnesia Syndrome. This is a very rare condition brought on at any mention of the names Haughey, Burke, Flynn or Gilmartin. It becomes particularly prevalent if the Tánaiste mentions these names.'

But it was Cowen who bore the brunt of Fine Gael's verbal assault that night. The mere mention of Cowen's name in Bruton's speech drew hisses from the audience, with Frank McNally of the *Irish Times* stating that the delegates reacted as if Cowen were 'the wicked witch in a pantomime'. In his address, Bruton said: 'Let me turn to another minister, Brian Cowen – the Tyrannosaurus Rex of Tullamore – all sound and fury but soon to be extinct.' Cowen apparently shrugged off the criticism as typical opposition banter. But people back in Clara were apparently far more offended by Bruton's attack – not because of the jibe at Cowen but rather because he'd labelled the minister as being from Tullamore instead of his true home town!

In one of his very rare slip-ups when speaking in public, Cowen caused uproar in Waterford when, during a Dáil debate on 14 October 1999 about the strike at Waterford Regional Hospital, he made an off-the-cuff remark about the city being 'known for its ability to come up with strike action'. Cowen immediately issued a retraction and apology. But it was later argued by a succession of callers to the local radio station, WLR, that Cowen's comment had the potential to damage the city's ability to attract new inward investment. During the same heated Dáil debate, Cowen appeared to confuse two different disputes and the opposition accused him of not knowing what the dispute with non-medical staff in the Waterford hospital was about, requiring his press secretary later to issue a rebuttal to the media, insisting that Cowen did indeed know the subject of the dispute.

The real thorn in Cowen's side during his time in charge of

health was the nurses' strike. In September 1999 the nurses rejected a Labour Court pay offer which would have cost the government about IR£110 million a year. This prompted the then Minister for Finance, Charlie McCreevy, to state on RTÉ that pay demands by the nurses and others in the public sector would 'wreck the Celtic Tiger'. This comment generated strong resentment among nurses, particularly when critics were quick to point out that the government expected an exchequer surplus of €5.8 billion for 1999. McCreevy's comments also came the day before the government was due to meet business and trade union representatives about a new national agreement, and – coinciding with damaging revelations at the Dáil Committee of Public Accounts of widespread tax evasion and suspect dealings – prompted Peter Cassells of the Irish Congress of Trade Unions to declare that if McCreevy intended to lecture them on wages then perhaps it would be best to cancel the meeting altogether.

The tension was defused when Ahern made a deal that any wage claim should be considered within the remit of Partnership 2000, the national agreement based on the 'social partnership' between government, employers and employees. But then, as it emerged that the social partners wouldn't be able to rein back the nurses' unions, Ahern decided to change tack, causing uproar when he criticized the nurses over their pay demands at a parliamentary party meeting in Galway. He declared that the government would stand firm in its rejection of the nurses' latest pay demands, a tough stance echoed by Cowen. On 12 October Ahern told the Dáil his plans for addressing the nurses' unions' pay claims under Partnership 2000, but then added that 'we cannot pay any more' than the Labour Court ruling offered.

A motion of no confidence in Cowen was then put before

the Dáil by Pat Rabbitte of the Labour Party, and was defeated. On the day the nurses set up their picket lines, 21 October, Cowen appeared at the Carers' Association's awards ceremony in the Westbury Hotel in Dublin, at which – perhaps somewhat ironically, as media commentators pointed out – he announced a substantial increase in annual funding for family carers. As he was entering the hotel, one of his constituents, up to Dublin on a shopping trip, was passing by and affectionately patted him on the shoulder, saying, 'Good luck, Brian!' She then told the assembled journalists that she fully supported her local TD's stance against the nurses' pay demands.

The awards ceremony was compèred by the broadcaster Pat Kenny, who quickly pointed out to the audience that the increase in funding which had just been announced was approximately equivalent to a 400 per cent rise. 'If the nurses hear about that percentage increase, they'll be out for the next five years,' joked Kenny, which prompted the room to explode into laughter, and even drew a smile from Cowen. Joking aside, Kenny then acknowledged that the carers' event co-incided with 'probably the most unfortunate day' for Cowen to be presenting awards to five people who had been nominated for their unpaid caring efforts. 'The minister had many excuses he could have used not to be here today, but we are delighted that he honoured his long-standing commit-ment,' said Kenny.

Cowen received a warm round of applause as he got up to make his speech. Eddie Collins-Hughes from the Carers' Association thanked the minister for the additional funding. 'I have worked closely with this man for quite a while and he has never broken his word once, and I think he should be complimented on that,' said Collins-Hughes.

During that same week, some ten thousand nurses turned

up on coaches from all parts of the country to march through the streets of Dublin. During their demonstrations and rallies, the nurses would shout out 'We're not bowing to Mr Cowen!' and some held placards bearing the obvious pun 'Mad Cowen Disease!' It was a scene that would strike fear into most politicians, mindful that they would have to canvass these same disgruntled nurses in the future for votes. And the nurses were mindful of this too. 'McDaid needn't come back to the hospital in Letterkenny looking for our votes,' one of the nurses told TD Liz McManus, who was handing out flyers declaring the Labour Party's support for them.

As a mark of respect at the passing of Jack Lynch, who had died on 20 October, the nurses decided against picketing the Dáil. On the morning of the former Taoiseach's requiem mass, Cowen decided to visit his widow Máirín, who was at the Royal Hospital Kilmainham, where her husband's remains were lying, to express his heartfelt sympathy. As his car pulled up near the hospital, Cowen felt it would not be appropriate simply to drive past the nurses' picket positioned there. On the spur of the moment he decided to get out of the car, walked up to the gates and had a conversation with some of the nurses – to gauge their own views on the situation – before walking into the hospital. Later, he attended the requiem mass at the North Cathedral in Cork. Lynch had been one of Cowen's political role models and the younger man was acutely aware of all they had in common. Apart from the obvious factor of both men coming from rural, republican backgrounds, they both also had a passion for the Irish language and a love of GAA, as well as having family members in the clergy: Lynch's brother Father Charlie Lynch had served as parish priest in Inchigeela, west Cork.

Days before the nurses began their strike, Cowen told the

Dáil that the threatened industrial action was 'a blind alley, leading nowhere', adding: 'There is no possibility of improving upon the terms of the Labour Court finding.' But within a week of the action commencing, the nurses' unions had won a substantial pay deal of IR£190 million, an increase of IR£80 million on the Labour Court's original offer. The nurses' unions argued that their agenda was about more than pay and working conditions – it was also about achieving public recognition that nursing was a real profession. It appeared that the government had taken on the nurses and lost; but some political commentators argued that its initial obduracy was necessary, because if the final offer had been made before the strike it might have encouraged other public sector employees to make extravagant demands.

Cowen was particularly frustrated by one particular repercussion of the nurses' strike action. It had inevitably increased pressure on already stretched waiting lists. Public sympathy for the nurses diminished significantly when it began to emerge that some critically sick children and pregnant women had had to be transferred to hospitals in Belfast and Glasgow. Added to that, some nurses sought wages for days not worked while they were out on strike. That demand and the negative impact of their action on vulnerable patients, together with the threat of complete withdrawal from hospitals if their demands were not met, all detracted from public support for the nurses' cause. As Fergal Bowers, editor of the *Irish Medical News*, pointed out, 'Patients should never be used, either by government or health professionals, as pawns in a battle for better pay.'

During Cowen's time in the health department, Albert Reynolds opted to seek the party's nomination for the upcoming presidential election. Back in January 1997, he had told Bertie Ahern that he planned to step down at the next general election because he didn't warm to the idea of spending his twilight years as a backbencher. Ahern urged his former boss to think again, fearing that without Reynolds Fianna Fáil could lose a valuable seat in the Longford–Roscommon constituency. Reynolds felt that Fianna Fáil would never lose the seat but reluctantly agreed to mull over Ahern's request, and eventually agreed, persuaded by Ahern's offer to make him a special 'peace envoy' to Northern Ireland and believing that he had Ahern's support for his presidential candidacy.

However, when the time came for the party to choose its presidential candidate, Reynolds found that his nomination was not, in fact, the formality he had understood it would be, and in the event he lost the vote to the young Northern Ireland barrister Mary McAleese. Out of the fifteen cabinet members, only Charlie McCreevy, David Andrews and Brian Cowen supported Reynolds in the vote. Both Reynolds and Cowen were surprised that the Minister for the Environment, Noel Dempsey, who was abroad, had decided not to vote. Reynolds shook his head in disbelief when he learned of Dempsey's decision: he saw Dempsey as one of his protégés, having given him his first big political break by bringing him into his cabinet. In his biography of Mary McAleese, *The Road from Ardoyne*, Ray Mac Manais points out that Dempsey 'had a fierce personal loyalty to the former Taoiseach, but felt that his candidacy for the presidency might not be the best thing for Albert himself'. He later said he envisaged a Reynolds presidential campaign as 'weeks of wall-to-wall Beef Tribunal re-runs'. However, it should be remembered that Reynolds had already been vindicated by the tribunal's findings.

Ahern knew that Reynolds' loyal supporters would have to be brought round. In what was widely seen as an 'ameliorating move', according to Mac Manais, he offered Fianna Fáil's presidential candidate a choice of Cowen or Dempsey as her campaign director. But McAleese probably knew that Cowen would not have relished the task, considering his obvious loyalty to the former Taoiseach, and opted for Dempsey.

Dempsey himself confirmed that he was the original choice for the role of campaign director, but he also recalls suggesting that perhaps Cowen should be considered. 'I was approached by Pat Farrell on the cabinet corridor and asked would I be Mary McAleese's director of elections. Pat went on to say that both he and the boss wanted to pull the Albert Reynolds faction on board, and that I was the man best suited for that job. I said I would have no problem doing whatever they thought best for the party, but if they wanted to bring the Albert faction on board they might think of asking Brian Cowen to take the job, as he would be more closely identified with Albert than me. I also suggested that they ask Mary McAleese herself,' recalled Dempsey.

Years later, Reynolds is still, understandably, bitterly disappointed at not getting the presidential nomination, not so much because he particularly wanted the job as because so many of the cabinet failed to support him; and because he felt badly let down by Ahern. He quietly retired from public life and is now writing his autobiography.

It is arguable that his time as health minister was the most disappointing period of Cowen's cabinet career, under the unrelenting pressure of the constant problems facing the public health sector in Ireland. But he can probably take some solace from the fact that the nurses' strike was the only major crisis to mark his tenure. Moreover, he did make some valuable progress, particularly with the 'Cowen package' for people with intellectual disabilities, which was highly praised, and his introduction of a multi-annual budgeting system for large capital projects such as hospitals. The established system was that the Minister for Finance would reveal the budget on a yearly basis, but Cowen felt that this needed to change. He wanted to be told exactly how much his department could expect over the next three years in order to plan a better long-term strategy. 'All previous Ministers for Health up to my time had this crazy situation where you only knew this year what money you had to spend on capital projects – even if you gave approval for a project that could take several years, you could only know how much it would get for that particular year. It wasn't a very good planning framework,' says Cowen. 'I went to see [Charlie] McCreevy and I said, "Look, Charlie, tell me what money you are going to give me over the next three years on capital projects. Let's come to an agreement now, so I can go off and plan – rather than coming back year on year, not knowing what I'm going to get." By doing that you could actually begin to plan the development of some hospital services in a far more certain and far more professional way. It's a much better framework in which health policy can be planned,' points out Cowen. Under the new arrangements, Cowen secured funding for new buildings at St James's and St Vincent's hospitals in Dublin, as well as hospitals in Galway, Tullamore and Cork.

Furthermore, rather than simply washing his hands of the problems facing the public health service once relieved of direct responsibility for it, Cowen has indicated that it is one of the main issues he intends to tackle during his period as

Taoiseach. In one of his first speeches after being appointed leader of Fianna Fáil in April 2008, Cowen outlined his ambitious plans to cut back the number of administrators in the health service in order to create scope for employing more front-line staff. He spoke about setting up a possible voluntary redundancy programme once the Health Service Executive's management and administration audit was complete. Cowen made his thoughts clear while speaking at the AGM of Inclusion Ireland – the national association for people with intellectual disabilities – which was held in Tullamore. The crowd observed how passionately Cowen spoke about his vision to transform the health system from one that revolves around the hospital service to one that focuses on being a health service. He pointed out that this was particularly important for people with intellectual disabilities, many of whom suffered a lack of attention because of the emphasis placed on the acute hospital sector.

Cowen has some interesting theories on how best to improve the public sector health system. He doesn't subscribe to the idea of change merely for change's sake; but he does consider it vital that his government drastically change the way services are delivered. He believes that the right leadership at all levels within the hospital sector – coupled with greater flexibility and a disciplined adherence to budgetary constraints – will bring about dramatic improvements. 'The fact is there aren't infinite budgets,' explains Cowen. 'The fact is we won't be growing at the same rate as in recent years. We have to get better outcomes for the very considerable resources we are putting in. Therefore getting more efficiency from the much increased spend is the constant challenge. Reform of service delivery is key to sustaining the improvements in the health service and, over the long term, switching spend from hospitals to the community and primary care sector is vital.'

When Cowen was Minister for Health, from 1997 to 2000, his final budget allocation was about € 3.2 billion; eight years later, the government is now spending five times more than this, some € 15 billion. This, argues Cowen, demonstrates that if it were simply down to resources the health crisis would have been solved. He acknowledges that there are structural problems that need to be addressed. Cowen also wants to build up primary care in the community, believing that for too long the A&E department of the nearest hospital has become the extension of all the GPs' dispensaries in the area; sometimes, in fact, patients simply bypass their GPs and head straight for A&E. Cowen is adamant that getting all the appropriate issues dealt with in a primary healthcare setting will ensure that hospitals will then be able to focus on the acute cases that require their attention. 'In ordinary person's terms that just means giving everyone the best possible chance of surviving. That's what it means when you cut through the jargon. Patient safety has to be our first concern. And that we have services that can be regarded as world class in due course. That's what we have to do,' says Cowen. 'It is the great challenge in the social partnership process. Focusing on solving the problem, rather than prolonging arguments over vested interests – that's the key issue.'

Judging by Cowen's passionate words, there is no disputing that he fully intends to rectify the structural problems in the public health service. If – unlike his predecessors – he is able to achieve a modern, fully functional health system, it will be his crowning glory as Taoiseach.

7

Minister for Foreign Affairs

Cowen's appointment as Minister for Foreign Affairs in January 2000 made him the third graduate of Cistercian College to hold this key position within twenty years. The first of the trio was Dick Spring; the second, David Andrews, his immediate predecessor. Back in July 1999, Andrews had announced that he would not be seeking re-election to the Dáil in the next general election, having held the foreign affairs portfolio for a little more than two years since Ray Burke's resignation over planning corruption allegations back in 1997. At the age of sixty-five – and after spending thirty-five years in politics since first being elected as a TD in 1965 – Andrews felt it was in the party's best interests for the Taoiseach to face the impending general election in a position to present his future cabinet team to the electorate.

It was widely speculated that Ahern had given the foreign affairs portfolio to Cowen as a reward for holding the fort through a difficult time in the Department of Health. However, some political pundits reckoned there may have been another motive for Ahern's decision: that Ahern may have felt that a conciliated Cowen would act as a counterweight to Micheál Martin, who saw himself as a potential party leader in waiting. But even if Ahern was acting in his own best interests, he must also have realized that Cowen would be the ideal heavyweight to deal with the British Northern Ireland Secretary, Peter Mandelson, in the tough negotiations ahead. 'I was particularly interested in foreign affairs because of the Northern Ireland issue,' says Cowen.

Regardless of Ahern's exact reasoning, Cowen was privately delighted to learn that he would be moving to foreign affairs. It was reported in the media that Andrews had called Ahern on 21 January 2000 to inform him officially of his decision to step down. Six days after Andrews' announcement, Ahern revealed the full line-up of his new cabinet, which also included Micheál Martin at health, Michael Woods as Minister for Education, and Frank Fahey as Minister for the Marine and Natural Resources. He also promoted Eoin Ryan to Minister of State for Tourism, Sport and Recreation, and appointed Mary Hanafin as Minister of State for Health and Children.

Not everybody welcomed news of Cowen's ascent. Journalist Vincent Browne was particularly vocal in his criticism of the move, arguing in a commentary piece for the *Irish Times* that Cowen had no relevant expertise for the job and doubting that he'd have any thought-out opinions on major international issues. Sixteen months later, however, Browne revised his opinion, acknowledging that Cowen was enjoying a successful tenure as a combative Minister for Foreign Affairs.

While Cowen immensely enjoyed his new role, it took a heavy toll on his home life, the constant travelling abroad preventing him from spending as much time as he would have wished with his family. But he took solace from his wife's tremendous support and encouragement during these very hectic years. He could remember visiting four capital cities in one day alone. Even so, any time Cowen felt tired from his gruelling schedule he would remind himself that it was a job that would only last for a few years. Cowen has never taken anything for granted in politics, and he knew there might never be another opportunity to hold so senior and significant a cabinet position. He is an extremely ambitious politician but has never been presumptuous or calculating. His father's death at only fifty-two had had a profound effect on him, making him reluctant to plan too far ahead; you never know, he says, where you will be in five years' time. 'Because of the fact that my own dad died so suddenly,' he says, 'I genuinely don't get up in the morning wondering about future cabinet positions.'

Cowen may have held the foreign affairs portfolio for less than five years, but they were years that brought especially heavy responsibilities: the political climate was febrile both close to home, in Northern Ireland, and globally. Not only did Ireland gain a seat on the UN Security Council after a long campaign, but Cowen found himself chairing the Council in the aftermath of September 11. Back in Offaly, it was feared that Cowen would be too busy with global matters to give time to constituency issues. However, Cowen was conscious of this potential problem and decided that he'd simply have to put in longer hours to ensure a balance between government and local duties. Cowen would never pass up an opportunity to ensure the contentment of his constituents. A good example of this was when – during one of his first official trips abroad as Minister for Foreign Affairs, to the White House for Bill Clinton's swansong St Patrick's Day reception – Cowen was on his way to meet a prominent politician but became delayed when he bumped into some Offaly immigrants. Naturally, he stopped for a chat and appeared to forget that he was now behind schedule for his important appointment. When one of his aides approached him to explain that they were running late for their meeting with the American politician, Cowen quipped: 'He can't vote for me! But these people here all have relatives back home that can!'

Naturally enough, Cowen also ensured that he was available during that same trip when invited to open an Irish bar which was owned by a fellow Offaly man. After all, as Cowen would admit himself, here again was an opportunity to canvass for potential votes. Cowen believed firmly in the Tip O'Neill adage that 'all politics is local', and as he worked the bar he impressed his expat constituents with his ability to remember their names and other, obscure details. A prime example of Cowen's relentless canvassing for votes occurred some time later, when he was invited as a guest speaker to a Muslim cultural convention in Tullamore. As he went up on to the stage, Cowen quipped to the audience, many of whom were foreign nationals: 'I know you're all Fianna Fáil!' Declan McSweeney, who was covering the event for the local weekly paper, could see the rationale behind Cowen's promotion of his party: 'He was astute enough to realise that many of those present were Irish citizens, while others would become citizens in the following years, and he lost no opportunity to canvass their votes.'

On the home front, it was a difficult time to be taking the helm in foreign affairs. Cowen was plunged straight into the uncertainties surrounding the precarious Northern Ireland peace talks. Albert Reynolds – who had been the instigator, alongside John Major, of the peace process – had built up an impressive number of contacts in Northern

Ireland. He immediately went to see Cowen in order to give him some valuable advice about the situation north of the border; later, too, he introduced Cowen to some of the key figures within the republican movement. When it came to the peace process itself, while obviously the highest-level contacts would take place between the British Prime Minister and the Taoiseach, much of the behind-the-scenes work was conducted by Cowen, who was determined to push the process forward. He kept in close contact with Ahern to keep him abreast of developments, but also spent much of his time working alongside other senior figures on the British side, above all the three different Secretaries of State for Northern Ireland during Cowen's time at foreign affairs: Peter Mandelson, John Reid and Paul Murphy. 'It was interesting that John Reid had Offaly connections on his mother's side and Paul Murphy came from an Irish background as well,' reflects Cowen.

Unfortunately, Cowen's relationship with Mandelson, the UK government's key negotiator, did not get off to a good start. It appears that both Ahern and Cowen were irritated by Mandelson's decision in February 2000 to pay an official visit to President McAleese, to brief her on the continuing developments in Northern Ireland. They were wary of the symbolic figurehead of the Irish state – particularly one with a Northern background – being drawn into the discussions at such a precarious moment in the peace process.

Bizarrely, Mandelson felt that Cowen was not supporting him during heated confrontations with Sinn Féin's delegation during tense talks about the suspension of the institutions. An irate Gerry Adams told Mandelson that the Republican movement would 'go to town over this'. Jonathan Powell, the Prime Minister's chief adviser, observed in his memoir: 'Certainly, the Irish government did little to palliate this campaign of abuse, and when Adams attacked Mandelson in the presence of Brian Cowen, the Republic's Foreign Minister would not support him.' But Cowen dismissed Mandelson's suggestion that he should have assisted him. Cowen says that he hopes that his role will be assessed as one that was carried out honourably. He is adamant that he did not, at any stage, seek to undermine anyone else in the process.

That particular relationship deteriorated further when a record of a conversation between the two men at a dinner was leaked to the press – making it transparently obvious what Mandelson thought of Cowen. 'Relationships were distinctly frosty for a while after that,' recalls Powell.

During a meeting in the Irish Government Buildings, the British delegation was pushing for the RUC insignia to be incorporated into the proposed new police service, but Cowen rightfully pointed out that this would not 'meet with the parity of esteem requirement'. He painstakingly explained that policing was a 'very fundamental issue' and there was a need to 'make a clean break', as had been suggested in the Patten Commission's report.

'I was very strongly of the view that we needed to ensure that the reforms that were envisaged in the Patten report were actually implemented, rather than diluted. This was a crucial issue. There was always a tendency on the British side to accommodate the unionist perspective more easily than they were able to accommodate the nationalist perspective. I very much saw my role – as part of the agreements the governments had signed – to ensure that we would, in fact, meet the requirements of the agreement. What the leak indicated was that there were elements on the British side who felt I was overly forceful on this issue and perhaps being inflexible, but that was from their perspective. I knew in my heart and soul that if we got this wrong – if we didn't meet with the ambitions of the Patten recommendations – it would undermine the agreement,' explains Cowen.

Cowen believes that the timing of the leak of the British internal document, which made references to him being 'troublesome or whatever', 'was interesting': it was passed to the press just as Cowen and Ahern were arriving at Hillsborough Castle for vital talks on the peace process. 'I was being characterized as the source of the problem. It had no impact on changing my views – in fact, it had quite the opposite effect,' he recalls.

In July 2000 Cowen gave a very revealing insight into his edgy working relationship with Mandelson to the *Guardian* newspaper, which ran the interview under the headline 'My Spats with Mandelson, by Ireland's Bruiser', the writer unkindly and needlessly describing Cowen as having the face of a 'bruiser'. Cowen revealed in the interview that while there was some tension between him and Mandelson he believed this was having a very positive effect because, instead of wasting time with small talk, they just got straight down to matters of business. Even though their relationship was frosty at times, Cowen went on to acknowledge Mandelson's role in the peace process as a valuable one. Commenting on Mandelson's surprise resignation on 24 January 2001 (for reasons unrelated to his role in Northern Ireland), he pointed out that it came at a bad time because the two governments and the parties in favour of the Good Friday Agreement were engaged in the 'most intensive efforts to achieve the full implementation of outstanding aspects of the agreement'. Cowen has always held the view that in politics you fight hard but fair – and you always shake your opponent's hand in the aftermath. Even though some critics would beg to differ, Cowen doesn't believe in holding political grudges. 'Life's too short for that,' he would often say. Speaking of the many tense dialogues he has had with political colleagues and opponents alike, he says: 'I may have disagreed with them vehemently from time to time but I dealt with the matter professionally. I always feel that while there were disagreements, there were difficult times, there were tensions with these political relationships, while they may have been strained from time to time, there was never anything personal; it was business.'

Even though Cowen had been placed at the heart of negotiations dealing with the collapse of devolution at Stormont and decommissioning of IRA weapons, he appeared to be disliked by many leading unionists, who considered him nothing more than a staunch republican. Writing in the *Irish Times* about Cowen's first trip to the White House as Minister for Foreign Affairs, Dick Walsh seemed to sum up this sentiment when he wrote: 'Cowen, on a charm offensive in Washington, has succeeded in appealing to the unionists as he once appealed to the nurses – by showing an exasperating indifference to their case.'

The leader of the Ulster Unionist Party, David Trimble, was not enthusiastic about Cowen's appointment, telling his aides privately: 'We may now have to start paying more attention to the Department of Foreign Affairs.' Trimble had several sharp exchanges with Cowen and his deputy Liz O'Donnell. But Cowen believed that what others called heated arguments were simply 'straight dealing', which he felt was ultimately respected by Trimble and other leading unionists. Yes, he acknowledges, there would be times when the issue would come to the boil during serious discussions with people who held a different point of view; but Cowen saw himself as a man with a job – and that job was to uphold the Irish government's side of the bargain.

The British government, which had initially welcomed Cowen's appointment, began to view him less warmly. According to Trimble's biographer Dean Godson, they thought Cowen's 'apparent lack of sympathy for certain unionists made things worse (as a leaked memorandum from the British ambassador to Dublin, Ivor Roberts, made clear)'. But Cowen rejects any imputation that he breached confidentiality; he is adamant that he never at any stage manipulated the media or attempted to use the media, as he put it, 'to try and anticipate discussions I was to have or subsequently breach confidentiality or anything like that'.

Eventually certain unionists decided to take the step of publicly attacking Cowen. On 29 April 2003, Ian Paisley Snr cruelly insulted him during a DUP election press conference. 'Somebody told me the other day that the reason his lips were so thick was that when his mother was bringing him up, he was a very disobedient boy. So she used to put glue on his lips and put him to the floor and keep him there, and that has been recorded in his physical make-up,' stated Dr Paisley.

Many of the DUP members roared with laughter at this hurtful jibe, while others in the crowd gasped in disbelief that a senior politician should make such personally insulting remarks.

Paisley continued: 'What right has a foreign minister from Dublin to have a say in our affairs, our internal affairs? None whatsoever. Yes, away with him. If he wants to use his lips to better effect, he should do it somewhere else and do it with people of similar physical looks.'

Initially, Cowen sensibly deflected several media requests to respond to Paisley's comments. Ignoring the badgering from the press, he focused his own comments instead on the need for political stability and how vital it was for the elections to go ahead. The press also approached Cowen's younger brother Barry for a quote, but he said the family would not pay Paisley's remarks the compliment of a reaction. 'He's the type who trades in insults, we've all seen that from him over the years. We're just ignoring it, not dignifying it with a response,' he said. Eventually, later that week, Cowen reluctantly gave a response himself: 'Those comments have been made, and I'm quite prepared to allow the discernment and judgement of the Irish people to decide their merits or otherwise.' Later, he added: 'We've gone beyond the failed politics of insults and we have a far more substantial issue to address.'

Shortly after this episode, during a speech to launch the publication of *The Tallyman's Guide to the Northern Ireland Elections*, Cowen said: 'I welcome the fact that political contests are not beauty contests and it's great to be successful in that respect.' The media speculated that this remark was directed at Paisley's insults, but Cowen insisted: 'No. It was an attempt at humour.' Later still, during an interview in 2007, Cowen insisted that Paisley's jibes had not hurt him on a personal level, but said he considered them not 'very sensible'. While admitting that he had been perplexed by the outburst, he diplomatically brushed the incident aside: 'Look, I have said a few things myself in my time maybe I shouldn't have said, so let's forgive and forget. I have met him since and he never brought it up. It is not an issue for me. It was an unfortunate comment.'

Others were less disposed to let the incident pass, and Paisley was heavily criticized for his abusive comments. SDLP Assembly member Alban Maginniss said the comments were 'very personalized and ugly', adding: 'These are offensive remarks by Ian Paisley who purports to be a man of God. No one could regard those as godly remarks. They are quite ungodly. But we are never surprised by the DUP or its leader in terms of the sort of lurid language they use.' Paisley's bizarre outburst also drew a response from the British Prime Minister Tony Blair, who actually cited the insults as a contributory factor in the postponement of elections to the Northern Ireland Assembly.

On 5 May 2003 Cowen turned up at the Brewery Tap in Tullamore to sing a Christy Moore tune at a concert in aid of the Offaly Hospice. Locals rallied around him to express their disgust at the insulting remarks made by Paisley. As Cowen sang that night, the pub's owner, Paul Bell, remarked that Cowen appeared to have put the incident behind him. 'He's a down-to-earth kind of fella with a good sense of humour, so I'd say if anyone mentions it, he'll just make a joke about it or laugh it off,' said Bell. And mention it people did: one man in the pub said he'd been watching the press conference live and promptly switched off the television in disgust. 'It is not a big deal,' Cowen would say when locals conveyed their outrage to him. 'My mother wasn't upset – that's the important thing.'

The year after Paisley's juvenile comments on Cowen, the two men met again at the Irish Embassy in London. This time, Paisley decided to insult the Irish government delegation once again – as he had done in 1999 – by not shaking hands with any of them, including Taoiseach Ahern. Paisley had refused the cordial gesture with Ahern back in 1999 because, as he explained, he would not 'shake hands with a prime minister of a country which still has a claim over my country'. But this was not the reason for his impoliteness in 2004, because by then the Irish claim to the North had been amended in its constitution. The true explanation was that Paisley feared a backlash from unionists who weren't ready to see their leader shaking hands with the 'enemy'. When the DUP delegation met with Ahern, Cowen and Michael McDowell in the embassy, none of the Irish contingent rose from their seats when Paisley walked into the room. They then got up and shook hands with the rest of Paisley's team – including Peter and Iris Robinson, Nigel Dodds and Gregory Campbell – who had no reservations about shaking hands with members of the Irish government.

'I think previous foreign ministers have often been characterized in an unfair way by unionists,' reflects Cowen, 'when, in fact, all they were doing was trying to do their job and make sure the agreements we had were lived up to and that the spirit and letter of the agreement were understood and lived up to. There was always an attempt, in my view, in the negotiation for those with opposing points of view to get away more lightly from their side of the bargain if we weren't robust and rigorous in insisting on certain things happening the way that had been envisaged in the agreements we'd signed.'

But for every disgruntled unionist there were others who sang Cowen's praise, most notably Ken McGuinness, who acknowledged Cowen's contribution to the peace process. Others also argue that Cowen had a good rapport with the unionists. Interestingly, Cowen believes that there were many attempts by various people to portray him 'in a certain way'. He explains: 'I always saw that as part of the psychology that goes on and I wasn't distracted by it in any way. A lot of it is set as a test to see how you'd react.'

Nor did Cowen discriminate between unionists and republicans in his robust approach. During one heated argument Martin McGuinness (now Deputy First Minister of the Northern Ireland Assembly) is reported to have told Cowen: 'I'll have to go see the IRA about what's being offered here.'

Cowen apparently looked at the straight-faced McGuinness and retorted: 'There's a mirror in the bathroom if you want to talk with them.'

Despite all the quarrels endured during the peace process, Cowen is proud of his input and is adamant that the mandatory coalition arrangement under the Good Friday and St Andrews agreements is helping slowly to bring together a divided community. Cowen believes that, if nothing else, the peace process gives the lie to the sceptics' dismissive claim that 'politics is irrelevant'. On the contrary, argues Cowen, 'Politics works.' He hopes that the success of the peace process will be seen as a beacon of hope by and for other countries experiencing conflict. Ireland, he maintains, is an example of how a seemingly hopeless situation can actually be resolved.

However, like his predecessors, Cowen has no intention of going into coalition with Sinn Féin in the Dáil. During an interview in May 2007, Cowen spoke about people's lasting suspicion of Sinn Féin's possible connection with republican groups still allegedly involved in illegal activities. But the main reason he is reluctant to do business with Sinn Féin in the Dáil, it seems, is that he doesn't believe its policy positions are sufficiently compatible with those of Fianna Fáil. And while he concedes that it would be churlish not to acknowledge the progress Sinn Féin has made towards peaceful democratic politics, there remains a question over its long-term performance and its ability to ensure that none of the residual paramilitaries ever re-emerge. In Cowen's view, Sinn Féin still has a long way to go before the party can claim to have proved to the Irish electorate its commitment to exclusively democratic politics. Therefore it is highly doubtful that Cowen will even consider negotiating with it for any type of coalition during his tenure as Taoiseach.

'Is the World Ready for Brian Cowen?' ran the headline of an article published in the *Irish Times* on 16 September 2000, referring to Ireland's imminent anticipated election to the Security Council of the United Nations. Cowen was certainly ready to take his place on the world stage: up until the point when he delivered his first speech to the UN General Assembly, he had been almost inactive on the international political scene, the first nine months of his tenure as foreign minister having been dominated by the peace process in Northern Ireland.

Cowen was adamant that Ireland would make a significant contribution both at UN level and equally within the EU. He felt that it was important from Ireland's point of view to contribute 'where we can, when we can', as a modern democratic state. But despite growing fears that Ireland might eventually focus its resources on the EU project instead of the UN, Cowen insisted that Ireland would be 'absolutely committed' to the UN and that there would be no change in this policy. For Cowen, the UN was the most important organization in international relations and the promotion of peace and prosperity. He insisted that Ireland would use its UN position 'not for the purpose of grandstanding', but as a platform from which to engage constructively with other Security Council members to tackle many of the intractable problems that bedevilled international relations.

Cowen considered Ireland's election to the UN Security Council an historic moment in the country's history. The intense campaign for a seat, which had been pursued for two years under David Andrews prior to Cowen taking over at the

Foreign Ministry, was evidence of the government's commit-ment to this goal. But it was a campaign that newspaper reports at the time claimed was costing the state huge amounts of money that, some argued, could be better spent. Perhaps Cowen himself best summed up the benefits of the UN seat when, in an address to the Irish–Portuguese Friendship Society on 6 October 2000, he said: 'Our foreign policy is about much more than self-interest. It is a statement of the kind of people we are.'

In other words, Cowen saw Ireland's enhanced status within the UN as an opportunity to establish the nation's brand, so to speak, in the eyes of the world. But Cowen also saw Ireland as a nation of participators, endowed with what he described as 'the nature of taking on political responsibility'. He didn't want Ireland and its people characterized as a nation which would stand aside, sit on the fence or turn a blind eye to injustice or poverty, doomed to inaction out of an unwilling-ness to offend. During Ireland's two-year stint on the Security Council, Cowen wanted his country 'to stand up and give amplification to the values that we claim on behalf of what makes us Irish'. He argued that the whole purpose of Ireland's fight for freedom was to enable it to take its place among the nations of the world. He would tell critics at the time: 'Here's an opportunity for us to do that and to be a voice for smaller and weaker countries that haven't had the opportunity to develop and prosper that we have.'

In April 2001 Cowen faced his first major criticism in foreign affairs when Ireland was condemned by an Amnesty International report for having failed, in its presidency of the Council of Europe during the first half of 2000, to deal adequately with the growing crisis in the Russian state of Chechnya. Cowen rejected Amnesty's accusation –

particularly the charge that Ireland didn't take effective action against the Russian Federation when the crisis in Chechnya deteriorated during its presidency. Nor was he alone in repudiating the criticism, which surprised the Council of Europe's Secretary-General Walter Schwimmer. 'Ireland's presidency, in the first half of last year, was a key moment in our action on Chechnya,' he said.

May 2001 is probably a month Cowen doesn't care to remember. At the start of the month, as he was crossing the road outside Iveagh House, he was knocked down by a motorbike. For a split second, as the motorbike came speeding towards him, Cowen says he feared he'd be killed. Luckily, the motorcyclist – in an attempt to avoid Cowen – brought the bike down on its side, but still managed to hit Cowen's leg. Miraculously, Cowen picked himself up off the ground and managed to walk, slowly, with jolting pain in his leg, back into his office while waiting for an ambulance to take him to St James's Hospital. He was fortunate to have suffered no more than a badly bruised ankle. But the doctors told him he should take some time off work to recuperate. Reluctantly, he obeyed their advice and cancelled two imminent diplomatic trips: one to Sweden that weekend, and one to China for a meeting of ASEM and a summit of Asian-based ambassadors. Even so, Cowen was back in the office by the middle of the month. 'I might be hobbling, but at least I can still do my desk work,' he would quip to parliamentary colleagues when they enquired about the accident.

At the end of the month, Cowen's ministerial colleagues had a good joke at his expense when he failed to turn up for a special cabinet meeting in Kerry. He might have travelled thousands of miles around the world without any hitches, but he could still make a mistake when it came to taking a domestic flight from Dublin to Kerry: inconceivably, Cowen was on his way to the wrong airport before he discovered the error! While the rest of the cabinet arrived on time at Dublin airport on 28 May for the flight to Farranfore on the government's Gulfstream IV jet, Cowen mistakenly had his government car take him to the Baldonnel military airport.

Things got progressively worse in June with the Irish electorate's rejection of the Nice Treaty, which reformed the institutional structure of the EU to accommodate its eastward enlargement. Of those who took part in the referendum, 54 per cent voted against. It was a bitter blow for Cowen, who had been the government's election campaign director, commending the treaty to the people. The government's embarrassment was compounded by the admission from the Minister of State for Agriculture, Éamon Ó Cuív, that he had actually voted against the treaty. Cowen was annoyed by the admission; along with other cabinet ministers, he felt that went against the ethos of party loyalty. Nor would he quickly forget it. When he eventually became Taoiseach, Cowen said at the launch of his party's 'yes' campaign for the referendum on the Lisbon Treaty that support for the treaty was settled and that it was party policy for any parliamentary party member voting against it to lose the whip.

The resounding 'no' vote on Nice was the last thing that Cowen wanted. He felt it would be detrimental to the country's interest, fearing that – certainly in its bilateral trade and economic relationships with the applicant countries – Ireland would be remembered as the country that said 'no'. Cowen didn't want Ireland to be accused of putting a brake on enlargement of the EU. He was also angered by the suggestion made by opponents of the treaty that the electorate had the luxury of voting 'no' because the government could then renegotiate its contents, which Cowen described as 'just naïve in the extreme'. He told the press at the time: 'If we vote down this referendum, there is no legal basis for the ratification of the Treaty of Nice. That is the situation.' But perhaps Sinn Féin leader Gerry Adams summed up the reason for the government's failure in the first Nice Treaty vote when he said: 'The government tried to rush through the referendum without a debate. They tried to do it quietly.'

Bertie Ahern later acknowledged that the 'yes' campaign had been unsuccessful because of the government's failure to counter fears and negative perceptions, many of which were generated around issues that lay largely outside the treaty but nevertheless influenced people's voting decisions. 'While I am certain that the vast majority of the Irish people remain strongly committed to the European Union and enlargement,' he said, 'it is clear that there are genuine anxieties and concerns about the future, which go well beyond the terms of the treaty itself. We are going to have to reflect deeply on how those may best be addressed.'

It appears that the question of Irish neutrality had a huge impact on how people voted, many believing that acceptance of the Nice Treaty would mean Ireland signing up to participate in the EU's Rapid Reaction Force. Cowen saw this as nonsense, put about by opponents of the treaty as a scare tactic. 'Do the same people who are talking about a European army believe that Kofi Annan has an army? Because he has a signed-up capability submitted by sovereign governments throughout the world in eighty-eight countries for 147,500 people to be available at the disposal of the UN? Is someone suggesting to me that he gets up some morning and gets them all together on some plain in Massachusetts and goes off to take on China? What are they talking about? These are capabilities that are available and the EU position is simply mirroring that UN standby system,' he told Vincent Browne in an *Irish Times* interview.

Cowen would be the first to acknowledge that, despite his best efforts, he had failed to get the government's message across clearly enough to reassure the electorate that ratifying the Nice Treaty would not result in any changes to the Irish constitution. He knew that a new referendum – eventually scheduled for November 2002 – was the only solution, and vowed to double his effort behind the government's pro-treaty campaign. They would have to treat the second referendum as if it were a do-or-die election campaign. More immediately, Cowen was kept busy with his efforts to reassure his European counterparts that the Nice Treaty would indeed be ratified. He held meetings, as part of a damage limitation exercise, with the accession states' ambassadors to Ireland in an effort to quell their frustration and assuage their real anxieties about Ireland's rejection of the treaty having the potential to delay the date for their admission.

The EU summit in Luxembourg the week after the referendum was a tense affair. Cowen flew over with Ahern to reassure the other EU leaders that the Irish rejection of the Nice Treaty would not influence the schedule for the planned accession of new members. Speaking to reporters before he entered the vast, wood-panelled conference room in the Council of Ministers building, Cowen said: 'I came here to explain the circumstances as best I can. I didn't come here expecting a solution.'

As soon as the meeting started, the Swedish foreign minister, Anna Lindh, who was in the chair, bluntly told Cowen what he had already told the Irish electorate: 'There is no possibility to open the text of the Nice Treaty again. There is no possibility to change the treaty.' Cowen instantly knew that it was going to be a difficult conference. He later diplomatically described the meeting with the other fourteen ministers as 'a mature political discussion'; newspaper reports described further meetings between Cowen and the candidate countries as 'polite but frosty'. Cowen revealed to his European counterparts that the Irish government had been taken aback by the result of the referendum. 'We are still trying to interpret last week's vote,' he said. 'But I accept – without hesitation – that if a second referendum were to be held it would be on the basis of an unchanged Nice Treaty.'

After the conference finished, Cowen came into the Irish delegation's room and told the press that ratification of the Nice Treaty was vital. Ireland needed to be united with the EU; therefore another referendum was the only option. 'I don't intend for Ireland to be isolated in Europe,' he said. 'That is not in Ireland's interests, and it's my job to protect Ireland's interests.'

Immediately after the meeting, the anti-Nice Treaty group, which was called The National Platform, released a statement calling for Cowen's immediate resignation. Their secretary, Anthony Coughlan, alleged that Cowen was embarking on a course of 'high treason' by 'conniving' with other EU foreign ministers to 'overthrow' the result of the vote. The 'no' campaign group rejected wholesale the unanimous statement issued by EU foreign ministers ruling out renegotiation of the treaty, and argued that Cowen's subscribing to the statement was a grave insult to the Irish people and to the democratic process.

Matters were not helped by an embarrassing slip-up the following week, when Cowen accompanied Ahern to an EU summit in Gothenburg. Cowen and Ahern were attempting to calm the mood by reassuring their EU colleagues that they would deal with the situation – only for Charlie McCreevy to nullify their efforts by declaring that the 'no' vote was, in fact, a 'remarkably healthy development'.

By the end of June 2002, the government had published the wording for the second referendum on the Nice Treaty. It differed significantly from the first in including a prohibition on Ireland's entering into an EU defence policy system without a further amendment to the constitution being required. Cowen had learned from the mistakes of the first referendum and was adamant that they would not be repeated. He realized that, apart from undertaking a major canvassing campaign, it would be necessary to jolt the electorate into recognizing the hard facts of a 'what if' scenario: what would happen if Ireland didn't ratify the treaty. At a press conference in the Burlington Hotel in Dublin at the start of October 2002, Cowen explained that 875,000 jobs in Ireland depended on economic ties with, and participation in, the EU. He warned his audience that it would be 'extreme foolishness' to assume that Ireland had left behind the possibility of high unemployment. 'We live or die by our exports,' he said. 'We have now reached the situation where fully fifty per cent of everything we produce is exported to the European Union. More trade has brought more jobs for Ireland.' He also strongly criticized the scare tactics used by the anti-treaty campaign. His hard-hitting words struck home with the electorate, who voted positively with a resounding 'yes' at the second referendum, in which 60 per cent of votes were cast in favour of accepting the treaty.

In an unusual political move during the campaign, the former Fine Gael Taoiseach Garrett Fitzgerald decided to endorse the government's pro-treaty stance in public canvassing

ABOVE: **The young hurler** Brian Cowen, end left standing, on the Cistercian College Roscrea senior hurling team.

BELOW: **The young candidate** Brian Cowen, flanked by Charles Haughey and Brian Lenihan, with Ger Connolly in the background, after his victory at the Fianna Fáil candidate selection convention for the Laois–Offaly by-election, in the Bridge House Hotel, Tullamore, May 1984.

ABOVE: **Minister for Foreign Affairs** Receiving the seal of office from President Mary McAleese in January 2000. *Back row, left to right:* Eoin Ryan, Michael Woods, Brian Cowen, Frank Fahey, Micheál Martin, Mary Hanafin. *Front row, left to right:* Bertie Ahern, the President, Mary Harney.

RIGHT: **'Straight dealing'** David Trimble, First Minister of Northern Ireland and leader of the Ulster Unionist Party, and Brian Cowen, Minister for Foreign Affairs.

ABOVE: **Implementing the Good Friday Agreement**
Left to right: Cyril Ramaphosa, former Secretary-General of the African National Congress; Brian Cowen, Minister for Foreign Affairs; Peter Mandelson, Secretary of State for Northern Ireland; Martti Ahtisaari, former President of Finland.

ABOVE: **Good relations** Brian Cowen and Jack Straw, British Foreign Secretary.

RIGHT: **In earnest mode** Brian Cowen with Colin Powell, US Secretary of State.

LEFT: **Received at the Vatican** An audience with Pope John Paul II in November 2001.

RIGHT: **International diplomacy** Brian Cowen in discussions with the President of Afghanistan, Hamid Karzai.

BELOW: **Seeing the funny side** *Left to right:* European Union Commissioner Chris Patten, Brian Cowen, and China's Minister for Foreign Affairs Li Zhaoxing during the Asia European Foreign Ministers' meeting in Straffan, April 2004.

ABOVE: **The world stage** Brian Cowen with the US President, George W. Bush, following an EU–US summit at Dromoland Castle, Co Clare, June 2004.

BELOW: **Representing Europe** Brian Cowen with Kofi Annan, UN Secretary-General, Brussels, January 2004.

ABOVE: **With Yasser Arafat** Hand in hand in Ramallah.

ABOVE: **Budget Day, 2006** Brian Cowen, his wife Mary and their daughters Maedhbh and Sinead on the steps of Government Buildings.

LEFT: **The amicable handover** Brian Cowen and Bertie Ahern shake hands as, unopposed, Cowen is declared leader of Fianna Fáil.

BELOW: **First day at the office** On 8 May 2008 the new Taoiseach meets Ian Paisley, First Minister of the Northern Ireland Assembly, and his Deputy, Martin McGuinness.

ABOVE: **Homecoming**
Celebrations in Tullamore,
May 2008.

BELOW: **Light relief** 'Our Brian'
enjoying the 2008 Grand National
in the local pub in Tullamore.

ABOVE: **Vote for Lisbon**   Campaigning for a 'yes' vote in the Lisbon Treaty referendum with former Taoiseach and leader of Fine Gael, Garrett Fitzgerald.

BELOW: **Sombre faces on a bad news day**   Flanked by his ministerial colleagues, Micheál Martin, Mary Harney and John Gormley, the Taoiseach addresses a press conference outside Government Buildings in Dublin immediately after the announcement of the Lisbon Treaty referendum result.

ABOVE: **An Taoiseach** In Government Buildings, July 2008.

BELOW LEFT: **Still time to smile**   Sharing a joke with the President of France and of the European Council, Nicolas Sarkozy, on his visit to Dublin in July 2008.

BELOW RIGHT: **Crisis in Europe** Brian Cowen and the British Prime Minister, Gordon Brown, at the European Council meeting on 20 June 2008, days after the Lisbon Treaty referendum result.

with Cowen in his home constituency of Tullamore and with another minister, Micheál Martin, in Cork. Tullamore-based journalist Declan McSweeney jokingly described Fitzgerald's visit to the constituency as resembling a moment when 'civil war divisions were put aside'. He recalled that Cowen's introduction of Dr Fitzgerald at a public rally was a 'most unusual event on the Tullamore political scene'. Fitzgerald said he had taken the surprising step of canvassing with an opposition party to show how vital it was that Ireland voted in favour of the treaty. 'For this is far too important an issue both for the applicant countries and for us in Ireland to allow it to become bogged down in party politics,' he wrote in an opinion piece for the *Irish Times*. He felt that the treaty had been used for the wrong purposes by some voters who were dissatisfied with the government 'for one reason or another and who irrationally see this referendum as a way of lodging a protest – clearly unaware of the dangers to our national interests of alienating our partners in Europe by blocking enlargement for such a domestic political reason'. From the vantage point of canvassing on the streets, Fitzgerald came to the conclusion that the opinion polls were showing a significant swing to a 'yes' vote because large numbers of the electorate were annoyed at having been misled by the 'no' campaign.

A couple of years later, in 2005, Cowen repaid Dr Fitzgerald's gesture of solidarity during the Nice campaign by launching his book *Ireland in the World: Future Reflections* at a reception in Dublin Castle. Cowen delivered his speech with passion, speaking highly of the former Taoiseach and describing him as 'the greatest advertisement against ageism that I know'. Cowen spoke about how Fitzgerald symbolized a 'rational approach' to which he, and other politicians, aspired. Interestingly, Cowen then spelt out the ethos for his future tenure as Taoiseach when he spoke critically of contemporary politics in Ireland, castigating the current political mindset as a 'short term opportunistic point-scoring' mentality, which produced nothing more than a theatrical type of politics. 'We really do need to engage in the affairs of the state in a way that is far more challenging and far more inspiring,' he told the audience.

Fitzgerald has made no secret of his admiration for Cowen, and even has a framed picture of the two of them together as they emerged from a bookie's shop in Tullamore during his visit to canvass for the Nice Treaty. Speaking at the launch of his book, Fitzgerald could be heard telling acquaintances: 'He's very able. He was a very good Minister for Foreign Affairs and, as far as I can see, he's a very good Minister for Finance.' Furthermore, he was acknowledging to the press even then that Cowen would make a good Taoiseach, which must have surely raised eyebrows back at Fine Gael headquarters. Fitzgerald was one of the first opposition politicians to congratulate Cowen publicly when he was appointed leader of Fianna Fáil and has described Cowen as clearly the ablest of his generation within his party.

As preparation for Ireland's chairmanship of the UN Security Council the following month, in September 2001 Cowen went to the Middle East on a scheduled five-day tour. His visit coincided with a surge in violence in this volatile region. It was a disturbing situation that appeared to be deteriorating further almost day by day.

Cowen was a member of a mission to stress the need to implement the recently published report of an international committee chaired by US Senator George Mitchell, which was calling for a ceasefire, as part of a confidence-building measure, in an effort to restart political negotiations in the continuing Israeli–Palestinian conflict. Cowen felt his visit should highlight the fact that the EU had played a strong and increasingly effective role in the process in recent years. He planned to tell Arab leaders that the Mitchell Report was a unique beacon of hope, offering an opportunity to halt the spiralling tit-for-tat violence in the Middle East.

On 10 September, Cowen had a fruitful meeting with the Egyptian President, Hosni Mubarak, in Cairo. After this he jetted off to Jerusalem for a meeting with Israeli foreign minister Shimon Peres. On the morning of 11 September, Cowen was in Bethlehem meeting Arab leaders. He visited a school there and recalls 'these beautiful kids' looking up at a bullet-ridden blackboard. The classroom was in half-darkness from sandbags piled up against the windows in an effort to prevent random shots coming in and hitting the pupils. Cowen attempted to hide his horror at the situation, smiling at the children. As he left the school, Al-Qaeda terrorists were in the process of hijacking four planes in America. The events that were about to unfold would put Cowen in a pivotal role during the aftermath of the devastating attacks in New York. As the first aircraft crashed into the Twin Towers, Cowen was in a convoy speeding along the dusty highway towards Gaza for a meeting with Yasser Arafat. He was halfway there when his phone rang with the terrible news. He could barely comprehend the information being relayed to him from Dublin. Cowen ordered his driver to pull over to the side of the road. The rest of the motorcade – mostly jeeps carrying security personnel and a few members of the Irish media – followed suit. Cowen stepped out onto the sun-baked asphalt and paced up and down as he spoke to government officials back in Ireland.

At the time, Cowen found it 'most unusual' that a plane would hit an iconic building in Manhattan, but he didn't automatically assume that it was a terrorist attack. Of course, when he was informed that a second plane had hit the Twin Towers, it became clear that this 'was something very serious' – a deliberate attack on American territory. For the next fifteen minutes, Cowen was in deep conversation with various political advisers, as well as the Taoiseach, who had been in a meeting with the new US ambassador at the time of the first attack. Cowen told the Taoiseach that he was just about to visit Yasser Arafat. A lot might hang on that meeting: a potentially groundbreaking further meeting with his Israeli counterpart was being lined up in an effort to stop the violence. So, after a brief discussion with Ahern about the situation, Cowen decided to continue as scheduled. 'I didn't really hesitate about continuing on to Gaza,' he recalls.

As he got back into the car, Cowen's mind attempted to grasp the 'obscene acts of hatred', as he would later describe them, that had been committed in America. Later, he watched the video footage of the planes plunging into the buildings, a sight that left him shaken. In an article he wrote later that month for the *Irish Times*, Cowen mused: 'Nobody who has followed the endless television coverage of the dreadful events of September 11th and their aftermath can be unaware of the deep sense of violation felt by the American people at these savage attacks on their nation. We all watched in sympathy as a people in turn passed through fear, bewilderment, anger and finally to steely resolve.'

Cowen could feel the tension in the air when they finally arrived at Arafat's compound. As their motorcade stopped, Cowen noticed that the media were already swarming to the vicinity. Cowen – accompanied by the local Irish representative, Isolde Moylan – went in to meet Arafat, and spent a little under three-quarters of an hour with the Palestinian leader. Cowen observed that Arafat was visibly disturbed by the events in the United States. It seemed that his expression was asking, *Who would think of carrying out such a brutal attack?* Even the most extreme Palestinian terrorist faction had never contemplated an assault on so large a scale. 'He was shaken. Visibly shaken,' recalls Cowen.

Cowen knew that he had to urge the Palestinian leader to condemn the horrific attacks. It was not a hard task. Arafat immediately stated that he was 'absolutely adamant' that these attacks had nothing to do with his cause. 'No person in my organization has been involved in such an atrocity,' he vehemently stated. 'My country has much sympathy for the American people.'

Cowen looked into Arafat's eyes and saw genuine sorrow.

Cowen then spoke about the huge significance of this moment. 'It is very important for the Palestinian cause that you announce an absolute and immediate condemnation of all of this. You must also state that the Palestinian Authority's cooperation will be available to everyone,' he pointed out.

Mindful that the meeting had been originally planned to discuss possible routes towards a resolution of the conflict between the Palestinians and Israel – and even though it was hard to steer the conversation in this direction in the light of the devastating breaking news – Cowen did the best he could to include some discussion of that original subject.

Emerging from their brief meeting, Arafat and Cowen held a press conference for the waiting media, who bombarded the Palestinian leader with questions about the New York attacks. Did he know who would do such a horrible thing, or why?

Arafat stressed that he had no prior knowledge of the

attacks. He then made the precise points that Cowen had advised him to make only minutes earlier. Arafat would later go on publicly to endorse America's 'war on terror'; at one point the Palestinian police even shot and killed demonstrators who had protested against the Anglo-American invasion of Afghanistan.

Nevertheless, early reports in the American media suggested that a Palestinian splinter group was involved in the attacks. Scenes of allegedly jubilant Arabs from Palestine were being beamed around the world. When Cowen looked at the pictures of balaclava-covered men shooting off guns to 'celebrate' the atrocity, he immediately felt there was something amiss with the images. It later transpired that the scenes, including a woman screaming in joy, had actually been recorded in Lebanon. 'I have often wondered about this subsequently because there was no basis for that,' Cowen recalls. 'All of that had been portrayed very quickly, which was doing great injustice and damage to the Palestinian people. What I observed in Gaza City was not celebratory at all; on the contrary, it was just as stunned as you would expect from people looking at the television screens on the streets of Dublin. Because I was the only one in there, I felt it was my responsibility in the hours and days after to dispel that fake notion that people in Palestine were revelling in what happened – because these two separate and isolated pieces of television footage of maybe six people were being made representative of the whole Palestinian people when nothing could be further from the truth.'

As Cowen's motorcade took off back towards Israel, word reached them that Jerusalem airport had been shut down as a precautionary measure, the local authorities fearing similar attacks being carried out on the city. Thankfully, the Israeli government agreed to allow Cowen's private jet to take off; it was the only plane to leave Israeli airspace that night.

Instead of continuing on his scheduled sequence of visits to Syria and Beirut, Cowen immediately headed back to Europe for an emergency meeting of EU foreign ministers in Brussels. After the meeting, the European Commission President Romano Prodi emphasized the EU's solidarity with the US and stated that terrorism must be defeated. The former Italian prime minister told the waiting press: 'This criminal act was intended as an assault on all our shared values and on freedom itself. It is a true watershed and nothing will ever be the same.'

In the aftermath of the terrorist attacks Ireland held the chairmanship of the UN Security Council. Under normal circumstances, chairing the Council was, while a prestigious and demanding task, one filled with an almost endless influx of routine paperwork, and Cowen had originally planned to attend only the start and end of the chairmanship, with the Irish ambassador to the UN, Richard Ryan, deputizing for him in the meantime. But in the events now unfolding, Ireland would be in the hot seat – with changes anticipated to laws on terrorism and America's increasing talk of going to war, the Security Council would be playing a pivotal role – and Cowen was determined to ensure Ireland's chairmanship was deemed a resounding success.

'Richard Ryan was the man on the spot with his team in New York. He chaired most of the events, but we liaised with him on an ongoing basis,' recalls Cowen. 'I went out to chair the agreement to grant independence to East Timor. That was interesting because here you were chairing a debate about the establishment of a new country – after all the hardships and difficulties they went through. It was a proud moment for East Timor.'

At the end of September, Cowen travelled to the US 'in sadness but also in hope', as he put it, 'wondering about how much the US will have changed since my last visit'. He expected to arrive in a 'different America from the one I have known; less ebullient, more sombre, but an America determined to right the injustice that has been inflicted upon it'. One of his first ports of call was Washington, where he was to see Colin Powell; the meeting of the UN General Assembly was postponed to allow this crucial meeting between the US Secretary of State and the incoming President of the Security Council to take place. Cowen brought a threefold message to America on behalf of the Irish people: 'That we fully share America's grief; that we will join America and others in the long struggle to eradicate global terrorism; and that we must work together to resolve conflict and injustice, and respond to the challenge of poverty and hunger wherever they exist.'

Cowen told Powell that Ireland recognized the 'inherent right' of the US, under Article 51 of the UN Charter, to defend itself against terrorist attacks, 'including the right to defend itself against regimes who shelter and protect those carrying out or planning such atrocities'. But he also stressed to Powell that military action should be 'proportionate, measured and focused on the pursuit of justice'. Cowen also reassured Powell that Ireland, when it assumed the presidency of the UN Security Council in October, would stress the need for the international community to unite in the face of terror. 'We will be working with our partners on the Security Council to strengthen the obligation on UN member states to cooperate in the fight against terrorism,' he pointed out to Powell.

Cowen also used his meeting with Powell as an opportunity to encourage the US administration to maintain its constructive pressure on Israel and the Palestinian Authority to engage in negotiations. 'It behoves each and every nation to use its influence in the interest of furthering peace, stability and reconciliation,' he said.

But the government's agreement to facilitate the landing and refuelling of American military aircraft at Shannon airport was contentious to some back home. Cowen argued that Ireland was doing so in pursuit of UN Security Council Resolution 1368, which condemned the September 11 attacks and urged international cooperation against terrorism, but critics pointed out that allowing foreign soldiers onto Irish soil clearly contradicted Ireland's neutrality. Heated protests ensued, and an attack was even made on an American military plane by a campaigning activist at Shannon airport. Former MEP Patricia McKenna even went so far as to suggest that Ireland 'had blood on its hands' for allowing the stopovers. Cowen made no concessions to the critics, but he did acknowledge that the offer of facilities to US forces had 'caused concern to some'. Writing in the *Irish Times*, Cowen attempted to argue his case: 'I would emphasize that our offer is appropriate and legal. This offer has no implications for Ireland's traditional policy of neutrality by non-membership of military alliances. And it is, above all, the right thing to do when such a friend has been so grievously attacked.

'Looking to the longer term, the Government is determined that Ireland will play its full part in attempts to eliminate terrorism, through improved security, increased co-operation between police and security services, and by choking off the funding required to finance terrorist organizations. In this regard, the Government has decided to accelerate work on ratifying international anti-terrorism conventions.'

Fast forward to June 2006, when the Council of Europe's Committee of Legal Affairs and Human Rights accused Ireland, along with thirteen other EU member states, of 'intentional or grossly negligent collusion' in facilitating the American government's secret 'global spider's web' of detentions and unlawful transportation of terrorist suspects. The report stated that Ireland was guilty of 'negligent collusion' for allowing these so-called rendition flights to pass through Shannon airport. The Swiss senator Dick Marty, who had spent six months drawing up the report, said that Shannon was 'involved in an indirect fashion' because 'planes landed at Shannon after rendition operations, when they no longer had detainees on board'. The chair of Ireland's Human Rights Commission, Dr Maurice Manning, also called for the introduction of a new monitoring system for any US flights making stopovers in Ireland. 'The only effective way of ensuring that we do not become complicit in dispatching people to be tortured or ill-treated is through establishing an effective regime of monitoring and inspection,' he said.

Cowen dismissed suggestions that the Irish government had given any assistance to American rendition flights via the stopover facility at Shannon. 'We have made it very clear we didn't willingly or unwillingly aid any renditions. I don't accept we were involved in any renditions whatsoever and we have assurances to that effect that we find satisfactory,' he stated.

Back in October 2001, while in New York Cowen held discussions with the UN Secretary-General, Kofi Annan, and the other members of the Security Council. But the most poignant moments of his trip occurred during his meetings with people who had lost loved ones in the destruction of the World Trade Center. Cowen was told by one of the relatives of a missing firefighter at Ground Zero that he had been identified by a claddagh ring – a traditional Irish friendship ring – that he had been wearing.

Cowen can still vividly recall his visit to Ground Zero, accompanied by the then Mayor of New York, Rudolph Giuliani. Cowen was very familiar with this part of the city – he'd worked on the building sites in this district of New York during his student days – but now he was taken aback by the sheer 'stillness of the place', which he found 'very eerie'. As they were brought across to the sealed-off area by the harbour police, Cowen was overcome with a profound sense of sadness. 'It was a hellish scene,' Cowen later recalled. 'The smoke was still rising, two weeks later.'

As Cowen was taken through the horrific wreckage, which he could only compare to a scene from a war movie, he turned to the chief of the New York Police Department and asked if his officers had come across any more examples of the traditional Irish friendship ring.

'Minister,' the chief replied with a genuine tone of sadness, 'we found two hundred claddagh rings here.'

Cowen was left speechless by this fact. His heart sank as his eyes gazed sadly out over the rubble of the collapsed buildings. He says he pondered on how many more such rings would eventually be recovered in the wreckage. Later, the Governor of New York, George Pataki, said that the discovery of such a substantial number of claddagh rings in the ruins underlined 'the loss suffered here and in Ireland'.

Cowen arrived back at his hotel that night, as he recalled, 'very reflective, silenced by the horror of it all'.

Two months after the Twin Tower attacks, Cowen was back in New York to address the UN when a plane mysteriously dropped out of the sky in the borough of Queens. With tension and unease still very near the surface throughout the city, such a disaster naturally led to presumption that Al-Qaeda had struck again – prompting the city authorities immediately to shut down the three airports of JFK, Newark and LaGuardia. For some time it was uncertain whether the meeting of the UN's General Assembly would be cancelled; eventually, after much deliberation, it went ahead as scheduled.

During his passionate speech at that meeting, Cowen appealed for the military action by then under way in Afghanistan to be carried to a quick resolution. He urged that every step be taken to ensure the minimum number of casualties during the intense bombing campaign; he added that it was vital that a 'concerted international effort' be made to establish a new, stable government in the country. 'It is crucial that the military campaign be accompanied by a visible and effective humanitarian strategy. The long-suffering people of Afghanistan deserve no less,' he said.

But Cowen also made it clear in his speech that the US had the support of the Irish government. 'Ireland's position has been steadfast and clear – we stand with the United States and with the rest of the international community in asserting that the barbarism of September 11 cannot be allowed to succeed,' Cowen told the UN's fifty-sixth General Assembly.

Cowen realized that Ireland would not end its time in charge of the Security Council with 'all the world's problems solved', but he did believe 'that people will look upon our record and our membership as being one of a principled contribution which is also pragmatic in its approach'. While the general consensus was that Ireland's chairmanship of the UN Security Council could be deemed a success (particularly in the light of the September 11 crisis), Cowen still came in for some criticism. In particular, the Dublin-based TD and former Lord Mayor of that city (later leader of the Green Party and now a minister in Cowen's first cabinet) John Gormley alleged that Ireland's chairmanship of the Security Council was 'a period of total and abject failure'. The Minister for Foreign Affairs, he claimed, 'went out of his way to facilitate the US and Britain in their misguided war' against Afghanistan.

'Innocent people have died and a humanitarian crisis is now looming. Osama bin Laden's position has been strengthened and the whole region has been destabilized yet the Government continue to give unequivocal support to a failed strategy,' said Gormley.

In the following year's general election, the Greens vowed not to enter a coalition government with Fianna Fáil unless the US military were refused further access to Shannon airport. In the event – and much to the dismay of a significant number of their grassroots party members – they eventually opted to strike a deal with Fianna Fáil's negotiation team, which was headed by Cowen, without any such concession being made.

One encounter and another exchange provide two humorous footnotes to Ireland's chairmanship of the UN Security Council. Cowen was approached by the representative of a poor third world country who said he had been offered financial assistance for his country by 'one of our rivals' and wondered what to do. Without even pausing for thought, Cowen immediately replied, 'Keep the money – and vote for us.'

At another point during Ireland's month at the helm of the UN, the *Irish Times* received a complaint from the Department of Foreign Affairs because one of its journalists had jokingly referred to Cowen as Clow-en. Harry Browne later wrote: 'Three months ago, as the Republic took over the chair of the UN Security Council and the US started to pulverise Afghans, a senior official in the Department of Foreign Affairs found the time to complain to my boss that this column had referred to his boss as Brian "Clow-en" Cowen. In the extraordinary circumstances, it was a wonderful if incongruous compliment to be read so carefully, and taken so seriously, even when making the stupidest of jokes.'

At the end of November 2001 Cowen had the honour of an audience with Pope John Paul II in the Vatican. Cowen briefed the Pope on the latest developments in the conflict in Afghanistan and explained how, during Ireland's chairmanship of the UN Security Council, he had emphasized the need for humanitarian aid in the region. Cowen would later have a similar conversation with the Italian minister with special responsibility for Afghanistan, as well as meetings with the Secretary of State for Foreign Affairs in the Vatican, Archbishop Thuran.

Out of the hundreds of meetings Cowen had during his time as Minister for Foreign Affairs, it was probably the meeting with the Pope that touched him the most. 'History will record how influential Pope John Paul II was when the record of the twentieth century is written,' he reflects. He knew that his mother and his uncle, the Cistercian priest Father Andrew, were thrilled to know that he had had an audience with the Holy Father. Cowen himself was particularly struck by the Pope's enquiry about developments in Northern Ireland, noting that it was an issue about which His Holiness was particularly concerned. The Pope told Cowen that he still had fond memories of his only visit to Ireland in 1979; Cowen had been in America at the time, but his wife Mary could vividly recall the excitement the Pope's visit had generated, and how the streets of Offaly, like others all over the country, had been decorated with papal insignia and bunting in the papal colours for the occasion.

Straight after that visit to Ireland in 1979, Pope John Paul II visited New York. Cowen and his ex-Vietnam veteran friend Al both took a half-day off work to see the Pope at St Patrick's Cathedral in Manhattan. Cowen can still vividly recall his friend's amazement at 'seeing this little guy in white with a little biretta on his head'. He nudged Cowen and told him that the Pope was wearing 'a bad lid', which was American slang for a 'good hat'. Afterwards, when they were leaving, he bought a similar cap from one of the hucksters outside the cathedral. It was a comical experience for Cowen, watching his African American friend insist on wearing the white cap on his Afro haircut for the remainder of the day.

In Cowen's view, religious belief can play a positive role in people's lives, which is perhaps a surprising position for a politician to take in today's Ireland. During an interview in 2007, Cowen was asked if he believed in God, and replied: 'I do. Being a good Christian is a difficult thing. I don't believe in the secularization of the country. I believe that religion has its place. Spirituality has its place for people. It can bring a bit of meaning to life and a purpose. I respect those who don't believe; I also respect very much those who do. It is certainly part of my life. You fall along the way from time to time, but you do the best you can. For me, one struggles with one's faith all the time. It is like everything, you have to renew it. You have to work at it. You have a different perspective at different times of your life. But I am not a person who is dismissive of religion.'

Cowen would be the first to acknowledge that the Church's image in Ireland has been greatly tarnished by the sexual abuse scandals of recent years. But he believes that people in the Church were just as appalled by these horrific revelations as those outside, and that it is wrong to create a 'them and us' attitude, casting the Church as villain, on the basis of these discoveries. Cowen is adamant that the Church remains firm in its commitment to move forward in Ireland. 'There is a need also to acknowledge the great good the Catholic Church has done in the past and continues to do in the present day,' he maintains. As an example, he cites with pride Ireland's tradition of missionary vocational work in poorer countries, particularly in Africa. 'Many people went with the right motivation to many parts of the world to help those who hadn't a voice, those who were very poor,' he says.

One secondary effect of the extensive missionary work carried on throughout the world by Irish Catholics is the great amount of goodwill towards Ireland it has generated. Many Irish business leaders have made reference to this bank of goodwill, and the wide-ranging networks and personal contacts which exist because of the work of those missionaries in the remotest parts of Africa and elsewhere. The same legacy has also generally served Ireland well at the UN, Cowen maintains. He is repeatedly struck by how frequently political leaders in Africa mention their appreciation of the Irish missionaries whose predecessors educated them. Cowen says there is a great fund of goodwill for Ireland 'as a result of what those people did and achieved'. This is something that Cowen believes Ireland should be proud of.

During his time as foreign minister, Cowen had to face a tricky general election in 2002. According to former Progressive

Democrat TD Tom Parlon, it is an election that will be remembered as a bitter one in the Laois–Offaly constituency. Fianna Fáil is normally guaranteed an impressive three out of the five available Dáil seats in this constituency, but the party organization apparently feared the potential threat of the PDs taking one of these precious seats. The former *Irish Times* editor Conor Brady described the tension between the two parties as 'war to the knife'. As the election got under way, the local paper the *Leinster Express* ran the headline 'FF out to shaft Parlon'. In the accompanying article, local reporter John Whelan wrote: 'All political posturing went out the window in Portarlington this week when over four hundred FF supporters were warned that Parlon posed a real threat to their third Laois–Offaly seat and their ambitions to form the next government. In a direct affront to the party's publicly-stated policy of a vote transfer pact with the Progressive Democrats, delegates packed into the GAA centre in the Fianna Fáil stronghold were directed to omit Parlon from their ballot papers.'

Cowen had taken a break from his UN duties to attend the party's election rally, at which he gave a speech described by the *Leinster Leader* as one that brought 'the audience to their feet for an enthusiastic standing ovation' with its 'infectious passion and conviction'. Regardless of the hostility between his party and the PDs, Cowen still managed to top the poll in the constituency, as he would do again in the following general election in 2007. In 2002, the announcement by the returning officer of Cowen's top position was met with thunderous cheers from party supporters. Parlon recalls that there was real passion in the ear-piercing roar from Cowen's entourage. 'My crowd were looking at them and just for a second I thought, "There's going to be a mill here!" Genuinely. There was that sort of rawness in it . . . I started to clap. Two more joined in. And then others joined in. But just for a second it was that intense. You wouldn't know if all hell was going to break loose,' he told Katie Hannon in an interview for her book, *The Naked Politician*.

After the election Cowen was appointed deputy leader of Fianna Fáil, following Mary O'Rourke's decision to step down from the role after eight years, having lost her Dáil seat to Donie Cassidy. Even though the post of deputy leader is seen as a largely ceremonial role, Ahern's decision to appoint his Minister for Foreign Affairs was perceived by many political pundits as an unspoken acknowledgement that Cowen was now heir apparent to the leadership of the biggest political party in the country. Explaining why he selected Cowen, Ahern said: 'Brian is held in very high regard throughout the Fianna Fáil organization and has gained vast experience over the past number of years in the Irish electoral system.'

While the appointment was widely and enthusiastically received by the party's grassroots members, some did express surprise that both the Minister for Finance, Charlie McCreevy, and the Minister for Sports, John O'Donoghue, had been passed over. However, one TD, speaking off the record to the *Irish Times* political reporter Mark Hennessy, said: 'Frankly, it would have been a surprise if it had gone to anyone other than Brian.'

'We'll do it with a smile.' So said Cowen in December 2003 when questioned at a press conference as to how Ireland would conduct its forthcoming six-month presidency of the EU. After the press conference, at the Justus Lipsius Building in Brussels, a lavish reception of smoked salmon, Irish cheese and Guinness was put on for the European journalists. As they knocked back a few beers, many remarked on Cowen's astonishing ability to brief the press in minute detail without a script. Reynolds had once told Cowen that it didn't matter if you had the best-prepared speech in the world, nobody would listen if you were going to stumble over the words. Reynolds believed that you needed to look the audience in the eyes and speak confidently – without a script. It was advice that Cowen took to heart. The foreign press were amazed that day as he rattled off, apparently without effort, what he perceived as a list of key areas that needed immediate attention at EU level, including everything from the need for an EU-wide identity card system to tackling the problems of sub-Saharan Africa.

During his time in foreign affairs, Cowen showed great interest in contributing constructively to attempts to resolve the intractable conflict between Israel and Palestine. At one stage, it was even alleged in the UK's *Daily Telegraph* that Ireland was 'one of the most anti-Israeli democracies'. There appeared to be a general consensus that Cowen was biased towards the Palestinians, which is a perception that he has rejected publicly. 'Ireland', he once said, 'fully subscribes to the position that the Palestinians have a right to their own homeland and the state of Israel is entitled to live in peace and security. It is true that successive governments have been very supportive of the Palestinian cause for all the right reasons, in my opinion, which is not an anti-Israeli position, it is a pro-Palestinian position. We are not saying that the rights of the Palestinians must be vindicated in a way that compromises the right of Israel to exist.'

Israel, nevertheless, made no secret of its displeasure that Ireland should be holding the EU presidency during a very tense period in the negotiations over the so-called 'road map for peace'. Just as Ireland took over the presidency, the negotiations had stalled. Israel stated on the one hand that it was planning to withdraw unilaterally from part of the occupied West Bank, but on the other that it would continue with its erection of a fencing corridor dividing Palestinians from Israelis – a policy that had been attacked by the Palestinian government, who saw this as an attempt by Israel to renege on its obligations under the road map. The Palestinian prime minister Ahmed Korei warned his Israeli counterpart Ariel Sharon that he was prepared to consider a 'one-state solution' and demand equal rights, which could have resulted in an Israeli state with a Palestinian majority, given the demographic facts of rapid growth in the Palestinian population of the occupied territories and rapid decline in Jewish immigration since the influx of one million Russian Jews in the early 1990s. Sharon for his part would never agree to a settlement that opened the way to this outcome, which his political analysts compared to the transition from apartheid to democracy that had occurred in South Africa.

Against this backdrop, it was Cowen's mission as representative of the EU presidency to kick-start the peace talks in the hope that both parties would agree to a two-state solution. In 2004 he visited Israel in an effort to help push the peace process further along. The previous week he had held a meeting with the Palestinian negotiator and Minister for International Planning and Development, Dr Nabil Shaath, who described the EU as the Palestinians' 'ally of choice'.

At the end of April 2004 Cowen was present at a two-day conference on anti-semitism in Berlin, organized by the EU and attended by representatives of fifty-five countries, including the US Secretary of State, Colin Powell, and the Israeli President, Moshe Katsav. Cowen gave a powerful speech on behalf of the EU. As well as calling for much greater action to tackle the 'vile phenomenon of anti-semitism', Cowen also stated that European governments had every right to criticize particular policies of the Israeli government, free speech being 'an essential feature of democratic political systems': 'Anti-semitism must be addressed by firm measures. But, while we do so, we cannot and should not expect reasonable criticism and fair comment about specific Israeli government policies to fall silent. The exploitation of race for political purposes by any government or any politician ... is quite simply unacceptable.'

Shortly after this speech, diplomatic relations between Israel and the EU came under severe strain when, on 22 May 2004, Cowen made a strong statement arguing that Israeli military forces had shown 'a reckless disregard for human life' during a brutal attack in the Rafah area of Gaza that resulted in eight casualties, including four young children – all apparently killed by an Israeli tank shell. Cowen was disgusted by the Israeli decision to deploy helicopters and tanks to confront a Palestinian protest. He described it as being 'completely disproportionate to any threat faced by the Israeli military'.

As a result of Cowen's comment, the Irish ambassador, Patrick Hennessy, was summoned to the Foreign Ministry in Jerusalem to be handed a letter by the department's deputy director-general, Ran Curiel. It stated that the Israeli government was 'sickened' by Cowen's words. The letter, which apparently rejected 'any insinuation aimed at sullying our soldiers that hints they deliberately targeted children', was described by Israeli government sources at the time as being the most furious protest letter ever sent to a foreign official. The letter unfairly criticized Cowen for comparing the slaughter of these young children – or, as the letter put it more gently, the 'regrettable events' – to what the Israelis described as the 'foul murder' earlier that month of a pregnant Israeli woman, Tali Hatuel, and her four daughters by Palestinian terrorists. The letter also alleged that Israel 'makes every effort' to prevent civilian casualties (even though Israeli officials did admit that a shell was fired off at a so-called abandoned building, which may have gone straight through it and into a crowd of thousands of demonstrators) and warned Cowen 'to be more careful' about making comments on the basis of what it claimed was 'biased and false information'.

Cowen was forceful in his condemnation of attacks by either side, but he also feels it is important for Europe to 'balance out' the American bias towards Israel. 'I was always quite rigorous that Europe needs to find a balance – and it is a difficult balance to find. Let's be clear: Israel has the right to exist – peacefully. But, equally, Palestine has the right to exist too and I felt very strongly that keeping that balance there is a critical role for Europe to play. It's a somewhat counter-balancing role, in some respects, to the United States role. The US political culture is very uncritical of Israel in terms of the obligation it needs to show towards the two-state solution. We need to be objective on that and we need to call it when we need to call it,' Cowen says.

One of the highlights of Ireland's EU presidency for Cowen was surely the day in April 2004 when many of Europe's leading political figures visited Tullamore. The scene was a festive one: all the town's main streets were festooned with bunting and the national flags of all the EU member states were hoisted at the town council building, where Cowen had started his political career some twenty years earlier. They made an unusual sight: as Deaglán de Bréadún pointed out to readers of the *Irish Times*, 'Authoritative sources said the last big event with a European flavour in Tullamore was a row at the local barracks in the 18th century, when some German mercenaries tragically fought to the death for the affections of a local lass. The lovelorn Hessians are remembered with a plaque in Kilcruttin Cemetery.'

There was a huge international media contingent at the event, which Offaly reporter Declan McSweeney later described as a 'strange experience for local journalists'. The media centre was in McSweeney's former school, Coláiste Choilm, where he recalls the Gardaí conducting airport-style security checks in the classrooms. He found it a surreal experience to see the Greek foreign minister giving a TV interview in the playing field, while high-profile international journalists from *Le Monde* and the *Financial Times* rubbed shoulders with the local reporters working on provincial titles. 'I recall the then British Foreign Secretary Jack Straw being interviewed by reporters as he entered the Tullamore Court Hotel, saying, "I'm glad to be here in the constituency of my good friend Brian Cowen,"' says McSweeney.

Perhaps McSweeney best sums up Cowen's tenure as Minister for Foreign Affairs: 'Always proud of his local roots, he was at the same time a citizen of the world, a quality most clearly seen when he was at Foreign Affairs.' It was also the portfolio that Cowen appears to have relished most, more than any of his four other cabinet posts. 'Foreign affairs was a brilliant time,' he enthusiastically recalls. 'During this period, I had the opportunity to undertake Ireland's membership of the Security Council of the United Nations for two years. I was also honoured to be at the helm of Ireland's presidency of the European Union – with all that entails, including the negotiation of the draft constitution, which really was a major diplomatic and political achievement. I was also very proud to be there in the heart of the peace process negotiations and developments. That was also a very gratifying experience. To have experienced any one of these would have been special in terms of political challenge, but to have all three – in a tenure that lasted less than five years – means that, for me, it was a great time.'

One of Cowen's 'truly proud moments' during this period occurred during Ireland's presidency of the European Union, when the draft of the EU Constitutional Treaty was signed in Rome. 'Our whole objective was to get to a point where the Taoiseach would deal with the last five or six big outstanding issues at heads of state and government level. My job was to get agreement on all the other parts of the treaty. It was a genuinely proud moment for me when we went in for the last session and we got agreement on the draft of the EU Constitutional Treaty, which was subsequently amended to the Lisbon Treaty. But ninety per cent of what was in the Lisbon Treaty was agreed during the Irish presidency,' explains Cowen.

'It really was a magnificent achievement – a great team effort by the Taoiseach and many officials across a number of departments in the Irish government. I don't think there was any other presidency as well equipped as we were to get that through. It shows the goodwill for Ireland in Europe. To be able to broker that deal – and to be coming to the table as an honest broker and a fair-minded country that would try and get agreement – Ireland picked up a lot of goodwill because of that achievement. I would hate to see it dissipated now because we find ourselves in a situation where we voted "no" on a treaty that we negotiated during our presidency.'

8

Finance

The likelihood that Cowen might one day become Taoiseach was greatly increased when in September 2004, following Charlie McCreevy's departure to Brussels as Ireland's EU Commissioner, he became Minister for Finance, often viewed as the key preparatory position for the top job.

The move gave Cowen the opportunity to work closer to home. While he had hugely enjoyed the challenge of the foreign affairs portfolio, the constant travelling disrupted his home life more than he liked. But the Department of Finance had its own difficulties. As Cowen explains with wry humour: 'Finance has probably been the ultimate challenge because you're "Doctor No" in some senses. It's quite demanding in terms of the tension that exists between spending departments and Finance.'

It was a demanding time to take over the running of the department, with a budget to be prepared immediately for release in December. That first budget was universally deemed a success; but Cowen soon ran into controversy when he made the decision to reform aspects of the generous tax provisions enjoyed by artists and writers in Ireland. An innovative and progressive measure originally introduced by Charles Haughey, it had enabled many struggling artists and writers to secure a livelihood by exempting them from income tax. Cowen sought to place a cap on the amount of income which could be deemed tax-exempt in order to bring very high-earning artists and writers into the tax net. This move drew strong criticism from the arts community: several prominent Irish authors urged Cowen not to withdraw or restrict the scheme, and a report drawn up by the Arts Council also argued that the scheme should be retained.

Many artists were concerned that putting a cap on the amount of income which would qualify for exemption would compromise what they felt was the original intention of the scheme, that is, to encourage the flourishing of arts and culture in Ireland. Some felt that there was a misplaced public perception that the scheme was only established to help *struggling* artists. There were also fears that if the cap was introduced with immediate effect it would permit no time for artists to reassess and reorganize their tax affairs to allow for the change. Cowen, on the other hand, was adamant that the intention of the scheme was to assist artists who were struggling financially.

The renowned author John McGahern, who had penned modern classics such as *Amongst Women* and *The Dark*, visited Cowen as part of an Arts Council delegation to urge the Minister to retain the exemption. Prior to his meeting with Cowen, McGahern had added his voice to the objections raised by his fellow artists. McGahern argued that 'the vast majority of artists who benefit under this scheme earn very little from their work . . . [It] is a simple principle and costs little to administer.' However, Cowen recalls being satisfied after their meeting that McGahern 'understood' the thinking behind his proposed tax change. Sadly, in 2006, just a few months after this meeting took place, McGahern died. Cowen still treasures the signed copy of the novel *That They May Face the Rising Sun* which McGahern presented to him when they met.

The Irish publishing industry predicted that many Irish writers would leave the state if the tax exemption were abolished, and that in consequence it would become, as Michael O'Brien of the O'Brien Press put it, 'increasingly difficult to find new Irish authors, particularly in the less commercial areas of children's fiction, fantasy, poetry and biography'.

Protests from writers and publishers were accompanied by a letter from Cowen's cabinet colleague, the Minister for Arts John O'Donoghue, pleading the case for those who would be seriously affected by any dramatic changes. 'Most of those benefiting from the scheme are on very modest incomes,' O'Donoghue explained. 'We have good reason to believe that terminating or even capping the scheme is more likely to result in high earners legally leaving the jurisdiction, or structuring their earnings in a way that avoids or greatly reduces any tax liability, than in any revenue windfall for the Exchequer.'

Cowen had originally contemplated scrapping the scheme completely, but having reflected further on all the cases put to him and after weighing up all the arguments, he decided instead to put a cap of €250,000 on non-taxable earnings, which he argued 'met the equity rule'. This decision met with a mixed reaction from the arts community. But regardless of any criticism levelled at him for changing the system, Cowen remains adamant that his decision was the correct one. 'This measure will help eliminate the phenomenon of tax-free millionaires,' he said at the time of the announcement. For when he 'did the figures, did the study of who exactly benefited from this exemption', Cowen argued, he discovered that by placing the cut-off point at €250,000 per year he was exempting, in effect, 95 per cent of the people already covered. According to figures for 2001, more than half the writers and artists availing themselves of the scheme earned less than €10,000 a year, while another third earned between €10,000 and €50,000; just twenty-eight writers and artists earned more than the cap that particular year. As Cowen explains: 'What I wasn't prepared to continue on – because it had gone beyond what was contemplated in the first place when Charlie Haughey introduced it in 1969 – was people on €7 million, €8 million. This was brought in for struggling artists! As you know, in some areas of art now – including music and other businesses – the commercialism issue is as much a part of success as the artistic content.'

Cowen argues that he was prompted to introduce a cap because the government had to show that its tax system was credible and fair. 'I didn't get rid of the exemption – the modification I introduced, and the motivation behind it, was the right one. And I don't think, in any way, it should decrease the level of artistic endeavour in the country. There is a certain level beyond which one should – despite one's artistic contribution – make a financial contribution,' he says.

Shortly after Cowen's controversial amendment to the income tax rules, Ireland's most successful music group, U2, decided to move part of their multi-million-euro business interests abroad to the Netherlands in an effort to avoid pay-ing excessive tax under the new regulations. The band's manager, Paul McGuinness, defended the move by pointing out that 'the reality is that U2's business is ninety per cent conducted around the world. Ninety per cent of our tickets and ninety-eight per cent of our records are sold outside of Ireland.' He added in an interview with *Hot Press* magazine: 'It's [Ireland] where we live and where we work and where we employ a lot of people. But we pay taxes all over the world – of many different kinds. And like any other business, we're perfectly entitled to minimise the tax we pay.'

U2's move was criticized by several high-profile politicians, but Cowen was philosophical. In fact, he had anticipated that some high earners would take this course. 'This is a response that people the tax planners – can come to,' he points out. 'In fairness, I met Bono at the Ireland–England game in Croke Park, the rugby match. He brought it up; it was a private discussion on a social occasion, but I got the impression that he recognized what I was trying to do – and I have no adverse comment to make on their decision either. Hopefully, maybe that situation might change in the future in terms of where they locate some of their business.'

Even ahead of his first budget, Cowen had had to weather controversy when he revealed that the Irish government would not be able to achieve the target of donating 0.7 per cent of GNP to international aid by the year 2007, as Ahern had promised at the UN Millennium Summit in September 2000. Cowen's admission was one of a series of announcements emerging from the government following the reshuffle indicating that, for varying reasons, many of the key promises made before the general election of 2002 were being cancelled or deferred. Thus the Minister for Justice, Michael McDowell, announced that a pre-election promise of two thousand extra Gardaí couldn't be met owing to lack of sufficient funding; the Education Department let it be known that a promised schools refurbishment project wouldn't be

fully implemented; and the promise of ending hospital waiting lists within two years was revealed to be an unrealistic goal
by the health minister Micheál Martin.

Cowen's declaration that the government would not meet
its overseas aid commitment came under fire in March 2005
from Sir Bob Geldof. At a press conference in London to
launch the report of the British government's Commission for
Africa, Geldof, standing alongside British Prime Minister
Tony Blair, said Ireland's stance was 'shameful' and a 'cop-
out'. Geldof continued: 'Now that we're well off, please let's
spare us going into this economic trickery, these false, broken
promises. It ill becomes us . . . We have a specific role to play
within Europe. We are a serious voice, a dynamic economy, a
people who have moved out beyond Africa and the rest of the
world. Go back to what we said. Let's not break our word . . .
In a world where prosperity is increasing and more people are
sharing each year in its growing wealth, it is an obscenity that
should haunt our daily thoughts that four million children will
die in Africa this year before their fifth birthday.'

But Cowen rejected the criticism, arguing that Ireland was
'unique among donors' and pointing out that it was the first
donor country to support the objective of total debt cancellation for heavily indebted third world countries. 'Ireland is
one of the world's leading aid donors on a per capita basis. We
are currently in eighth place among OECD member states and
our performance is well above the EU average,' Cowen told
the press.

In September that year, during a diplomatic trip to the US,
Ahern announced a new date of 2012 by which his government would reach the aid target. Cowen insisted that this new
commitment was a 'demanding but achievable' goal, warning
that it would require significant financial commitments from

the Irish government. Speaking at the International Monetary Fund–World Bank meeting in Washington on 25 September, he said: 'This will be achieved in 2012, some three years earlier than the agreed EU target date of 2015. Given current economic projections, this will mean a tripling of Ireland's ODA [overseas development aid] above current levels. This commitment is very demanding. But my Government believes that it is achievable.'

Cowen also declared that Ireland was willing to contribute its share of the cost of the recent decision by the G8 countries to cancel the outstanding debts of a group of the world's poorest countries to the World Bank, International Monetary Fund and African Development Bank, stating that the agreement 'represents very significant progress towards solving the so far intractable problem of third world debt'. But he also argued that, while the cancellation of third world debt had been the Irish government's policy since 2002, 'the key to underpinning growth' was trade reform, which he felt was 'within our grasp'.

Fine Gael's leader Enda Kenny and Pat Rabbitte of the Labour Party declared it a 'disgrace' that Ireland had reneged on its self-imposed 2007 deadline for meeting the 0.7 per cent aid target and vowed that, if elected, they would immediately restore it in their joint programme for government. But Cowen pointed out that neither of them had actually provided money for this in their respective election campaign promises. Dismissing the claim that the target could be reached earlier than 2012, Cowen stated: 'They haven't found out where they are going to get the money . . . there are significant resources going to be provided for this, and we have put them into our plans. The others haven't. If they are saying they are going to do it anyway, even if they haven't provided for it in their budgets, could they kindly tell us then what falls out of the budget?' Cowen is still adamant that the 2012 target will be reached.

More reflectively, Cowen suggests that the promised 0.7 per cent aid commitment is 'really our generation's response beyond the missionary zeal of those who went before'. He continues: 'It is a modern manifestation of that continuing, I think that's the best way of putting it. That's why it is an important issue and the Irish people expect our government to come up to the plate on this. Thankfully, we now have the prosperity and the resources to show ourselves to be in the top four or five or six countries in the world. We don't tie our aid to a benefit for the country in terms of our bilateral relations with these countries. That's another defining characteristic which emphasizes the genuineness of giving.'

Cowen believes that because of the changes that are occurring in contemporary Ireland – particularly the decline in religious vocations – it is inevitable that less emphasis will be placed on the institution of the Church; the corollary of this, he insists, is a need for 'a greater personal commitment on the part of us all towards the fundamentals of Christian living, to enable us to move beyond these difficulties without losing methods that served us well in adversity.' He continues, using care of the elderly as an example of his wider point:

'I would be very strongly of the view that these values that have served us well – historically – are just as relevant in this era of prosperity today. It's important that we don't become a "me" generation – that we don't become a selfish individual-istic society that fragments. It's important to maintain values of solidarity, love and dignity towards our elderly. We must provide facilities that enable them to improve their lives. These are important values that we need to give expression to more effectively. That involves us giving up ourselves to others. I think it is true that you gain more by giving than by receiving. This is a fundamental concept that needs to be continually manifested by all in society, for all of us to use this prosperity to make sure we are bringing more people from the margins into the centre – that our policies are effective in these matters rather than being rhetorical.'

Cowen feels that it's important for contemporary Ireland to look at how best to nurture a more humanitarian society. 'I think expanding opportunity is the best way of doing business – providing work for our people is the best poverty buster of all because it enhances people's own sense of self-empowerment and ability to change their circumstances.' Cowen is worried by the growing trend in Irish society to, as he puts it, 'overdo the state approach'. He dislikes the mentality that assumes that the state will provide for all society's needs.

'I think there's a huge sense of self-worth in people themselves,' he says. 'I have seen it in communities – people making sure communities are connected, that they work, that the whole volunteer effort of providing for our kids' recreation and being engaged in clubs and sports and community activities keeps going. These are as important in improving quality of life as the idea that someone from the Department of Something is going to sort out some problem. I don't think that works. Obviously, there's a role for the state and we have it through our various schemes and resources. But it's active communities on the ground that are really important – I've seen it everywhere throughout the country – people who feed into what the state can provide and places where localized solutions are built from the ground up, where social capital is built up in communities. These are important. These are the issues that matter for me.'

One achievement in which Cowen takes pride is that, as Minister for Finance, he set up the Social Finance Foundation. This fund supports social finance providers on the front line who help people gain access to social benefits. Cowen believes in the sort of governance where citizens interact very positively with state institutions and the state apparatus, 'so that localized solutions are found and that the flexibility is there and the creativity is there to address these issues. I suppose in the past it could be said that the Church played that role before the state provided these resources, in its own way. It was part of the leadership of the locale – and now we need to try and make sure that, in the event that that power is receding – and some of it for good reasons – that we replace it with something that's also positive, or has the potential to be positive. That's the transition. That's the change I see that's happening on the ground,' he says.

Cowen feels that it's important to ensure that the Ireland of the future does not turn away from the values derived from the Church as a result of these changes. Ireland needs to be conscious, he says, 'of what it is that motivates our people, what is the sort of society that we all want. People don't articulate it very often. And I think these sorts of things are important. Our young people, who are coming into this new era now, obviously come unburdened with the mistakes of the past, but they also must come with a sense of direction for the future. I would be conservative with a small "c" in that sense. I don't believe in throwing everything away. I think there are things which have brought us to where we are and served us well. They may not have brought us material wealth but they do encompass many of the attractive characteristics that make us well liked as a nation and well respected in the world.'

*

In April 2005, Cowen caused something of a controversy on a trip to Derry when he publicly endorsed the candidacy of Mark Durkan for the leadership of the SDLP. Cowen denied that he was 'trying to put anyone's nose out of joint' by endorsing Durkan, who was in the process of defending the seat vacated by Nobel Peace Prize winner John Hume. During the trip, journalists asked Cowen if his public backing of Durkan could be seen as a snub to Sinn Féin.

Cowen easily sidestepped that trap by diplomatically answering: 'Mark Durkan is an excellent candidate to succeed John Hume. They will vote for whomever they wish and obviously I am here to support who I would like to see them support. I am not here to put anyone's nose out of joint, I am here to support Mark Durkan. I think he has been an outstanding finance minister in the Assembly and he is a good personal friend of mine. He is here to contest and to hold John Hume's seat and I am delighted to be here to be associated with his efforts.' Sitting alongside Durkan, he told the press that, were he eligible to vote, 'I would be voting for the man beside me. He espouses some of the economic republicanism that is relevant to twenty-first century Ireland.'

Later that day, Cowen further endorsed the SDLP when speaking to representatives of Derry's business community, telling them that it had the 'most economically literate agenda' of the Northern parties. Cowen also emphasized that, following a period of stability in the North, he envisaged that €100 billion could become available to spend on an all-Ireland basis during the next decade. 'It is my firm contention that the huge progress that has been made economically in both parts of Ireland in recent years is due in part to the peace process and the Good Friday agreement, but we are only scratching the surface of its potential to bring mutual benefit for all of our people,' he said.

It is interesting to note Cowen's description of Durkan as a close personal friend, particularly in the light of current speculation that an historic alliance, or even a merger, between the two parties might develop, possibly even before the next general election in the North. If the SDLP did decide to merge with Fianna Fáil, it would result in Cowen being the leader of the biggest political party on an all-island basis.

Speaking on the subject of the SDLP's future, Durkan has revealed that the possibility of 'doing business' with Fianna Fáil is still being discussed at the grassroots level of the party and could take time to evolve. 'As I said to our own party members – change changes things. We now have a settled process. The template that we set out to achieve many, many years ago is now a given. These arrangements are here to stay and I don't believe we are going to see the collapse of institutions or we are going to see the sort of instability that we were witnessing a few years ago. That stability creates new opportunities. And those new opportunities will involve, I believe, political and electoral realignment. I believe there are prospects of change over time within the North – and, I believe, on a North–South basis as well; and we want to foster and cultivate those prospects.'

Cowen hit the headlines yet again in June 2005 when he threatened to take legal action against Labour TD Joan Burton if she repeated outside the chamber allegations she made against him in the Dáil (deputies have full privilege when speaking in the House). Cowen also warned Dan Boyle of the Green Party that he would have a 'chat' with him if he repeated allegations outside the Dáil.

The controversy arose when, during a heated Dáil exchange, Cowen insisted that non-residence for tax purposes did not mean that people were exempt from paying tax in the state, but rather meant that they would be liable to pay tax only on their Irish-sourced income. At this point Burton, who eventually became deputy leader of the Labour Party in 2007, snapped at Cowen: 'Non-residency enables them not to be subject to tax on worldwide income,' before alleging: 'Almost none of them has Irish-sourced income – and the Minister knows that. He is protecting his rich friends again.'

This raised Cowen's hackles. It appeared to him that Burton was constantly making allegations that he had inside knowledge of the tax affairs of individuals in Ireland's business community. Her suggestion that Cowen might in some way have been less than honest, that he might have shown undue favour to rich supporters of the government party, stung Cowen, who insists that he has always sought to espouse high standards of integrity and probity in public life. Indeed, in one of his first acts as Taoiseach, Cowen declared plans to order a full review of the Fianna Fáil party organization, with particular emphasis on its fundraising. Speaking on 22 May 2008 to the Fianna Fáil national executive in Leinster House, Cowen revealed that he had decided to abandon the party's controversial fundraiser tent at the Galway Races – one of its most significant fundraising events, normally attended by many of the country's leading property developers, building firm proprietors and affluent businesspeople. Although the cancellation was announced as applying for that year only, while the review was under way, it is unlikely that the tent will ever reappear. It appears that this decision was a clear signal from Cowen that he intended to distance the party from the kind of contributions that had become the subject of so many allegations made in the Mahon Tribunal. 'The Taoiseach's edict will be seen as an important change of tone, with Mr Cowen intent on emphasising a different style to his predecessor Bertie Ahern,' pointed out Mark Hennessy in an *Irish Times* piece the day after the announcement.

Cowen called on Burton to withdraw her inflammatory remarks. But she refused, and went further, retorting: 'The eminent Minister is at every race meeting in this country where people who are non-resident for tax purposes are walking around.'

Cowen then pointed out that the non-residency rules were agreed under a Fianna Fáil *and* Labour government in 1994. 'My integrity is not going to be challenged under privilege. If the deputy wants to challenge it outside the House, she should do so. I would gladly sue her,' he told the Dáil.

Dan Boyle then decided to add his voice to the challenge to Cowen. He stated: 'Regarding the residency rules, the Minister is being economical with the truth. Not only is he exempting a wide swathe of tax relief schemes that are not examined by the current review, he is failing to treat the resident reviews as the obvious tax expenditure that it is.'

'The deputy can throw his jibes,' fumed Cowen. 'I would advise the deputy to keep using the privilege of the House when he does so, because if he ever does it outside the House, I will have a chat with him.'

It was probably the first time that a minister had offered to have a proverbial 'chat' outside with an opposition TD – in what amounted, in the words of Drapier in the *Irish Times*, to 'the Dáil equivalent of a punch-up outside the pub'.

In December 2005 Cowen unveiled his 2006 budget – one which he felt reflected not only the priorities of the government but the 'needs and hopes of the Irish people as well'. As he pointed out during a lengthy and wide-ranging speech, this budget was about the 'facilitation of sustained economic growth' and 'improved equality and opportunity for all in society'. Cowen had always argued that economic prosperity 'is a means to an end and not an end in itself'. He explained:

'My aims for this Budget are straightforward. I want to improve equality and opportunity for all in our society. I want to help those on lower incomes and to support families at all levels. I want to develop our infrastructure so our firms can compete better while helping to secure our environment and our heritage. I am also determined to pursue value for money for consumers and for taxpayers.'

The response to his budget was generally favourable; but Cowen did come in for criticism from the opposition over the length of his speech. Dan Boyle, the Green Party's finance spokesman, pointed out that Cowen's speech would come in at seventy-five minutes – compared to other budget speeches during the previous three years which had been no more than about forty-five minutes long. In effect, Cowen's overlong speech was making it impossible for the opposition to respond in time for their dissenting opinions to be carried by the primetime RTÉ news at six o'clock. 'You try to make a comment in this house after six o'clock and see what type of media coverage is given to you,' Boyle fumed.

The row was eventually resolved when the Labour Party's whip Emmet Stagg generously suggested that his party would use up only forty-five minutes of their allotted seventy-five minutes, thus allowing more time to the Greens, Sinn Féin and the Technical Group.

Cowen shaved fifteen minutes off his following year's

speech, introducing the so-called 'giveaway' budget for 2007. As part of this budget, he introduced a €1.25 billion package of tax changes that included the widening of tax bands and a cut of one percentage point in the top tax rate. There were also substantial increases in the basic state pension – which was pushed over the €200-a-week barrier, to a round of applause from coalition TDs – and in welfare payments; and a doubling of mortgage interest tax relief for first-time buyers. It had been widely speculated that Cowen would announce plans to scrap stamp duty for first-time buyers, but he was reluctant to do so because he thought cutting this tax would result in the figure saved simply being included in the house price – with the extra money simply ending up in the seller's pocket, and house prices rising further. 'Our firm aim is to help first-time buyers directly and substantially, not only those who are in the market now but also those who are already paying their first mortgage. The best way to do this is by way of mortgage interest relief,' Cowen insisted at the time.

Having spoken for an hour, Cowen sat back down to the sound of deafening applause both from his cabinet colleagues and from backbenchers behind him. Ahern quickly turned to Cowen, who appeared slightly embarrassed by the sheer volume of the enthusiasm, and clasped his hands.

One backbencher, Conor Lenihan, the son of the former Tánaiste the late Brian Lenihan Snr, shouted out: 'Ten more years!'

It was hard to recall a more enthusiastically received budget.

The opposition, however, accused Cowen of using this budget as an attempt to 'buy' the next general election. Speaking in the Dáil, Labour leader Pat Rabbitte alleged that the budget, which he described as lacking imagination, was designed merely as 'a safe targeting of interest groups that might show an electoral dividend'. Not for the first time, Rabbitte argued that the government had orchestrated the budget to favour the 'the super-high earners in our economy' and had 'failed to use the resources to relieve the strain on our society'. He pointed out that a 1 per cent cut in the top rate of tax delivered more than €2,000 to a person with an annual income of €250,000, but gave absolutely nothing to someone on €32,000. 'One of the most striking elements of the Budget is that the Government has decided to completely jettison its promise to the electorate, that only twenty per cent of tax-payers would pay tax at the higher rate,' he added.

Cowen's decision to retain stamp duty for first-time buyers was heavily criticized by the estate agents Sherry Fitzgerald. Their chief economist, Marian Finnegan, said that the punitive rate of stamp duty applicable to first-time buyers in the second-hand housing market was acting as a barrier to entry into the property market for this group. 'The decision to increase the threshold for stamp duty from €190,501 to €317,000 in Budget 2005 went some way to addressing this situation but it is not far enough. The divergent treatment of first-time buyers in the new homes and second-hand market has for too long created an unnatural bias against investing,' she said.

Ahern defended the budget by stating that the changes introduced by Cowen were designed to sustain the strength of the Irish economy. 'The Budget is an entirely responsible one, designed not to overheat the economy and to give us a sub-stantial safety margin, if the existing environment should disimprove,' Ahern told the Dáil.

Ahern then lambasted the opposition for making

contradictory demands on the public coffers. 'On the one hand, they have argued that our strong performance showed that taxes should be lower, that the Government did not need the money because public spending was high enough and could be funded through lower taxes. On the other hand, they argue that there should be higher public spending, because the resources are now available for an unlimited spending spree, except, of course, that it would be irresponsible of the Minister to embark on such a pre-election splurge,' said Ahern.

Cowen dismissed the accusations that he was attempting to buy the electorate with a giveaway budget. When interviewed on RTÉ's *Today with Pat Kenny* radio show, Cowen asked a rhetorical question: 'How high a surplus am I to have before that charge is not levelled against me? Thankfully the public finances are in a good shape, and we had a surplus to deal with . . . One-third of the windfall gain is being spent on immediate priorities and two-thirds retained as surplus because we can't put all that money back into the economy without having inflationary effects and affecting the cost of living.'

However, when Cowen presented his budget in the Seanad there was at least one dissenting voice within his own ranks. In March 2007 Senator Margaret Cox clashed with Cowen during a second-stage debate on the Finance Bill. Furious because she felt her Galway constituency had not got its fair slice of the cake during the previous two budgets, Cox repeatedly interrupted Cowen during the debate and, at one stage, declared: 'I will not stand here and say this is good enough for Galway.'

While accepting that there were challenges facing Galway, Cowen rejected her claims and pointed out that Galway was the fastest-growing town in Ireland. 'I was glad, as minister for health and children, to invest over €70 million to develop that area,' he explained. Cowen then pointed out that there were universities and multinational companies in the west of the country, and that University College Galway was doing extremely well, receiving much-needed research money through excellent relationships with those companies; but Cox interjected again, retorting: 'They cannot get to the university because the road system is failing us.'

She then called for a vote on the Finance Bill, which incensed Cowen, with his strong belief in party unity. But when the time for the vote came, the Cathaoirleach of the Seanad Rory Kiely said that it could not proceed because the required two tellers had not been provided by the caller of the vote within the prescribed time. Cox then wanted it put on record that she did have two tellers.

At Fianna Fáil's 2007 Ard Fheis, Ahern announced a set of promises that dwarfed anything the opposition had included in its election manifesto – including, unexpectedly, a commitment to implement stamp duty reform for first-time buyers. The other key promises included the halving of Pay-Related Social Insurance (PRSI) for employees and a reduction for the self-employed, a cut in the standard rate of income tax from 20 per cent to 18 per cent, and a 1 per cent cut in the higher rate. Political pundits immediately described the package as 'auction politics' – despite the avowals of Fianna Fáil in the run-up to the Ard Fheis. Cowen said on 16 February 2007 that 'we in Fianna Fáil will not participate in auction politics ahead of this year's general election'. Ahern echoed these sentiments the following day when he declared at the Ógra Fianna Fáil conference: 'We're not going to participate in an auction.' Even the Minister for Social and Family Affairs,

Séamus Brennan, said: 'We certainly will not be matching the unprecedented scale of the promises given by Fine Gael and Labour.'

The day after Ahern's speech, Pat Rabbitte described it as one of the most remarkable U-turns in recent political history. 'As recently as last Tuesday, the hapless Séamus Brennan was sent out to warn the country of the dangers of auction politics. "We will promise less because our approach will deliver more," he solemnly told a press conference. Then five days later his leader makes a speech reminiscent of Fianna Fáil's irresponsibility in 1977, in which he promises everything bar a partridge in a pear tree for every family in the country,' said Rabbitte.

Ahern defended his promises at the Ard Fheis by stating that he and Cowen had been working on the tax reform package with party advisers for several months. 'I am in a different position to all the other parties on tax reform because we have the credibility: we do it, the others talk about it,' said Ahern.

But it was Ahern's announcement of stamp duty reform that really turned heads. It was rumoured that he had made it without prior consultation with his finance minister – simply because he feared the opposition was out-promising the government with its pre-election pledges. Cowen dismisses the suggestion: 'What I said very clearly – which is consistent with everything I've said; the U-turns here are on the other side – was that, as Minister for Finance, I couldn't speculate on what I would do or not do, because the market reacts to what the Minister for Finance says. And I said that at the time, "I refuse to speculate." Secondly, I said that I would do nothing that would disrupt the market – not that there would be nothing done. The third thing I said was that if people wanted to have an idea of what I would be thinking about, I asked them to look at the two initiatives I had brought forward in this area of my previous three Budgets, which were exclusively for the benefit of first-time buyers. Those were my three holding statements, if you like, because I am very strongly of the view that speculation is, in fact, destabilizing the market. And I also felt that the policy position was daft because the people who U-turned here are the other side. We came up with our proposal at the launch of the Fianna Fáil manifesto, which is affordable, which is targeted, which is, as I said, exclusively for first-time buyers. It has always been the policy of successive governments to get that person on the first rung of the ladder.'

In June 2007 Cowen published his legislation to abolish stamp duty for first-time buyers, the provision being back-dated to 31 March of the same year. It exempted first-time buyers – providing the property was purchased for residence – from paying any tax on new or second-hand properties up to the value of €317,500. For first-time buyers of properties valued between €381,000 and €635,000 the rate of stamp duty would be 3 per cent; and for all properties valued above this level, stamp duty would be set at 9 per cent.

Cowen dismissed the opposition's objection that his stamp duty reform contained a flaw that allowed parents to avoid paying tax on a house purchased for their child as a gift. He explains: 'The point now is, we are saying, "OK, we'll abolish stamp duty for first-time buyers – costs €44 million. I'll do it to bring certainty to the market if the first-time buyer is assisted in all circumstances. To kill any controversy that might be arising about that. That's the end of that." Then Mr Rabbitte comes up and says, "This means that rich Daddy can buy young son a house for €3 million and he'll pay no stamp duty on it." Not true – he'll pay twice as much gift tax on it. OK? So, again, there is a nonsense argument. The point is, we have brought certainty. Everyone knows that if Fianna Fáil's elected, all stamped deeds presented to the Revenue Commissioners by first-time purchasers after the first of April will be exempt. That's a certainty. Everyone else knows we are not going to mess up the market. So, I brought certainty. It is affordable; and it is consistent with everything I have said.'

One of Cowen's last acts as finance minister attracted criticism from the Catholic Church. This was his decision in February 2008 to reduce the rate of VAT on condoms from 21 per cent to 13.5 per cent. The move was warmly welcomed by health campaigners, but the director of the Catholic Church's Communication Office, Martin Long, absurdly alleged that Cowen's VAT reduction was 'effectively promoting [the] widespread use' of condoms and thus encouraging promiscuity. 'The Church's teaching is clear: within the sacrament of marriage, the use of condoms as contraceptives is wrong, though there may be mitigating circumstances,' stated Long. 'Outside of marriage, the use of condoms encourages sexual activity, which is always gravely sinful. This decision sends the wrong signal to our young people as the promotion of condoms promotes promiscuity.'

But the director of the Crisis Pregnancy Agency, Caroline Spillane, defended the move. She pointed out that a recent study had shown that a staggering one in five people aged between sixteen and twenty-four had stated that the cost of condoms discouraged their use of them. 'While the reduction in cost to the consumer is not large, it will have an impact on the purse of the low-waged and younger persons who report that cost is an issue for them,' she said.

In May 2007 Cowen had found himself the target of more serious criticism when he, as Ahern later put it, gave the 'wrong figure' for the cost of proposals to encourage developers to build private hospitals on public hospital grounds. Speaking on *Questions and Answers*, Cowen stated that the scheme would cost €70 million a year in tax forgone to the exchequer. The following day the three ministers – Séamus Brennan, Dermot Ahern and Mary Hanafin – attending the party's final pre-election press call came under pressure from journalists to clarify the figure; after they were unable to do so, Cowen's adviser, Colin Hunt, intervened to offer an explanation. Ahern then went on the *Six One News* on 22 May to explain that the correct figure was actually €56 million gross. 'Brian Cowen gave the right figures a week ago. In the middle of a programme it is very hard to get every figure right. He just said the wrong figure last night. What's in his document is €400 million over seven years: €56 million gross, 40 net. Last night, he gave a higher figure for the gross,' Ahern explained.

But the slip-up by Cowen, though soon cleared up, was used as ammunition by the opposition in its attack on the 'co-location' project, under which the government planned to relocate government departments to other parts of the country. Labour leader Pat Rabbitte stated that Cowen had given 'a very definite answer' on *Questions and Answers* and asked: 'Who is the real Minister for Finance? Brian Cowen or Colin Hunt?' Fine Gael deputy leader and finance spokesman Richard Bruton also alleged that the co-location plan was a 'sham' and even accused the government of pretending to have provided for the costs. 'First, it was going to be costless; then the costs were, what, €70 million a year, €490 million over seven years. Then it had dropped by the press conference down to €40 million. Then, in the middle of the press conference, it surged again,' stated Bruton, who argued that co-location was a tax-driven scheme that would allow private investors to receive tax relief at up to 42 per cent on the investment in hospital beds.

Probably Cowen's most significant policy initiative during his time as Minister for Finance was the implementation of the National Development Plan (NDP), which was prepared in consultation with other cabinet ministers. The original NDP – which covered (mainly) national infrastructure over the years from 2000 to 2006 – was deemed to be a resounding success. 'It was an important policy because it set out a long-term view of a multi-annual framework – instead of deciding on a year-to-year basis – of strategic direction for the country,' recalls Cowen.

For the period 2007–14 Cowen and his ministerial colleagues set out a second, more ambitious, NDP entitled *Transforming Ireland – A Better Quality of Life for All*, which Cowen believes will build on the 'significant social and economic achievements of its predecessor'. The new plan, which is the largest and most ambitious investment programme ever proposed for Ireland, originally had a budget of €184 billion attached: €54.6 billion for investment in economic infrastructure, €49.6 billion for social inclusion measures (for example to help children and people with disabilities), €33.6 billion for social infrastructure (such as housing, health and justice), €25.8 billion for human capital (for example, schools, training and higher education) and €20 billion for enterprise, science and innovation. However, cutbacks now planned by the government in response to the downturn in the global economy will inevitably extend to the new NDP. Nevertheless, Cowen is adamant that the NDP is still a vital policy because it sets out the planning framework in terms of where the government intends to invest. He explains: 'The new economic circumstances mean we are going to have to prioritize to maximize the economic return in terms of building up the country's infrastructure and resources. What I said about it at the time was based on certain economic assumptions and growth – such as achieving 4 per cent growth – which are not going to emerge now, in the immediate term at least. The Development Plan was always subject to achieving certain criteria and, if not, you have to adapt the plan and prioritize the work you are going to do based on the resources that are available.'

Prior to the budget for 2008 – his fourth and last as Minister for Finance – Cowen came under fire when it was discovered that there was a pre-budget deficit, reported by the papers to be in the region of € 1.46 billion, though Cowen insisted it was much lower, more like € 622 million. At the time, Cowen was adamant that, while his spending might be a 'little ahead', it would come into line. He had predicted in his previous budget that he would end the year with a deficit of € 547 million; current projections were somewhat over that, 'but this was about a € 50 million difference on a total spend of € 50 billion,' he stated.

In planning the budget for 2008, Cowen vowed not to introduce any expenditure cutbacks because he wanted to maintain the National Development Plan's aim of 'modernizing the country'. In order to stay true to this budgetary philosophy, Cowen borrowed € 1.85 billion for his final budget. This was the first time since 2002 that the government had had to borrow to meet its budget commitments. He had warned in his pre-budget outlook statement that the economy had passed a 'turning point' and had forecast that growth in GDP would fall to 3 per cent in 2008. But perhaps even more worryingly, Cowen's budget documents also indicated that the government was anticipating the need to borrow further in 2009 and 2010. This was a very different outlook from the forecast of a €900 million surplus which Cowen had made in the 2007 budget.

'It is right and appropriate that we should run budget surpluses when the economy is performing very well,' explains Cowen. 'It is equally right and appropriate that we borrow when the growth outlook is less favourable. However, the move into deficit must involve productive borrowing, borrowing which will strengthen our economy for the long term.'

In introducing his fourth budget, Cowen described it as the first he had constructed 'against a challenging economic backdrop'. While emphasizing the 'extraordinary growth' of the economy during the previous decade, he warned that 'the global economy is beset by uncertainties, financial markets are highly volatile and the construction sector domestically is experiencing a slowdown'. However, he pointed out that 'we must not lose sight of the fact that the fundamentals of the economy are still good – a point often lost by some'. He emphasized that this budget was all about, as he put it, placing the country's 'economic objective ahead of any other – that we do things now that will position our country for sustainable development over the years ahead. This objective does not conflict with our commitment to make Ireland more environmentally friendly.'

Highlighting the vital aspects of his budget, Cowen went on: 'What this means is that the rate of increase on public current expenditure in 2008 has to moderate to take account of the resources available; but, even so, I am still providing almost €53 billion, which is a net increase of over €1.7

billion. This includes almost €960 million for welfare support in 2008, which is just over half of the total additional spending announced today. I am also providing over €8.6 billion in 2008 for investment on the capital side. When I compare that with the resources available to me, I am planning for a general Government deficit of 0.9 per cent in 2008, which is the appropriate response at this time. This is the context in which my Budget is set. This Budget is focused on the future challenges and addresses them now in a way which is sustainable.'

Speaking in the Dáil, Ahern praised Cowen's budget, stating: 'The confidence of the Irish people in the capacity of this Government to manage our way through difficult conditions has been fully vindicated by the terms of the Budget introduced by Brian Cowen, Tánaiste and Minister for Finance. This is a Budget that will sustain progress in the Irish economy through more difficult international conditions. Our ability to produce an innovative, progressive and socially caring Budget at this time reflects well on the strength and resilience of our economy which we have built up over many years.

'Today, we have the resources and the flexibility to respond constructively to less favourable conditions, in a way that would be the envy of our predecessors in the 1980s and of many of our European partners now. The Budget is prudent, and stays well within the margins of safety, but expresses the Government's determination, not just to hold what we have, but to maintain forward momentum.'

Cowen is proud of his achievements as Minister for Finance, arguing that his promise to reform the PRSI system – 'while others shy away from it' – was an important change. He says:

'I'm bringing in a progressive characteristic to the tax because I'm making sure that those who earn more pay more. At the moment, you pay the same PRSI if you are an employee if you are on €48,800 as someone on €148,800 – what the hell is that about?' he stated before the May 2007 general election.

'So, all of my taxation reforms and taxation priorities since I've became Minister have been geared towards the lower- and middle-income groups. There are now 40 per cent of people outside the tax net because they are on low pay. I'm proud of that. Eighty per cent of all our income-earners pay less than a fifth of their income on income tax. These are milestone achievements when you consider that when I entered politics we were suffering from a dysfunctional tax system – and we had tax marches on the streets, and rightly so. And we had tax rights that killed the incentive for people even to try to play it straight because the system was geared against ordinary families.

'At the end of the day I think we can be proud of what we've achieved. I'm proud of my four budgets. The direction of the budgets – promoting social equity, expanding opportunity, social inclusion, and, obviously, a strong economy, are the basis on which all of your social objectives have to be achieved.'

9

The 2007 General Election

In September 2006 Cowen declared that Fianna Fáil would have 'the bottle for the battle' in the forthcoming general election of 2007. He made this boisterous rallying call while speaking to the media following a two-day parliamentary conference in Westport, County Mayo. A little under nine months later, Bertic Ahern would attempt to become the first party leader since Eamon de Valera to be appointed Taoiseach for a third time. But the signs were ominous for Fianna Fáil: virtually every opinion poll was showing a surge in support for a Fine Gael–Labour coalition, following the decision of those two parties to announce the 'Mullingar Accord', their pact effectively to run as a team in the general election, hoping by this unusual move to attract the electorate to an alternative 'government-in-waiting'.

During that press conference in Mayo, Cowen acknowledged that the forthcoming election was an 'open race'. He blamed his party's poor performances in the opinion polls on shortcomings in communicating the progress the government had made. He had the foresight to realize that Ahern's appearance before the Mahon Tribunal, a public inquiry established by the Dáil in 1997 to investigate allegations of corrupt payments to politicians, coupled with the almost endless stream of negative stories in the press about the Taoiseach, would put pressure on Fianna Fáil's TDs to go out to the country and articulate clearly 'what we have been doing, and what we will do'. But as the general election drew closer, Fianna Fáil's main political candidates appeared reluctant to court national media coverage, which was focusing increasingly on the allegations being made about Ahern's unorthodox personal finances. The greatest number of these stories on Ahern's financial affairs, many based on information linked to investigations in relation to the Mahon Tribunal, were written by the freelance journalist Frank Connolly, a brother of one of the IRA members dubbed the 'Colombian Three' who absconded from South America after being arrested for allegedly training FARC rebels in explosive-handling techniques.

It had already emerged that Ahern had been in the habit of signing blank cheques – apparently without even asking what they were for – for Charles Haughey during the latter's period as Taoiseach. Ahern's admission to the tribunal that there was a policy of signing blank cheques on the Fianna Fáil party leader's account for reasons of 'administrative convenience' attracted some sharp criticism in the media. But worse was to come in September 2006, when the *Irish Times* printed leaked material concerning allegations that in 1993, while Minister for Finance, Ahern had received money from prominent businessmen. Ahern admitted receiving money, but said on being interviewed: 'What I got personally in my life, to be frank with you, is none of your business. If I got something from somebody as a present or something like that I can use it.' This was in complete contrast to Ahern's statement to the Dáil in December 1996: 'The public are entitled to have an absolute guarantee of the financial probity and integrity of their elected representatives, their officials and above all of Ministers. They need to know that they are under financial obligations to nobody.' It was a contradiction that the national media were quick to highlight.

After the payments were publicized, Ahern went on RTÉ television and admitted in an interview with Bryan Dobson that he had received two payments totalling IR£39,000 in 1993 and 1994, but explained that he regarded the money as a loan – a 'dig-out' as he put it himself, during a difficult personal time in his life, when he had just separated from his wife and was facing financial problems. The loan, Ahern insisted, 'was raised by close friends, people who were close to me for most of my life'. He emphasized that he had tried to repay the loan but that his friends would not accept repayment. He had, he insisted, 'broken no codes – ethical, tax, legal or otherwise'.

Ahern also admitted to receiving a payment of £8,000 from a group of twenty-five businessmen in Manchester. He pointed out that this money was an unsolicited 'gift' and therefore was not subject to tax as it had been received when abroad in the role of a private citizen and not in his capacity as Minister for Finance. The sum had been paid to Ahern after he had given an after-dinner speech at an unscheduled function. Ahern went on the record to state that he had received no other payments after speaking at other similar functions.

But on 30 September 2006 the *Irish Times* reported that part of this contentious payment to Ahern was actually a cheque drawn on an account of NCB stockbrokers. On 28 November 2007, former NCB managing director Padraic O'Connor contradicted part of Ahern's story at the Mahon

Tribunal by stating that the payment was not a loan and that he was *not* a personal friend of the Taoiseach. He said the payment of IR£5,000 made by his company was intended as a donation to Fianna Fáil. O'Connor told the tribunal: 'It is flattering to be described as a friend. I was not a close personal friend. Since I left NCB eight years ago, I have met Mr Ahern once or twice. I have no recollection of any mention made of the money paid. I made no personal donation to Mr Ahern.'

On 5 October 2006 it emerged that Ahern's residence in Drumcondra had been purchased by the Manchester-based Irish businessman Micheál Wall, who had been at the 'dig-out' evening for Ahern in 1994. It would later emerge that Wall had written a will in which he had left the house to Ahern.

The controversy continued to grow when it was pointed out that a number of Ahern's benefactors were later appointed as directors to the boards of various state bodies. But Ahern was adamant that no favours had been offered or received. 'I might have appointed somebody but I appointed them because they were friends, not because of anything they had given me,' he asserted. He must have hoped that the matter would be laid to rest for good when he gave an extensive statement in the Dáil to explain the unusual monetary payments to him. 'The bewilderment caused to the public about recent revelations has been deeply upsetting for me and others near and dear to me. To them, to the Irish people and to this House, I offer my apologies,' he said in his speech.

Further questions were raised about an amount of IR£50,000 which Ahern had lodged to his bank account in 1994 – money Ahern claimed he had saved over a substantial period of time from 1987 to 1994 when he had had no active personal bank account. But Ahern was able to weather the storm. He even managed to defend himself against some of the more serious allegations that had been made against him, most notably the claim he had taken a IR£50,000 bribe from a property developer, Owen O'Callaghan, in 1989 and a payment of IR£30,000, in connection with a shopping complex development of lands at Quarryvale in Dublin, in 1993. Ahern won a libel action against these allegations.

As the election approached, the outlook for Fianna Fáil seemed increasingly bleak. Bizarrely, however, the opposition parties decided not to raise the controversy over Ahern's financial affairs during the campaign. 'I can give Bertie Ahern one guarantee, there will be no descent into sleaze politics with me as leader of Fine Gael,' promised Enda Kenny. 'We will fight the election on the issues that are before the people – health, crime, value for money, and taxation. That is going to be a hard political battle but, for me, it will be a fair battle.'

Political pundits had anticipated that Fianna Fáil would suffer an electoral backlash following the serious issues uncovered by the Mahon Tribunal. The damaging leaks prompted Ahern to run for cover, refusing almost all requests for interviews during the election campaign. Apart from the leaders' debate on television, Ahern chose to restrict his engagement with the media to interviews with the *Sunday Independent*.

The electorate was perplexed by Ahern's personal finances, and the constant emergence of further allegations was making it next to impossible for Fianna Fáil to get its media campaign up and running. So far had the party been pushed on to the back foot that some of its press officers were refusing to return media calls or answer queries with the general election only four weeks away. Most political pundits were predicting with an air of inevitability that Enda Kenny would be the next Taoiseach.

At the time, Cowen felt that the 'well-orchestrated' leaks were designed to distract attention from the real issue of the day – the upcoming election. 'We are not naïve, we know where it is coming from,' he told one journalist at the height of the election campaign. 'And I know the Taoiseach is very anxious to deal with his side of the story in respect of some very serious and – as far as he's concerned – totally unfounded allegations that have been made against him.'

Cowen clearly felt that there was a certain bias in the media comment on the tribunal, though not necessarily a party political one. 'It takes some time before the person who assertions are made against comes in to give their side of the story. And, in the meantime, there's a certain version of events out there that gets a lot of prominence,' he said in the aftermath of the general election. Though he didn't subscribe to the point of view that there was an anti-Fianna Fáil agenda in the media, he felt that journalists had an appetite for change. 'Just take it as a premise, I'm sure that they'd like to see different faces . . . new faces. Different script. A new play, you know? They are the people who are sitting up there – theatre critics – looking in on the goings-on in government and when they see the same people at the head of things, you know, from a newspaper man or woman's point of view I'm sure they are saying, "Sure, it would be great if we had someone else to kick around!"'

Cowen was frustrated by his party's inability to mount an effective election campaign. He was equally frustrated by the fact that the opposition parties' political manifestos, particularly those of Labour and Fine Gael, were not being analysed or scrutinized by the media. At the beginning of May, faced with Ahern's obvious reluctance to front a media campaign, Cowen decided to come out fighting and to do media interviews himself. During the campaign Cowen was seen as the party's primary spokesperson and later was even credited with almost single-handedly winning the election for Fianna Fáil. There is no doubt that his robust intervention at this critical point in the campaign had a decisive impact in steadying the nerves of the party faithful and in galvanizing their efforts to get the campaign on to the front foot. Cowen's willingness to take the initiative set him apart from his peers and can be seen now as marking the moment when he did indeed become 'first among equals'. However, reflecting on the election campaign today, Cowen considers the televised debate between Enda Kenny and Bertie Ahern as a pivotal moment, with Ahern 'the clear winner'.

Cowen felt that the election needed to be about who was 'best equipped in terms of experience and strategic direction' to implement the best policies for the future development of the country; but he also felt that both Labour's and Fine Gael's political manifestos were deeply flawed, and pointed this out in his first major interview. Speaking at the start of May to *Hot Press* magazine, which had already obtained in-depth interviews with leaders of all the major parties apart from Fianna Fáil and the Progressive Democrats, Cowen declared: 'I have been saying this for a week but I can't get it into newsprint. This is the problem with this election campaign, which is the main point I want to talk to you about, which is – I don't have an economic plan or a fiscal plan in the name of Labour. What they have produced is seven promises in relation to health and pensions – two of which are flawed.'

As he would go on to point out during every media inter-view for the rest of the campaign, the two allied opposition parties had made different spending commitments out of the same €2.9 billion government spending fund. They were

making different election promises – but within the confines
of the same budget. 'They are not the same commitments, but
they are spending the same money twice. People need to
analyse what is going on here. This is a con job – plain and
simple. It is all dishonesty.'

Cowen's argument that when the election was over the two
parties would say 'Now we must negotiate the €2.9 billion'
clearly resonated with the electorate. He pointed out that all
the promises of the opposition would have to be 'funnelled
into this €2.9 billion magic can that they have, which they are
going to negotiate after the next election. So everything they
are telling you in the meantime, there's a rider on it. This is
treating people's intelligence now as if they're fools. You can't
buy that nonsense – that's a pig in a poke.' He was clearly particularly annoyed by Fine Gael posters declaring that they
would introduce two thousand more Gardaí if they got into
power. As Minister for Finance, Cowen was in the position to
point out that they had provided only €96 million in their
proposed government budget for those extra two thousand,
but would actually need €190 million to implement such an
increase. 'Then they say, "Sure, aren't you bringing in an extra
thousand this year?" So now they want to take credit for what
we are doing as part of their extra commitment. Again, it's
really dishonest,' he sighed during one interview.

There is little doubt that Cowen's formidable performance
during the general election had a major influence on its outcome. However, in one interview with *Hot Press* he
unintentionally introduced a lighter note into media coverage
of the campaign when he gave a typically straightforward
response to one of the magazine's stock questions: Had he
ever enjoyed a blast of an illicit marijuana cigarette?

Cowen wasn't anticipating the question, but he felt it would be best to be truthful – and by doing so, he became the first politician in Ireland to admit smoking cannabis when he candidly stated: 'Anyone who went to the UCD bar in the seventies that didn't get a whiff of marijuana would be telling you a lie. I would say there were a couple of occasions when it was passed around – and, unlike President Clinton, I did inhale! There wasn't a whole lot in it really – [it was like] a Sweet Afton, as a ten year old, under a railway bridge on a rainy day, in small town Ireland in the late sixties.'

The confession made the front pages of all the papers, as well as the leading story on TV and radio news, with the *Daily Mirror* giving Cowen the sobriquet 'Biffo Spiffo'. Some of the newspapers and political website forums even went so far as to print a photograph of Cowen with a superimposed marijuana joint in his mouth and a Rastafarian hat perched on his head.

But some sections of the media reacted less humorously, and Cowen did come in for sharp criticism. Some accused him of admitting to smoking marijuana in an effort to gain popularity among young voters. The morning after his admission became public, he walked into a press conference in Fianna Fáil's headquarters and noticed that many of the journalists seemed to be thinking: 'Here was this guy trying to buy into the youth vote!' Naturally, the subject was raised immediately. Cowen in fact felt the press had latched on to this in relief at finally having found something other than the Ahern saga to write about. But he does acknowledge that the controversial admission considerably changed the public perception – particularly among younger people – of him as rather a dour character. 'I'm not in any way being flippant about this. I wouldn't do that. The bottom line is I was asked a question and I answered it as honestly and forthrightly as I could. I didn't see any benefit in avoiding the question. In fairness, it was not just an accurate account but a verbatim account of what I had to say about it. I don't think people are unduly surprised that we were all young once. We all had a student life and, while I'm a politician now, I grew up in the very same environment in the seventies and eighties as anyone else. While I don't put that forward as an excuse for something that, on reflection, I certainly wouldn't do again, the fact is it's better to be truthful about these things and people see the human side. They see someone who's prepared to say it as it is, hopefully, in respect of that or any other matter, so far as one can.'

Ahern, probably delighted by the fact that the spotlight had been taken off him – albeit momentarily – defended Cowen's confession. When he was approached by a horde of reporters wanting to know if he supported Cowen, Ahern stated: 'I think as always Brian's been straight and honest. I've no big deal about it. I suppose a lot of people try it in school or in college' – and then added that he'd never tried the drug himself. The media then decided to ask all the cabinet ministers and prominent opposition members if they too had tried it, but no one else made a similar confession. Within a year, however, several other high-profile politicians, including John Gormley, Eamon Gilmore and Eoghan Harris, had admitted to having smoked marijuana at some stage – declarations that attracted no comparable media hysteria.

The polls were predicting that Fianna Fáil would lose between thirteen and fifteen seats in May 2007, but Cowen confidently dismissed these predictions: he believed that the momentum was behind them, and their canvassing confirmed this. Cowen was finding on the doorsteps of his constituency that the Ahern controversy wasn't a major issue. He found –

during this pre-recession period – that people were recognizing that the economy was performing well and were more concerned with local issues.

In the end, contrary to the mid-campaign expectations in some quarters, Fianna Fáil managed to return a total of 78 seats out of a total of 166. Cowen's performance in bringing home three out of the five seats in his own constituency vindicated his confidence throughout the campaign and clearly revealed his increased public standing. He was elected on the first count with 19,102 votes, the highest number any candidate received in this election.

Cowen is of the opinion that Fianna Fáil won the election because of its 'very good range of talents' throughout the party, coupled with a 'dearth of talent' within the opposition. 'If you take away Enda Kenny and Richard Bruton – you don't see many frontbench spokespersons arguing the case. The Labour leader seemed to dominate their campaign. But that was just my impression,' he says.

Following the election result, Cowen was given the role of chief negotiator on the Fianna Fáil team, tasked with entering into talks over a possible coalition with other parties. The decision to negotiate with the Green Party came as a surprise to many, particularly considering that the Green leader, Trevor Sargent, had vowed not to go into government with Fianna Fáil. He had earlier stated that he believed Ahern should resign; in fact, he had even suggested that his party would deal with Fianna Fáil only if they dumped Ahern and also agreed to block the American military from using Shannon airport. On hearing Sargent's suggestion, Cowen retorted: 'He can't choose our leaders. If he wants to negotiate with the party, he has to do it on the basis of mutual respect. As far as I'm concerned, I'm negotiating with a party and would demand that respect. And I will expect the size of our mandate to be reflected in any policy programme that would be negotiated with anybody. If people want to set such a pre-condition, I'm afraid they are opting themselves out of the process, rather than in. There are no circumstances in which such a precondition would be accepted.' And when, on the day of the election result, the Greens' Eamon Ryan spoke on television about the need to clean up politics, Cowen snapped: 'I don't need anybody to clean me up. Any negotiations have to be carried out with an air of mutual respect.'

Therefore it came as a surprise even to the Greens them-selves when the approach came. As John Gormley recalls: 'For a while we thought, "What's going on here?" When the call came from Fianna Fáil, we had a number of days where we thought, "Is this for real?" Once we found out it was for real, we then had to ask ourselves, "Will we go for this?" Because once we started negotiation – obviously it has its own dynamic, and we knew we might then be faced with the choice of going in with Fianna Fáil. That in itself was a very tense time for all of us.'

Gormley eventually became the Greens' new leader after Sargent honourably resigned in order to keep faith with his personal pre-election promise not to enter into government with Fianna Fáil. Sargent was later offered a junior ministerial position as Minister of State for Food and Agriculture, a position he retained in Cowen's first cabinet.

Initially, it appeared that it would not be possible to reach an agreement on a joint programme for government. The Greens found Cowen a tough negotiator who gave very little away: Gormley recalls that 'every single thing' Fianna Fáil conceded in the negotiations was given reluctantly. 'Everything was haggled over,' he says. He felt that Cowen was playing hardball with them, albeit 'all in a friendly way'. The Greens became increasingly frustrated by the tense negotiations. Finally they decided the offer on the table – in terms of ministries and Seanad positions, quite apart from the actual programme for government – didn't meet their expectations, and decided to quit the talks. Gormley remembers not being able to sleep a wink the night before the negotiations collapsed. He told himself, 'There is no way we can go through with this. Absolutely, no way. We are just not getting enough at all.' He said that it was the first time he ever had a sleepless night. The next morning he told his colleagues: 'Right, we're out of here. It is not going very well. We don't know if we can get an agreement.'

Gormley broke the news to Cowen and Noel Dempsey that the Greens were actually pulling out of the negotiations for government. Cowen remembers 'expressing surprise' when he was told of their decision. He pointed out that the method agreed for negotiations was that the negotiating teams would bring the talks as far forward as possible and anything they could not agree would be 'referred up to the leaders'.

'Has your leader told our leader that the negotiations have broken down?' Cowen asked the Greens' delegation.

'No,' they replied.

'I have to insist that that happens,' Cowen explained. 'You are now informing us that the negotiations have broken down, but the arrangement was we'd discuss things and if we couldn't agree to things we'd refer them up. You refer the issue you are not happy with up to the leaders. So you don't break down the negotiations.'

So the Green delegation then informed their leader Trevor Sargent. The Greens then got a number of text messages from Fianna Fáil, saying, 'Look, let's try and work this out.'

Gormley remembers the late Séamus Brennan, with whom he had a good rapport, contacting him and saying, 'What the *hell* is going on here? Do you not realize the way negotiations go? This is only the first bit of it . . .'

'I said to him that we do things literally – when we say things aren't good enough, we actually mean it. That was all very intense . . . We had a short and amicable discussion, and we shook hands and wished each other well. Actually, we got to like them, and Brian Cowen said he got to like us. It was a no-fault divorce,' recalled Gormley.

'On the Sunday, we sent them a paper full of stuff we really wanted, and that got it back on track again. But even then it was painful stuff,' recalled Gormley. There were 'very heated exchanges right up until the very end', as Cowen and his team argued every minute point with the Greens.

At one stage, Gormley was so exhausted that he got up and said, 'I have to get out of here.' As he was strolling down to the Green Party office, he got a call saying, 'You better get back up here. There is a bit of a row going on here. A major row.'

Gormley dashed back into the negotiations and found that a shouting match had broken out between the two sides. 'It was a row all right – shouting, and then a walk-out. People don't realize it, but that was just a few hours before the agreement was concluded.'

One of the major arguments surrounded the use of Shannon airport by American military personnel. At first, Cowen offered the Greens a deal on Shannon that would have stipulated no US landings 'without UN authorization', but the Greens did not want that set down in writing as policy. 'We argued about Shannon. We were offered this deal on Shannon and our lawyers said, "Don't agree to that. You are better off having nothing in than having that in." Then Fianna Fáil was insisting that the deal had to go in and we were saying no, we don't want it to go in. We rejected the wording. We said we'd be upfront with people – we'd prefer to have nothing at all than to have something that would actually make the situation worse, if it was in the programme for government,' confirms Gormley.

But Cowen bluntly told them some home truths: it didn't matter which party was in government – neither Fianna Fáil nor Fine Gael would ever make the decision to block the use of Shannon airport for transit purposes by the US military. At the end of the negotiations, Cowen pointed out to the Greens that it was a case of 'take it or leave it'. After all, he bluntly pointed out, Fianna Fáil could still go ahead and form a government without them. He accepted that Shannon was a moral issue for them; but surely, he said, it must be better for them to get into government and work on their climate change agenda? 'The troops are in Shannon. That's the reality. Nothing that we could have done would have made a blind bit of difference to how many men, women and children are killed in Iraq,' stated Gormley. 'We're in an unusual government, in that we are not propping up this government. The idea of a prop is that when you remove the prop, the whole thing falls. We could all resign in the morning and this government would still go on. Our support is not necessary for this government to continue. I feel that we are in a situation where we had to make choices. If we had gone into opposition, the troops would still be in Shannon.'

In retrospect, the Greens are content with the offer thrashed out. Gormley acknowledged that Fianna Fáil would argue – 'with a certain amount of justification' – that they had seventy-eight seats compared to the Greens' mere six TDs.

'Yet we are getting two people – one-third of our elected TDs – at the cabinet table. We would argue that we didn't clearly get as much as we wanted, but with six TDs, can you dictate? Can you get one hundred per cent? No, you can't. So, looking back at it, we may have seen them as tough negotiators, but they would feel, "Why should we give everything away?" You have to look at it from their perspective.'

After the negotiations had been concluded, the Greens had a difficult time selling the deal for government to their grass-roots members. At an emotional vote in the Mansion House, the party members endorsed the deal by the narrowest of margins – making them the first all-Ireland party to be in power since the foundation of the state. Cowen believes that bringing the Greens into the coalition was an 'important' necessity to help 'freshen up the government'. After the negotiations, he commented: 'We have listened and learned on the basis of mutual respect, and we have outlined a programme that will reflect the democratic mandates that both parties have.' He said the programme agreed would reflect the political realities of a mix of Fianna Fáil, the Greens and the PDs forming a government. 'We have here a very good policy platform building on the good experience of previous administrations and incorporating the perspective of the Green Party issues which are important,' maintained Cowen.

When the new cabinet was announced, Cowen kept the finance portfolio, but Ahern chose this moment to promote Cowen to the role of Tánaiste, making him his deputy prime minister. Jokingly asked by a journalist if the new role was a dream come true, Cowen responded: 'I don't have those sorts of dreams! You know, "There's the Tánaiste dream again! I hope that one comes true!"' He laughed, before adding seriously that it was 'a great honour to be asked by your

Taoiseach to become his Tánaiste'. He also noted that it was an honour not just for himself but also for 'my family, my constituency and my electorate'.

As an obvious acknowledgement of Cowen's significant contribution to ensuring Fianna Fáil's success in the general election and his invaluable input into negotiating the programme for government with the coalition partners, during an interview with the *Sunday Independent* Ahern declared that his new Tánaiste was his 'heir apparent' – which apparently annoyed some of the other obviously ambitious cabinet ministers, such as Micheál Martin, Dermot Ahern and Noel Dempsey, all of whom had designs on the highest political office. However, without any disrespect to their claims on the leadership, it must be noted that none of them had the same level of government experience as Cowen, who had held more ministerial positions than any of his cabinet colleagues. Political pundits did, nevertheless, find it unusual that Ahern should have decided, just days after the election, so publicly to endorse Cowen's candidature for the party leadership, thus increasing the likelihood of his becoming Taoiseach within the lifetime of the new government. In the immediate aftermath of the general election, Ahern even said publicly that he would not be making any major moves without first consulting with Cowen.

Ahern was surprisingly frank in acknowledging Cowen as his successor. When asked by Seán O'Rourke on RTÉ radio if Cowen was as obvious a successor as Seán Lemass was to Eamon de Valera, Ahern stated: 'I think that's fair enough. I mean, I could give you a lot of political answers about this one, but I'm not going to go down that road. Brian Cowen and I have been friends since the mid-1980s. We've worked together, he's a brilliant mind, and he's a great colleague. He has a vast amount of experience and is still not much beyond his mid-forties. He is a hugely experienced politician. Obviously the party will ultimately decide, but from my point of view, he is the obvious successor to me in five years' time or whenever.'

It was the general consensus among political pundits that Ahern, whom Charles Haughey had described as 'the most cunning, ruthless and devious of them all', would have his own motives for picking Cowen out in this way. He knew that he was likely to come under even more extreme pressure before the Mahon Tribunal within the coming months – and who better to have at his side under such circumstances than Cowen, who was dubbed the loyal politician from the loyal county? All agreed that it was an astute move on Ahern's behalf, as Cowen did indeed go on to defend his boss on several occasions before the Taoiseach's situation eventually became untenable.

The former Taoiseach Albert Reynolds has commented that a major contributory factor in Cowen's success as a politician has been the loyalty he has consistently shown to his leader and, more importantly still within Fianna Fáil, the loyalty he has always shown to the interests of the party. To Cowen, this is simply 'what I would call "straight dealing". You can't be a fair-weather friend,' he maintains. While it is a generally held view that 'straight dealing' is unusual in politics because of the widespread mistrust of political leaders, Cowen's ethos is one of straightforwardness. He believes that when a person does not live up to their best it is important that this is openly acknowledged and that person should say, 'I'll try to avoid that next time.' Mistakes and errors, he argues, happen to everyone – in all walks of life – and he thinks it's an 'unfortunate problem' that politics is judged according to a perfectionist model, so that 'if you don't live up to that then there's a reason to denigrate politics generally. I think that's a very absurd and false analysis to adopt because it's corrosive really. At the end of the day, we are all human, we are all fallible,' he says. 'There are times when we did things that we wouldn't be the proudest of. There are times when you should have been a bit bigger about things – that will happen – but you've got to be honest with yourself in those situations. Acknowledge it when it happens.'

But Cowen also disliked being labelled the 'heir apparent', as it inevitably led to constant questions from the media about his thoughts on the possibility that he might become Taoiseach one day soon. It was attention which he did not welcome. 'It is gratifying when your boss shows his trust and confidence in your ability. I'm glad that the Taoiseach has placed his trust and confidence in me. He was asked the question and he answered it in a certain way. In fairness, that is the Taoiseach's view as he sees it. I know it's a press pre-occupation because of the candid statement of the Taoiseach giving his forthright view, but that is not something that I want to entertain or speculate.' So spoke Cowen on more than one occasion.

In public, Cowen was adamant that it was never going to be a question of *when* he'd become Taoiseach: he felt that it would be presumptuous of him to be engaged in discussions that were not relevant at that point. When pressed, he resorted to what he described as a 'formulated way of answering that question', which was: 'My genuine view on that is this – because of the fact that my own dad died so suddenly at fifty-two, I genuinely don't get up in the morning wondering about that.'

Nor was this caution merely for public consumption. Even

though he was now dubbed heir apparent, Cowen was conscious of the fact that if Ahern did see out his full term it was highly likely that another candidate could challenge for the position. Moreover, Cowen was sufficiently realistic to know that his own popularity within the party might have significantly diminished by the time of a contest.

Ahern's achievement in winning a third successive term as Taoiseach was a remarkable and historic event in Irish politics. It was especially extraordinary in the light of the serious allegations about his financial affairs that had been circulating in the months before the 2007 general election. But despite his indication that he intended to see out a full third term in office, Ahern dramatically resigned a mere ten months after forming a new coalition government.

In retrospect, the opposition parties' decision not to challenge Ahern about his financial affairs during the course of the election came to be regarded as a tactical mistake by many within their ranks. Certainly, once the election was over it was not long before the opposition adopted a very different approach and relentlessly pursued Ahern at every given opportunity. On 13 September 2007 Ahern began four days of testimony before the Mahon Tribunal. He acknowledged that he had not hitherto been fully cooperative: when counsel stated that information supplied 'did not encompass all of the material questions that had been asked of you', Ahern replied, 'I accept that, yes.' The following day Ahern changed his story on the infamous 'dig-outs'. The tribunal chairman, Judge Alan Mahon, stated that there were 'significant gaps' in the money trail which 'would have made it impossible for the tribunal to follow the trail'. In a subsequent opinion poll, it was revealed that less than one-third of the electorate believed Ahern's accounts of his finances.

In the light of Ahern's appearance at the tribunal, Labour Party leader Eamon Gilmore called for the Taoiseach to resign; Fine Gael leader Enda Kenny was strongly critical of Ahern's 'rambling, incoherent' answers, accusing the Taoiseach of 'continually changing his story' while on oath.

When proceedings in the Dáil resumed on 26 September a motion of no confidence in the government was moved by Kenny, based on Ahern's statements to the Mahon Tribunal. A stormy debate ensued in which Ahern was accused of 'telling lies' and was called upon to resign; but in the end the motion was defeated by eighty-one votes to seventy-six, with all six Green Party TDs, two PDs and four Independents – Finian McGrath, Beverly Flynn, Michael Lowry and Jackie Healy-Rae – voting with the government.

The tribunal continued to uncover an ever-increasing number of questionable financial matters. In May 2007 it had been revealed that Ahern's former partner Celia Larkin had received IR£30,000 from Micheál Wall to contribute towards the refurbishment of the house in Drumcondra that Ahern had been renting from the businessman. On 2 February 2008 it emerged that Larkin had purchased a house in 1993 with money donated to Ahern's constituency organization in Drumcondra. But no documentation for this 'loan' was available.

By now Ahern was living on borrowed time. In an opinion poll in January 2008, 78 per cent of respondents stated they didn't believe Ahern had given a 'full picture' of his finances. The pressure mounted when it was revealed by the tribunal on 28 March 2008 that Ahern's former secretary Gráinne Carruth had made lodgements of IR£15,500 sterling on his behalf into building society accounts for Ahern and his children. She had stated ten days previously that she had made no sterling lodgements, and Ahern himself had told the tribunal in February that the lodgements into his daughters' accounts came from his salary as Minister for Finance, as he didn't actually have a bank account at the time. But when Carruth was reminded by Des O'Neill SC that she could face a two-year prison sentence or a staggering €300,000 fine if she was found to be lying under oath, Carruth broke down under the sustained pressure and asked if she could leave the room. She subsequently changed her testimony.

Ahern had said that he wouldn't be making any more public statements on the issue until his next appearance in front of the tribunal, but the very difficult position in which his former secretary had been placed was giving rise to public disquiet and presented Ahern with an embarrassing dilemma. Some of Ahern's cabinet colleagues were uncomfortable with the public seeing a distressed woman being placed in such a difficult position while testifying in an investigation into Ahern's affairs. Yet Ahern did not make any public statement to defend Carruth at this juncture, which gave the public the impression – rightly or wrongly – that he was now hiding behind his former secretary.

Immediately after his resignation, Ahern hit back at the tribunal, telling the press: 'I do feel very sorry about the way Gráinne Carruth was dealt with. That was just appalling. It was totally unnecessary. Talk about how not to do something, but anyway that's how it is,' he said. 'The way she was harangued. There was no need to harangue her. She just didn't remember something. I mean . . . she was concealing nothing. She was a mother of three – hauling her back on Holy Thursday. It's just low-life stuff.'

The depth of unease at Ahern's testimony having been

contradicted at the tribunal by his former secretary became clear when the acting party leader of the PDs, Mary Harney, who had traditionally been perceived as a steadfast supporter of Ahern, publicly called on the Taoiseach to make a statement. The Green Party leader John Gormley followed suit. Pressure also emerged within the Fianna Fáil parliamentary party for Ahern to make some statement on this latest twist in the tribunal saga when the Dáil reconvened after the Easter break on Tuesday 1 April.

Ahern realized that he was rapidly losing the support of his government colleagues. He was also aware of speculation in the media that a group of backbench TDs had made a discreet approach to Cowen to see if he might consider making a move to oust Ahern. Reports suggested that Cowen sharply rebuffed these approaches. 'We will remain loyal to our leader,' Cowen repeated time and time again when he was approached.

At this stage, Ahern was already, albeit reluctantly, considering his position. In a *Village* magazine interview in May 2007, he had said that he would step down as Taoiseach before the end of the current Dáil term in 2012, and made public his intention to retire from politics when he was sixty, which would be in 2011. But now he was thinking that perhaps he would have to go sooner. There had been talk of his stepping down some time after the 2009 local council elections.

Ahern was anxious to discuss developments with Cowen, who was out of the country, to get his view on what had to be done. If Cowen would remain loyal to his Taoiseach, Ahern knew that there was a possibility that he could once again weather the storm. But the opposition felt that loyalty to the Taoiseach could only go so far, and attempted to push Cowen on the issue. Labour's new leader Eamon Gilmore told the press: 'It is now time for Brian Cowen and other senior figures to put loyalty to the country ahead of loyalty to their damaged party leader; it is time to bring this sorry saga to a conclusion, so that the Government and the Dáil can now concentrate on dealing with the huge social and economic problems facing us.'

The message to Cowen was clear: it was time for him to tell his boss some hard truths. Just before Christmas 2007, Enda Kenny had decided to target Cowen as part of the opposition's attempt to oust Ahern. During a heated debate, Kenny asked in the Dáil: 'What is the Government's position on the Tribunals of Inquiry Bill which was on the Order Paper two weeks ago, but seems to have disappeared? Does the Tánaiste accept the Taoiseach's explanations as his previous evidence appears to be crumbling in the face of evidence being acquired by a tribunal? Does the Government intend to leave the Bill where it is until this module of the tribunals is completed?'

Cowen then pointed out that the second-stage debate on the bill had resumed.

Kenny then bluntly asked if the Tánaiste *believed* the Taoiseach's evidence at the Mahon Tribunal, and gave his own response: 'We will not get an answer to that question.'

Cowen decided not to dignify what he felt was an inappropriate line of questioning with a response, returning instead to address the matter under debate.

In February 2008 Kenny targeted Cowen again. The Fine Gael leader made a long speech in the Dáil, accusing the Tánaiste of being an 'accomplice to deceit' and declaring: 'As Minister for Finance, Mr Cowen sits beside a Taoiseach who has not paid his taxes. As deputy leader of Fianna Fáil, Mr Cowen sits beside a leader of Fianna Fáil who has not explained how a donation given for the party ended up in his own bank account. As Tánaiste, Mr Cowen sits beside a Taoiseach who has misled the Dáil in relation to his tax affairs and has refused to correct the record. When eventually Mr Ahern goes down in flames as the mounting evidence becomes unbearable, Mr Cowen will not be able to claim that he did not know or that he had no information or that he could not act.

'The reality is Mr Cowen does know the Taoiseach has not paid his taxes. Mr Cowen does know the Taoiseach has misled the Dáil and the Irish people. Mr Cowen does know that the Taoiseach has not given any credible explanation for his personal finances. If Mr Cowen does not act, and I believe act urgently, he too will bear his responsibility for Mr Ahern continuing in office despite the compelling case for his removal. Other Fianna Fáil Ministers are equally culpable in this farce. They are happy to condone a situation where money destined for Fianna Fáil was diverted for the personal use of Mr Ahern.'

At the time Cowen had retorted: 'I don't need lectures from you on my standards. My standards relate to fair play, to hearing the evidence, and they certainly do not relate to people being guilty before being proven innocent.'

By the time Gráinne Carruth gave her altered testimony to the tribunal, Cowen was in Asia. He received some phone calls from party colleagues, but he was 'noncommittal' about the news and simply stated that he was 'too far away to be making any judgements'. However, during Cowen's absence there had been behind-the-scenes manœuvring at senior levels of Fianna Fáil. Ahern was feeling under pressure to announce his departure date.

10

Taoiseach

By this stage, it has been speculated, Cowen must have been finding it difficult to support his Taoiseach in public. He knew the tide was turning against Ahern, and he also knew that, worse still, the constant stream of inconsistencies in information about his finances was having a negative impact on the party. While Ahern was still saying that he wanted to stay on, possibly until after the local elections in 2009, Fianna Fáil councillors were starting to fear that if he did they would lose their seats in an electoral backlash; and some in the party feared that the situation could seriously weaken the government's efforts to secure a 'yes' vote in the imminent referendum on the EU Lisbon Treaty.

Cowen returned with his family to Ireland on 26 March, following a short family holiday in Vietnam after his St Patrick's Day duties in Malaysia. Later that evening, he phoned Ahern to discuss some important issues concerning the financial markets (Cowen had even taken time out from his family holiday to contact his department and the governor of the Central Bank, John Hurley). The two men agreed to meet the following day in Ahern's home – not in his constituency office of St Luke's, as had been speculated in the press – in Drumcondra. After they had talked about the problems facing the financial markets, Ahern then 'discussed things generally', including the worrying allegations brought up in the Mahon Tribunal. As Cowen was leaving, Ahern said that he would be in touch shortly to discuss the situation further.

'I said that these were matters for himself. I know everybody has been speculating on our private conversation, but I put no issue to him. I was supportive of my Taoiseach,' recalls Cowen. 'I left it at that – I left it with him. I said he had my support in whatever he wanted to do. He wasn't indicating anything at that stage. He was reflecting on his own position.'

This was a difficult time for Cowen. Not only was the Ahern crisis coming to a head; his beloved uncle, Father Andrew, who had taught him in Roscrea, was dying. Leaving Ahern's home, Cowen jumped back into his car and sped towards a Mullingar hospital to be at Father Andrew's bedside. Two months previously, Cowen's other uncle, Michael, an engineer with the local authority and a former vice-chairman of An Bord Pleanála, had also died. Cowen thought it was very sad that neither man lived a 'short while longer' to see him become Taoiseach. He would later say that Father Andrew's death in particular brought an element of sadness and regret to what was otherwise a very special occasion. By the time he had made his affectionate farewell to his uncle – a man he loved dearly and for whom he had a great respect – late that night, Cowen was emotionally exhausted.

Ahern phoned Cowen the following day to discuss further the situation relating to the tribunal. He told Cowen that he was still reflecting on events and that he would be in contact. At this stage, Cowen had no idea that Ahern was considering stepping down after almost eleven years as head of government. Cowen didn't hear from Ahern again until the following Tuesday, 1 April, when his Taoiseach asked him to visit him that evening in St Luke's.

Ahern has always been known as a politician who kept his own counsel and rarely discussed issues with colleagues; but he trusted Cowen and respected his opinion. 'He told me in confidence of his intention to announce stepping down,' says Cowen. Even though they were now clearly discussing the end, this was sooner than Cowen had anticipated. Ahern revealed that he would announce his decision the following morning at the cabinet's breakfast meeting. Both men knew that the next day in the Dáil would be a difficult one, with the opposition planning to table another no-confidence motion against the Taoiseach. What if some of the coalition partners decided to vote against the government? Besides, Ahern didn't want to stand up in the Dáil and offer yet another explanation. He had grown weary of trying to explain himself. He really wanted to stay another year in office – but perhaps it would be best for Fianna Fáil if he outmanoeuvred the opposition by suddenly announcing his intention to resign. Ahern said it again: it was time for him to step down. Both men knew that such a move would catch their opponents unawares.

Cowen remembers telling Ahern that he shouldn't resign before the upcoming Taoiseach's address to the US Congress. It was, they both agreed, a perfect time for Ahern's swansong. With the tenth anniversary of the Good Friday Agreement approaching, Ahern already had scheduled formal engagements at Westminster and in the US Congress. There was never going to be a more apt time to step down with grace and to inevitable plaudits, both at home and abroad. It was also important that Ahern was seen to be choosing his own course of action, that he showed he was not being forced out of office, and was allowing both the government and his party due time to adapt to his decision.

'I want to make it very clear – genuinely and this is truthful – that we weren't at variance in any way. There was no acrimony or animosity or any problems between myself and the Taoiseach during those meetings. I had a good relationship with Bertie Ahern throughout his period as Taoiseach. At no stage did I indicate a withdrawal of support. He was obviously reflecting on the issues over the previous week. In fairness to Bertie Ahern, he came to his own conclusion himself in what he felt was in the best interest of the party. The Taoiseach came to his own decisions, in his own time, in his own way,' Cowen insists.

Later, when he resigned, Ahern went on RTÉ radio and stated that he'd been 'unlucky' with the tribunal: 'I feel very very unlucky and unfortunate in the extreme that Mr O'Callaghan and Mr Gilmartin fell out over a business deal, and we understand businessmen fall out over business deals, and unfortunately one of them decided to say the other fella had given me money and then everything comes down on top of me,' he said. 'But I got in the middle and I think I was unlucky to do that and I think I got a raw deal out of it all. But that's life,' he said. 'I was desperately unlucky to find myself in that position.'

It is not hard to imagine Ahern saying something similar to Cowen, who remembers empathizing with Ahern over the enormous stress he had to endure during his last few months in office as Taoiseach. Having worked closely with him for many years, on 'a personal level' he was sorry to see Ahern's tenure end in such a way.

But if Ahern did go 'in a month', as he now suggested, he would be standing down before the Lisbon Treaty referendum, scheduled for 12 June. Cowen knew that this was not ideal; it was an unenviable moment for any successor to be taking the helm. But first things first: he would have to ensure that he had the party's support as their new leader. Cowen was well aware that there were several very capable colleagues who could reasonably aspire to the role of Taoiseach. His ascent to power was probable but not certain. As he never tired of reminding people, a quarter of a century in politics had taught him that nothing in political life is certain.

On the fateful day, Wednesday 2 April, as the cabinet sat down to a hastily arranged working breakfast at Government Buildings, Ahern stunned his colleagues by breaking the unexpected news of his intention to resign. Some of his ministers did seek to persuade him to reconsider, but Ahern was determined.

'We've had a good run. I'm thirty-one years in the Dáil and over twenty-one years at the Cabinet table and eleven years of that as Taoiseach,' he told his dazed colleagues. He then told the cabinet that he would make his announcement after breakfast. Later, Mary Hanafin, Minister for Education at the time, would tell the media that the occasion was an emotional one, and that a few of the ministers had tears in their eyes.

Flanked by his cabinet, Ahern then went out to the waiting media and gave his resignation address to the nation live on television. In his speech, he reasserted his innocence: 'While I will be the first to admit that I have made mistakes in my life and in my career, one mistake I have never made is to enrich myself by misusing the trust of the people. I have never received a corrupt payment and I have never done anything to dishonour any office I have held. I know that some people will feel that some aspects of my finances are unusual. I truly regret if this has caused any confusion or worry in people's minds.'

One by one, Cowen's ministerial colleagues all publicly announced their attention to support his candidacy for the leadership of Fianna Fáil. Cowen submitted his nomination, which was formally backed by Brian Lenihan Jnr and seconded by Mary Coughlan, to the Chief Whip of the parliamentary party, Tom Kitt, for the position of Uachtarán Fianna Fáil from 7 May, Ahern's planned resignation date. After announcing his candidacy, Cowen spoke about his 'deep and abiding affection and respect for my party, its history and traditions'. He said that during his political career since 1984 he had come to appreciate the huge commitment and effort of the thousands of party members and supporters who made up the lifeblood of the organization. He said how 'deeply honoured' he would be if his parliamentary colleagues decided that 'I should succeed the Taoiseach as party leader'.

While it appeared that Cowen was going to get a clear run at the nomination, this didn't stop speculation mounting that somebody else – Dermot Ahern, Micheál Martin, Noel Dempsey – might enter the ring. Cowen wasn't so sure himself; though everyone was telling him he would be the only nominee, there was no certainty until the nomination process closed at 2 p.m. on 5 April. Cowen has always believed that you can never take anything for granted, and he wasn't going to start now. Reading between the lines of Noel Dempsey's statement that 'now that the procedures have been agreed and Brian Cowen has confirmed to me that he will be a candidate, I am happy to confirm that I will be supporting him in the vote for party leader and on the nomination for Taoiseach', it's easy to imagine that he would have run himself if by that point Cowen's position had not become unassailable. The future Minister for Finance Brian Lenihan was adamant that there were others within the party with the capability to lead.

On the day nominations closed, the national media descended on Tullamore. They observed that Cowen, as he strolled through the main street, seemed to be a bundle of emotions – happy and excited, but also tense and cautious. When the deadline finally arrived, Cowen received a text message confirming that he was the sole nominee. Now he could relax. He would be the unanimous choice of his party colleagues for the leadership of Fianna Fáil, a rare honour reflecting the popularity and respect he had achieved.

One of the first political correspondents to catch up with Cowen on that day was Harry McGee of the *Irish Times*. He later reported that Cowen, sitting in Digan's on the main street sipping a Lucozade, told him: 'The Cowens have been involved in politics locally and nationally for seventy years. There have been three generations of this family involved. Last week we buried my uncle, Father Andrew, who was a Cistercian monk in Roscrea. Two months ago, my father's eldest brother passed away . . . My dad is long gone. He would have been proud if he were still alive.' Cowen also told McGee that it was a special moment for 'all those supporters and activists' who had supported his family down the years. 'I am very aware and very proud of all those friends as this honour is bestowed on me.'

As the news sank in, Cowen decided to go for a stroll through the woodlands of Charleville Castle. After his ministerial car pulled up and Cowen stepped out, he was approached by a photographer from the *Sunday Tribune* who asked if he would pose for some pictures.

'No problem,' Cowen told him.

In the next day's edition it was observed that Cowen appeared to suffer 'mild mortification' at having to pose for the photographer. 'He smiled ruefully at his attempts to look natural while walking through a wood looking at nothing in particular,' the report stated.

Cowen assumed the mantle of Taoiseach-designate on 10 April 2008, when he formally replaced Bertie Ahern at a meeting of the Fianna Fáil parliamentary party in Leinster House. Afterwards, Ahern went on national radio to praise Cowen: 'He is highly intelligent. He is a powerful speaker, far better than I would ever dream of being,' he said. 'If there's a row on, he won't be as polite as I am. If somebody wants a row with Brian, if I was them I'd stay up late the night before preparing for it.'

After the formalities, Cowen walked down to the Royal College of Physicians of Ireland, a short stroll from the gates of Leinster House, to hold a press conference. As he entered the building, he was greeted with loud cheers and a standing ovation from a large Offaly contingent who had arrived by hired buses to attend the event. As Cowen read out his acceptance speech, his family, sitting in the front row, looked on with pride and tears in their eyes. Cowen told the packed auditorium that he was proud not only to be the first minister from County Offaly but now also to be its first Taoiseach. 'There has been great sporting success in this county. It gave a huge lift to everybody and there was also a great self-belief. I suppose something like this is a big talking point. I was the first minister appointed from Offaly. And obviously I'm the first to reach this position,' he said. 'On a personal level I am excited by the challenge, if somewhat daunted by the responsibility.'

After his speech, Cowen was asked what impact his accession to the office of Taoiseach would have on his personal and family life. Interestingly, he replied: 'I am, of course, in taking this position, fully aware that I am accountable publicly to the electorate, to the citizens of this country, for any decisions I make on their behalf. There is, as I have said last week, a private life and a family side to my life that I wish to see respected, and I believe the standards of Irish journalism are such that that will not prove a problem, as both of us set out to do our job in as conscientious a way as we can.'

Later, Cowen and his colleagues, supporters, family members and friends went across to one of his favourite pubs, Doheny and Nesbitt on Baggot Street, to celebrate in the privacy of the outdoor smoking area, which was sealed off on this special occasion.

Cowen made his first formal public appearance as Taoiseach-elect when he was personally requested by the family of Dr Patrick Hillery, Ireland's sixth President, who had died on 12 April, to give the graveside oration at St Fintan's Cemetery in the Dublin suburb of Sutton. Cowen considered this a great honour. At the cemetery, the band of the army school of music played the traditional melody to Thomas Moore's 'The Last Rose of Summer'; afterwards the Irish tricolour was removed from the casket and presented to the Hillery family. As he stood at the graveside, waiting to give his oration, Cowen thought about how he'd watched the then retired President shed tears of joy when his native Clare beat Offaly in the 1995 all-Ireland hurling final. Hillery was well regarded in Cowen's home town of Clara, to which he once made an official visit; to this day the town's people still talk about how the President had no air of superiority about him as he mingled with them in the square.

Cowen, giving his extended oration in both Irish and English, spoke passionately about Hillery as an 'exceptional figure in Irish life' who rejected self-publicity and instead could be found quietly working in the background, doing many great things for his country. 'He was part of a generation of Irish politicians who sowed the seeds of our current prosperity. He was the last surviving member of Seán Lemass's first cabinet,' said Cowen. 'Paddy Hillery would not crave statues or monuments to his legacy. Knowing that in some way he helped to shape our modern, confident and ambitious society was acclaim enough for a man who never lost touch.' He said that 'if greatness is judged by the content of character, we stand at the graveside of a great man today'.

Even before taking up the Taoiseach's mantle, Cowen found himself under fire from certain quarters of the media, as well as the opposition – particularly from Enda Kenny, who had during the past year increasingly focused his ire on Cowen. Rather than praise Cowen on his impending appointment, Kenny decided publicly to question whether his adversary was even competent to be Taoiseach. It appears Fine Gael wanted to 'set the bar' high for the incoming Taoiseach. One member of the party told the *Irish Times*: 'Brian Cowen has had a pretty soft run in the media for a long time: we don't see any great ministerial achievements.'

Then, on 5 May, as Cowen was working away on choosing his first cabinet, Kenny attempted to put pressure on him by calling on him to sack Mary Harney from the health portfolio. The new leader of the PDs, Ciaran Cannon, dismissed Kenny's call as a publicity stunt. 'It's a cheap shot. Mary Harney was the first politician to ask for the job of Minister for Health. No other politician from any party has had the confidence and courage and the tenacity and the sense of doing the right thing – and that's what Mary Harney's been all about – to go out and actually ask for that job,' he told *Hot Press*.

While Cowen was keeping his cards close to his chest as he reflected on how best to apply the talents of his colleagues, he had never considered taking Harney away from the Department of Health. In fact, when he was giving his first press conference as Taoiseach-elect, Cowen had emphasized his confidence in the former PD leader's ability. 'I believe many of the critics are in fact using their criticism to maintain and defend the status quo. The one thing that we do know about health policy is that the status quo is not sustainable in the long term. Mary Harney has shown her determination to proceed with that programme of reform and she does so on behalf of the Government and in compliance with Government policy,' he had said. Perhaps surprisingly, Harney was delighted to keep her hold on the so-called 'poisoned chalice'. 'I want to see it through and I am very pleased to have the confidence of the Taoiseach in my re-appointment,' she later stated at a health conference in Dublin Castle.

A few weeks later, just a few days before Ahern stepped down from office on 6 May, he was – perhaps somewhat ironically, considering the unfolding events – named 'Survivor of the Year' at the annual *Magill* Politician of the Year Awards; Cowen's former university lecturer Willie O'Dea became the first government minister ever to be given the light-hearted 'Heckler of the Year' award. Cowen was named by the magazine as its choice for 'Politician of the Year', being selected ahead of the Labour Party's recently appointed leader Eamon Gilmore and the Greens' John Gormley. In announc-ing Cowen as their choice for the prestigious award, the judging panel said the incoming Taoiseach was being acknowledged for his 'competent handling' of the previous year's general election, as well as his work in the Department of Finance.

Brian Cowen officially became the twelfth Taoiseach on 7 May 2008. Prior to going into Dáil Éireann for the formalities of being appointed head of the country's twenty-eighth government, Cowen ambled into a celebratory reception for his constituents being held at the nearby Alexander Hotel. Several hundred supporters from Offaly and Laois had gathered there to celebrate their local TD's appointment to the highest office in the country.

A deafening cheer went up when a proud yet sheepish Cowen walked in unannounced. Triumphantly, Cowen waved his arm in the air, and when the room eventually quietened down he told them: 'I just thought I'd come down and say hello to you all – and thank you for coming to share the excitement of this day.'

Again, there was thunderous applause and Cowen was immediately encircled by a group of well-wishers, seeking autographs and asking him to pose with them for photographs. Later, Brian's elder brother Christy described the atmosphere of the day as being akin to a football final. 'We came up in three buses from Clara, packed as usual. It was a great turnout and well supported. It was like another all-Ireland,' he recalls.

As Cowen was about to leave the hotel, he was approached by Eoghan MacConnell, a reporter with the local weekly newspaper, the *Offaly Independent*. He asked the Taoiseach-in-waiting: 'How are you feeling?'

'I'm feeling very relaxed and looking forward to it,' Cowen replied.

MacConnell noted that while Cowen did indeed look very relaxed, he also appeared to be 'somewhat emotional' as he posed with his mother for a photograph, surrounded by well-wishers. Senator Geraldine Feeney, who is a good friend of Cowen's wife Mary, recalled seeing a 'little tear trickle down' the Taoiseach's cheek as he took in his surroundings. 'He was very emotional. He got a huge reception and people came from all over,' she recalls.

As Cowen made his way into the Dáil for what would be his proudest moment in politics, he ignored the fact that protestors were holding demonstrations about the Lisbon Treaty and also about hospital conditions outside the walls of Government Buildings. Inside the chamber, Cowen's nomination was formally proposed by the acting Taoiseach Bertie Ahern and by the Minister for the Environment John Gormley. Ahern drew attention to Cowen's vast ministerial experience, which would equip him to undertake the obligations of the office of Taoiseach with 'flair and capacity'. He spoke of Cowen as one of the 'most successful contributors to partnership government over recent years and one who had an active role in the negotiation of the current programme for government' and so was 'well placed to lead a Government that will enjoy the support, commitment and energy' of all participants in the coalition. He also said in his proposal that Cowen was a 'fair-minded and straight-talking participant in the social partnership process and has all the necessary skills to lead the process towards the next stage of development in line with the needs of our economy and society'. Minister Gormley, who seconded the nomination, said: 'The Brian Cowen I know is tough but fair-minded, and gregarious but thoughtful. He is relaxed but always focused on the task in hand. He knows the task he now faces as Taoiseach is onerous.'

The opposition decided to do some mischief-making by nominating Enda Kenny and Eamon Gilmore for the post of Taoiseach, but there was never going to be any doubt of the outcome – and Cowen was duly elected by eighty-eight votes to seventy-six. Cowen then proceeded with his maiden speech as Taoiseach. In it, he said he accepted his position with honour and a genuine sense of humility. He went on to outline his vision of the country's priorities:

'Tomorrow, I will have the privilege of addressing the Investment Conference for Northern Ireland with Prime Minister Gordon Brown. It is appropriate that, on my first working day as Taoiseach, I will have the opportunity to advance relationships and deepen engagement, both on a North–South and an East–West basis. Consolidating the peace through economic development and mutual understanding will have my full engagement and whole-hearted support. Tomorrow's conference is a timely reminder that our destiny on this island cannot be secured in isolation from the rest of the world.

'We share too much from history and culture with our neighbouring island not to work for the deepest friendship and the most fruitful engagement. Our economic success on this island owes much to the strength and depth of our relationship with the United States, both through the very many investors who have found here a successful partner for investment, and through the scale of the trading relationship between the two economies.

'But it is in the context of our European identity, and membership of the European Union, that our place in the international arena, and our relationships with other nations, near and far, find their proper perspective and most potent context. As a member of the European Council, I will strive to

211

ensure that our European vocation is a live, engaged and creative thing, not a passive recipient of the fruits of the labours of others.'

Cowen also emphasized the need to ensure the ratification of the Lisbon Treaty. It was apparent that even on his first day in office as Taoiseach he was acutely aware of the negative repercussions that would follow if the electorate did the unimaginable and rejected the treaty. Cowen made it quite clear in his speech that one of his main priorities would be to ensure Ireland remained at the heart of the EU:

'The influence of the EU project has been all pervasive across every aspect of our lives. We have availed of the full range of opportunities of membership better than most. The political, economic and social landscape has been utterly transformed for the better in this country. The greatest mistake we could make now is to move away from that opening out to the world that has brought such benefits to our nation. I have been reading Des Geraghty's excellent book *Forty Shades of Green* in recent days. His thesis is that we are now in a new space. What was once one of the most dispersed nations in the world is now becoming one of the most diverse nations. The change is visible and real.

'We are now redefining ourselves in terms of both mending relationships with those of other traditions of long standing within the island and establishing relationships with the new Irish and migrants who have come to our shores to share in the economic miracle of the Celtic Tiger economy. We are also connecting in a myriad of ways through economic, social and cultural links with many peoples on the continent of Europe and further afield as the economic reach of our society is becoming truly global.'

Cowen referred to Ireland's Celtic heritage as a contributory factor to the country taking its place as a leading nation within the EU. 'We are admired and respected as a progressive country throughout the wider community of the developed world. In the developing world, the tradition of "giving" of our forefathers has been maintained by the contemporary missionary and development work of today's Irish men and women,' he told the Dáil.

'We have reaped benefits from the more confident Ireland as presented by its most successful people forging new opportunities at home and abroad. Overdone, this carries risks. Not correctly harnessed, this can sap the energy from our sense of community which is still strong and visible in so many ways. What we must prioritize is to turn the benefits of individual flair to the benefit of the community as a whole.'

He spoke about the government's responsibility of needing to 'fuel the engine of community'. It was important, he felt, for the people to dispense with an avaricious, self-interested mentality and, instead, focus on creating the 'superior value of a wider community interest'. He added: 'The pre-eminence of community and participation over self promotes social harmony and a better quality of life for all. This is what will allow us to develop a society of social inclusion. Our particular charge is to represent the interests of our young. The character of the generations that will build this century is still being formed. It is these generations that will decide the shape of the future.

'It is our job, as government and as parliamentarians, to take the steps that will make it clearer for that generation to help shape this Republic in a way that realizes its greater potential. I have referenced our economic progress and how that has translated into significant social enhancements. We have made great gains but we face great challenges. Our job as legislators is to provide leadership for society at this time of change. But we need society to engage with us in the process. Change of this nature cannot simply be driven by government.'

As he neared the end of his speech, Cowen reflected on what becoming Taoiseach meant to him at a personal level. He spoke about being excited and 'a little daunted' by this great sense of responsibility. 'I have been overwhelmed by the good wishes I have received from people the length and breadth of the country, and indeed from abroad. I want to particularly thank my family. I got my grounding in politics from my father, Ber, who had in turn got it from his father, Christy, a founding member of the Fianna Fáil party. Politics is about public service above all else.'

When Cowen ended his speech he received a standing ovation and thunderous applause. Once the formalities in the Dáil were complete, Cowen emerged to be greeted by the sound of 'The Offaly Rover' echoing throughout the grounds. Amazingly, some of his constituents had managed to find their way through the security cordon and were waving flags and singing with joy. After posing for photographs, Cowen was approached by former Taoiseach Albert Reynolds, who embraced him and said, 'Do you remember when I was leaving office and I pointed to the Taoiseach's chair and said, "I hope to see you in this chair some day, Brian"? Well, I am delighted to be alive and well to see this special day.'

Cowen was then driven to Áras an Uachtaráin for his formal appointment by President Mary McAleese. He had insisted that his wife and two young daughters, Sinead and Maedhbh, should be with him at this moment, and so became the first Taoiseach to have his family present during the ceremony. It was a decision for which he was highly praised in an editorial the following weekend in his local newspaper, the *Offaly*

Independent. Its editor Tadgh Carey noted: 'Brian's decision to bring his family with him to receive his seal of office was a fitting and lasting image of the day.'

After the presidential ceremony, Cowen stepped outside and gave RTÉ's Charlie Bird a brief interview. He spoke frankly about the pride his father would have felt had he been alive to see him become Taoiseach. He then returned to the Dáil, where he announced his new cabinet shortly after 6 p.m. before heading back with his new team to Áras an Uachtaráin in order to gain the President's formal approval of his administration.

Just forty-eight hours earlier, Cowen had still been mulling over his final decisions at home as he made phone calls to his colleagues who were anxiously waiting for news. He had decided to leave the two Green ministers in their portfolios of environment and communication, as it had been widely acknowledged that they were both doing a good job. Cowen's hand became slightly easier to play when Séamus Brennan, who sadly died only two months later, informed Cowen that he didn't want to be reconsidered for the Department of Arts because of his deteriorating health. Cowen opted to make less than subtle moves in most departments: having vacated the Department of Finance himself, he opted to give this key position to Brian Lenihan Jnr, who had nominated him for the leadership; Mary Coughlan, who had seconded the nomination, was awarded with the largely symbolic role of Tánaiste and also promoted to the Department of Enterprise, with her previous agriculture portfolio going to new cabinet arrival Brendan Smith; Micheál Martin was given foreign affairs and Dermot Ahern was appointed justice minister. Eyebrows were raised when Cowen promoted Batt O'Keefe – seen by many as a confidant of the Taoiseach – at the expense of Mary

Hanafin to the Department of Education and Science. The appointment of Pat Carey as Chief Whip meant that Tom Kitt was effectively sacked from the position; apparently disappointed to be offered nothing better than a junior ministerial role, Kitt soon afterwards announced his intention to retire from politics at the end of the current government term. Kitt denied that he had resigned to vent his anger at the demotion: 'Those people who would know me, know that there is no bitterness in Tom Kitt. There isn't an ounce of bitterness in me.'

There was no honeymoon period for the new government. As soon as Cowen's cabinet had been announced in the Dáil, Fine Gael's leader Enda Kenny passed on good wishes to its members, but then used his congratulatory speech to resume business as usual with a rapid attack on the government: 'The reality is that, out of the best times any Irish government was ever handed, Fianna Fáil has created catastrophe and chaos.'

On a similar note, Labour's leader Eamon Gilmore told the Dáil: 'The captain's armband has been changed, there are a few substitutions, and some positional switches, but this is essentially the same government that has been in office for the last eleven years.'

The next day Gilmore went on to complain in the Dáil that the timing of the key events – including Cowen and his cabinet getting their seals of office at Áras an Uachtaráin – had been stage-managed to coincide with RTÉ's news schedule, ensuring that the formal ceremonies appeared on television. An irate Gilmore said: 'It was clear what was going on. It was clear that the events here yesterday were timed to coincide with main news bulletins. That is very admirable news management and my congratulations to the people who organized that. If that practice continues into the future, the members of this Government will be going through those lobbies an awful lot more often than they may like to be.'

Tánaiste Mary Coughlan rejected the allegations: 'Luckily, as a woman of compassion I don't take threats. But I have to say I and the Taoiseach and this Government have the highest regard for this House.' Gilmore snapped back: 'I don't make threats but I do promise that if what happened yesterday is repeated, there will be a consequence for it.'

Gilmore also criticized the release of the Morris Tribunal report on allegations of corruption in the Donegal Garda during the formation of the new government. 'Publication of that report yesterday on the day when the Government was being formed was an act of political cynicism . . . It does not behove any new practices on the part of this new Government,' he fumed.

It was a tiring day for Cowen, but even so he popped back into the Alexander Hotel at 11 p.m. for an hour. Again, as he entered the hotel, the jubilant crowd greeted him with yet another chorus of their county's song, 'The Offaly Rover'. Cowen delighted them by taking his younger daughter's hand and spinning her around. He then enjoyed his first pint of Guinness that day, posed for some more photographs and listened intently to each individual congratulation. It was a day he'd remember fondly for the rest of his life.

11

The First Hundred Days

Brian Cowen began his tenure as Taoiseach on a buoyant note. Within a week of his taking office, the latest *Irish Times*/TNS mrbi poll showed a noteworthy increase of 8 per cent in Fianna Fáil's popularity among the electorate. The extent of the party's revival was a clear sign that the enormous positive publicity surrounding both Bertie Ahern's farewell celebrations and Brian Cowen's succession as leader and Taoiseach had converted into renewed support for the government.

'There can be little doubt that Brian Cowen's appointment has created a feel-good factor which has distracted voters from news of job losses and store closures which otherwise would have acted as a drag on support for Fianna Fáil. The almost carnival atmosphere created everywhere the new leader went last week served to confirm how capable he is of energizing his party and the public,' explained Damian Loscher, managing director of TNS mrbi.

But the so-called 'feel-good factor' soon faded. Unfortunately for Cowen, his immediate task as Taoiseach was a difficult one – to urge the electorate to ratify the EU Lisbon Treaty in a referendum. Only too conscious of the difficulty the government had faced in securing the ratification of the Nice Treaty, he dreaded a repeat of that first referendum vote. Initially, at least, the prospects seemed positive, as it appeared that the controversies prompting Ahern's resignation had not produced an electoral backlash. In fact, the anti-Ahern feeling in the country seemed to have dissipated since his departure from office. It was later suggested that Ahern's appearance in front of the Mahon Tribunal after he had stepped down had had a detrimental effect on the vote, but this was dismissed by Minister for Finance Brian Lenihan. During an appearance on RTÉ's *Week in Politics* programme, Lenihan admitted that Ahern's finances were 'not a pretty picture', but added: 'I think the transition to the leadership of Brian Cowen has been a very peaceful one. It has been a very constructive phase in the history of Fianna Fáil and it does put us in a position to tackle the economic problems and also to campaign for the "yes" vote.'

The preliminary opinion polls suggested that supporters of the treaty were twice as numerous as its opponents. They also suggested, more ominously, that almost half of the electorate were still undecided or would opt not to vote either way; and a highly organized and well-funded campaign against the treaty began to have its effects as voting day approached. Moreover, while the outcome of the Ahern saga did initially boost Fianna Fáil's popularity, it had negative effects too. Cowen and his cabinet were only settling in, and time was against them: the referendum date was set for 12 June, less than a month after Cowen's appointment.

The Lisbon Treaty, which had been in preparation under various different guises since 2001, was a complex document intended to streamline the workings of the EU. Among its main points were a revision of the EU Council's voting system; an increase in the European Parliament's involvement in the legislative processes of the EU Council; ratification of the Charter of Fundamental Rights; a reduction in the number of Commissioners from 27 to 18 (a particularly contentious point); and the introduction of two new positions at the highest level: a President of the European Council and a High Representative for Foreign Affairs. However, the treaty text itself was almost unreadable, and this played into the hands of the anti-treaty campaigners, who were able to highlight and sensationalize what they saw as the negative repercussions of a 'yes' vote to an increasingly weary electorate. 'The opponents had pressed a lot of buttons that raised fears and concerns among people,' says Cowen now, reflecting on the ill-fated campaign. 'There are an awful lot of places in Irish life where there are resisters to change – some quite organized, some quite eloquent, some who are good at distracting attention from the basic issue in order to protect their own interest.'

However, Cowen himself did not help matters when, with typical outspokenness, he admitted during an RTÉ radio interview that he had not read the current treaty text in its entirety. 'I haven't read it from cover to cover. I know exactly what's in it,' Cowen stated. As Minister for Foreign Affairs during the treaty's gestation, Cowen had read countless previous drafts and had been briefed fully on the treaty's final version; but that did not deter the tabloid newspapers from stating that he had not even bothered to read the document he was asking the country to approve. The media spin on Cowen's comment invigorated the anti-Lisbon campaign. The founder of the anti-treaty organization Libertas, Declan Ganley, stated: 'I have four young kids and I have read the treaty in full. Brian Cowen has not even read the entire treaty. You wouldn't sign a contract on a house unless you had read it in full.'

There is no doubt that Ganley's comments resonated with a now sceptical electorate, who – unable to comprehend the impenetrably worded manifesto attached to the treaty – would henceforth instead rely on the media debate for information and guidance on which way to vote. Libertas, moreover, was skilful in getting its messages across. Prominent among these were its allegations that a 'yes' vote would result in dramatic changes to the country's tax system and at the same time reduce Ireland's voting weight at the EU Council. Other opponents were equally forceful in advancing their arguments. The Socialist Party's leader Joe Higgins, a former TD for the Dublin West constituency, was adamant that the treaty would open the floodgates to the privatization of public services and would see the emergence of an EU military force. 'They do want to have military power and a disposable army,' Higgins stated at a press conference to launch his party's 'no' campaign. In other words, according to the 'no' campaign, if Ireland ratified the Lisbon Treaty it would place itself virtually at the mercy of the EU.

Regardless of whether these arguments were factually correct or not, the 'no' campaign was becoming more and more vocal; and the electorate were starting to listen. It did not help that Ireland would be the only EU country to hold a referendum on the issue. 'Ireland is the only place in the European Union to have a vote on the Lisbon Treaty, but there are tens of millions of people across the EU who have been denied a vote and who oppose this treaty,' Sinn Féin President Gerry Adams stated. 'The fact is that the Lisbon Treaty cannot proceed without the support of the Irish people so if it does not go through it will have to be renegotiated. A strong No vote on June 12th would create a huge opportunity for the Irish Government to address those issues which are clearly of concern to the public.'

The perception that the treaty would be open to renegotiation if it were rejected was widely held. Even though the
government insisted that there could be no renegotiating of
the Lisbon Treaty, the 'no' campaigners could counteract this
by referring to the Nice Treaty, in respect of which concessions had been made and elements rephrased in order to
get it ratified on a second attempt in Ireland. The 'no'
campaign shrewdly argued that the EU would respond in
similar fashion if the Lisbon Treaty were rejected.

However, Cowen stated categorically that Ireland had pro-
cured the best possible deal available on the Lisbon Treaty –
pointing out, moreover, that the Irish government had played
an instrumental part in drafting the document. 'Of all of the
European treaties, this was probably the most influenced by
smaller countries and Ireland can be very proud of its central
role in leading negotiations. This is reflected in the text of the
Treaty, which directly protects and promotes the interests of
the member states, irrespective of their size,' stated Cowen.

Cowen had the political foresight to anticipate that the 'no'
campaign would focus on the Lisbon Treaty's alleged
potential to damage Irish interests. Launching Fianna Fáil's
'yes' campaign in the Hugh Lane Gallery in Dublin's Parnell
Square, he told a press conference: 'During every European
referendum, groups have emerged which have claimed that
deep conspiracies are being hatched against the people of
Ireland. The most common tactic has not been to try to
persuade people, but to try and confuse them. There are some
shrill voices who always try to use this debate in an effort to
raise fears, raise the concerns, narrow the base, suggest that
there is a comfort zone where we can live in isolation from the
world, that we should step back, that we mightn't be able for
it, we might be overwhelmed. Those voices have been with us

since the European debate as far back as the sixties. If that is their view of the world they are entitled to put it.'

The first serious signs of unease within the 'yes' campaign came to light less than two weeks before the referendum, when Fine Gael and Labour both took offence at comments Cowen made at a public rally. Speaking in Portlaoise, Cowen had said: 'I'm glad to see our own party, the support of our own base, is certainly highest among all the parties and I'm sure the other parties will crank up their campaigns now as well.' Afterwards he was asked by reporters to expand on this statement, which he did by declaring: 'Well, from the Fianna Fáil point of view, what I think is a very important point is that you know we are the most pro-European party. We are getting most of our supporters out to support this thing in the hope that . . . colleagues in other parties now can crank up their campaign, which I'm sure they will, to make sure that we see the same level of support from other parties.'

But the following day Cowen insisted that his comments were not made with any intention of criticizing the opposition parties. 'I was not having a cut at anyone, obviously. I was saying I'm sure we will all be intensifying our efforts. I look forward to making sure we all get out there and get a Yes vote, that's all.'

A party spokesperson for Fine Gael described Cowen's comments in Portlaoise as the 'final straw'. This was a reference to an extraordinary confrontation between Kenny and Cowen that had taken place during a Dáil debate on 21 May. The row erupted when Cowen, while attempting to answer a question about the health service, was interrupted half a dozen times by the opposition during a Leader's Questions session. In retaliation, a clearly irate Cowen commented that he could arrange to have people 'roaring and shouting on this side' every time Kenny 'completes a sentence'. By this stage, the session was rapidly descending into farce, with the opposition attempting to taunt Cowen by interjecting every time he attempted to address the issue at hand, and Cowen growing visibly annoyed as the opposition shouted out: 'Answer the question!' or 'He can't answer the question!' every time he attempted to make a reply.

'Listen to me, I want to answer the question but I will make one point. If you keep that tactic up, I will make sure he—' Cowen said, pointing at Kenny '—will not be heard in this House . . . It can be organized.'

'The Taoiseach will not silence the people on this side of the House,' Kenny snapped back.

The Ceann Comhairle then asked for the House to allow the Taoiseach the opportunity to speak 'without interruption'.

But Kenny was now clearly riled. 'I am not going to take that from any Member of this House. The Taoiseach will not silence the Fine Gael Party or any of its members,' he declared.

'I will not be shouted down by the orchestrated tactic engaged in by the opposition for months. That will not work with me,' Cowen retorted.

Still the opposition continued to prevent Cowen from giving a detailed answer to the question. Afterwards, Cowen – who was clearly frustrated by the repeated interruptions – sat down and turned to Mary Coughlan, Tánaiste and Minister for Enterprise, Trade and Employment, to have a private conversation. Unfortunately, the microphone in the Dáil picked up the exchange word for word.

'Ring those people and get a handle on it, will you? Bring in all those fuckers,' Cowen told Coughlan. The media later speculated that Cowen was speaking to Coughlan about the National Consumer Agency and the current controversy over British retailers allegedly overcharging Irish consumers.

The Fine Gael leader later described Cowen's performance in the Dáil as 'quite astonishing'. He added: 'I have never seen any Taoiseach in my years in the house lose control the way that Brian Cowen did . . . and that's after thirteen days in office.'

The recorded comment elicited contrasting responses in the media. The *Irish Independent* declared that it was 'unbecoming' for a Taoiseach to use bad language and advised him 'not to let it happen again', while the *Irish Examiner* came out in Cowen's support: 'Voters like a bit of life in their leaders, and Mr Cowen's outburst will have done him no harm.' Later, Cowen apologized for the remark. 'A private comment was made to a colleague,' Cowen told reporters. 'It wasn't appropriate. It isn't appropriate whether it's inside the Dáil or outside the Dáil. I apologize for it.'

Ironically, shortly afterwards Cowen's lapse into bad language was used to support a legal claim to have a public order charge struck out of the Ballyshannon District Court. The *Irish Times* reported that when the Gardaí were called to a street disturbance in the town at four-thirty one morning back in January, a man named Jason McCormack had twice shouted 'fuck off' in front of the Gardaí. Now his solicitor, Paudge Dorrian, argued that 'This is the best parliamentary language we know. It was used in an exchange between the Taoiseach and the Tánaiste.'

'He [McCormack] runs from his house and tells everybody to fuck off and then sees the garda and turns and walks back into his house. He is entitled to the same consideration given to other people for the parliamentary language.'

However, the judge disagreed and fined McCormack € 600.

It was clear that Enda Kenny was still irked with Cowen when on 26 May he appeared on TV3's *The Political Party* and used the opportunity to continue the war of words between the two party leaders. 'Brian Cowen is having a problem being in control of himself and wants to set out to prove that he is a freak in control of the leadership of the party,' Kenny sneered.

These comments came in the wake of allegations that Cowen was perceived within his own party as having a 'dictatorial' style of leadership, with several unnamed back-bench TDs apparently claiming so in the press. However, the Minister for Finance Brian Lenihan later rejected Kenny's comments. 'Far from being a control freak, [the Taoiseach] has very much given me my head and I have been working in the department briefing myself on the issues, making my views known at Cabinet. But I think he is anxious that Government in this country should work in an orthodox way, that Ministers should debate issues among themselves, come to decisions and stick by them,' he said.

The day after his TV appearance, a clearly irked Enda Kenny brought up the comments Cowen had made in Portlaoise when speaking in the Dáil. 'We do need co-operation among those supporting the "yes" campaign in order to have everybody properly informed about what is in this treaty and how it can equip Europe to meet the challenges that lie ahead,' Kenny told the chamber. 'From that perspective, the Taoiseach's remarks at the weekend, as reported, have caused a great deal of antagonism and difficulty for people supporting the "yes" campaign who are not supporters of Fianna Fáil. In the interests of harmony and running a cohesive "yes" campaign by all parties that support the treaty, I ask the Taoiseach to withdraw those remarks and clear this matter up.'

However, after listening to Kenny's comments, Cowen opted not to make an apology. 'I do not understand what the issue is for the leader of the opposition. In response to a question I was asked about the opinion poll, I indicated that all the parties that support the referendum intend continuing to ramp up and intensify our campaign over the coming two and a half weeks,' he said. 'If people want to seek out offence I suppose they can take it, although I would not offer any offence to anybody – quite the contrary. I have plenty of reasons to have rows with Deputy Kenny on a range of issues, but I have no issue with him on this matter and never had. Rather than trying to find offence where none is intended, and none was actually offered, we should just get on with the campaign and proceed. That is the point and any inter-pretation to the contrary is mistaken.'

Several days later, the tabloid press speculated that Cowen had appeared to affront the Fine Gael party leader again by deciding to go out canvassing with Labour leader Eamon Gilmore. It later emerged, according to the *Irish Times*, that Kenny had prior commitments in Cork and was unable to attend the canvassing event with Cowen and Gilmore. 'We need to be working together,' Cowen urged, as he canvassed with Gilmore. 'This is a national issue, not a party political issue. There were some unfortunate issues earlier in the week. Whatever misunderstandings there were, we hope that we have left them behind us.'

Eventually, Cowen did make a joint appeal with Kenny and Gilmore – but this demonstration of unity took place only three days prior to the vote, inviting charges that it was too little, too late. Many political commentators have since pon-dered on how many Fine Gael voters – feeling slighted by Cowen's hostility towards their party leader in the run-up to the Lisbon referendum – opted to reject the treaty as a result. There is no doubt that the dispute distracted attention from the real subject of the referendum. On 5 June, the latest *Irish Times*/TNS mrbi poll suggested that 40 per cent of Fine Gael voters were planning to reject the treaty. The 'yes' campaign was by now in serious trouble, with this latest poll showing that the 'no' side was now in the lead. The proportion of voters intending to vote against the treaty had doubled to 35 per cent since the last poll, some three weeks previously, while the 'yes' vote had slipped down five points to 30 per cent. The *Irish Times*' political editor Stephen Collins predicted that it would 'take an unprecedented swing in the last week of the campaign for the Treaty to be carried'. He pointed out that the 'massive increase by the No vote since the last poll has mainly come through gains among undecided voters but, even more ominously for the Yes side, it has lost some support to the No camp'. It appeared that those 'no' voters questioned for the survey were deciding to reject the treaty because they did not understand what it meant. In the aftermath of the vote the Minister for Foreign Affairs, Micheál Martin, who was also his party's referendum campaign director, summed up what he saw as the reason for the result: 'People on the doorstep were saying, "I still don't know enough about this treaty."'

Cowen intensified his campaigning during the final days before the referendum. He even scored several significant political points, most notably by persuading the highly influential Irish Farmers Association, which had previously called on its members to vote 'no', to endorse the government's 'yes' campaign. He also persuaded the Irish Creamery Milk Suppliers Association to back the 'yes' campaign publicly. Cowen also visited as many cities and towns as possible. 'It's back to old-style politics and getting the vote out,' one unidentified senior Fianna Fáil figure told the press. But despite his hectic schedule, even Cowen could sense there was a lack of enthusiasm among the electorate. One man whose opinion he canvassed in Athlone responded: 'There's an awful lot wrong at the moment.' His reply seemed to sum up the electorate's increasingly gloomy mood, influenced by predictions in the media of an imminent recession that was going to drag Ireland back into a financial climate akin to that of the 1980s. Cowen clapped the man on his shoulder and told him: 'This is the important one at the moment. We'll get on to the other ones on the thirteenth.'

Later, a young man told Cowen he was going to reject the treaty because he simply 'didn't believe in it'. An exasperated Cowen replied: 'Have you looked at it? Have you looked at who is supporting the No vote? Sinn Féin, and others. Are you with the Shinners? Well, I hope that there'll be a job here at the end of it.' In the event, the Lisbon Treaty referendum turned out to be a major political coup for Sinn Féin and Libertas, who had pumped €1.3 million into their 'no' campaign – a level of funding similar to that provided by the government for its 'yes' campaign.

Across the European Union, other countries waited with bated breath on 13 June – which, ominously for the superstitious, fell on a Friday – for the results of the Irish referendum. The treaty was rejected by 53.4 per cent of the electorate, with 46.6 per cent voting in favour. In the immediate aftermath of this disastrous result, the Luxembourg premier and finance minister Jean-Claude Juncker declared that the Irish vote had caused a 'European crisis'.

A bitterly disappointed Cowen spent much of that day communicating with his EU counterparts, including the British prime minister Gordon Brown, France's President Nicolas Sarkozy, Chancellor Angela Merkel of Germany and the European Commission President José Manuel Barroso. Barroso told Cowen that the EU would 'respect the outcome of this referendum', but also that he would urge all remaining states, of which eleven out of twenty-seven had not yet done so, to ratify the treaty. Later, Barroso told a press conference: 'The European Council meets next week – and that is the place where joint decisions should be taken on issues that concern us all. The "No" vote in Ireland has not solved the problems which the Lisbon Treaty is designed to solve.' Barroso added that he hoped to hear at the conference Cowen's analysis and ideas on how to address the concerns expressed by the Irish electorate.

During a press conference in Government Buildings, Cowen said: 'I led that campaign and I take responsibility for the fact that it hasn't been successful.' He described the result as a 'source of disappointment to my colleagues in government and to me'. He spoke about the collective duty of his government to 'reflect on the implications of the vote to Ireland so we can move forward and keep this country on the path to progress'. But he acknowledged that there would be 'no quick fix', and that the crisis would not 'be resolved easily'.

The press immediately wanted to know if there would be a second referendum. Before the vote, Cowen had dismissed this possibility. But on that unlucky Friday the thirteenth Cowen gave a more cryptic answer. 'Well, that doesn't arise today because the people have just spoken,' was his quick response. 'A No vote brings uncertainty and therefore I must discuss with colleagues how we wish to proceed as a union in the light of this decision.'

As Cowen prepared for a tense European Council meeting in Brussels, the Irish government could feel the hostility growing among other EU members. The first shot came from Martin Schulz – the leader of the Socialist group in the European Parliament – who demanded that Charlie McCreevy be removed from his post of EU Commissioner.

Schulz was incensed by McCreevy's pre-referendum comments that 'no sane person' would read the treaty and believed – as did many others – that McCreevy's careless comments had contributed to his country's rejection of it. 'This man goes to Ireland and says he has not read the treaty and tells people there is no need to read it,' Schulz fumed during a heated debate at the European Parliament in Strasbourg on 17 June. 'Is that a way of instilling confidence? The best measure . . . for Europe is to take that portfolio away from Mr McCreevy. He has fallen down on the job.'

Later, the German foreign minister Frank Walter Steinmeier suggested that Ireland should consider taking a so-called 'break' from the EU, allowing the other twenty-six member states to proceed with the Lisbon Treaty. His compatriot Elmar Brok, a senior MEP, declared undiplomatically that if Ireland rejected the treaty in a second referendum it should be expelled from the EU.

On 19 June Cowen arrived in Brussels for what one newspaper editorial described as 'Ireland's unwanted day in the sun' – somewhat ironically, considering that it was a dreary, overcast day. Cowen's first appearance at the European Council as Taoiseach began with a brief meeting with José Manuel Barroso to make a quick statement. 'Clearly, I would not have chosen as my first task here to have to advise you that the Irish people have rejected the proposal to amend our constitution to allow us to ratify the Lisbon Treaty,' Cowen told a sympathetic Barroso.

He then faced the daunting prospect of meeting a room full of hostile representatives of other member states. But after the formalities, Cowen delivered his speech confidently. Recalling the situation later, he explained: 'The people had spoken and it was my job to explain the outcome – even though I had obviously campaigned for a different outcome. One of the attitudes you have to have when you do this job is: you play the ball as you find it. Whatever the situation is, you deal with it. You don't expect it to be easy or hard – it's just the way it is. You've got to handle it and deal with it. I'm very straightforward about that and I'm looking forward – I'm not looking back.'

Cowen spoke decisively to the meeting about his own personal commitment to the ethos of the EU, restating the position he had held all his political life. 'It is not some abstract commitment for me. It is because I have seen the powerful force for good our membership of the Union has been.' He went on to emphasize that the Irish people had 'spoken at the ballot box', which he described as the 'ultimate democratic forum'. It was a verdict, Cowen told the room, which his government accepted; but he made clear what that verdict was, and what it was not. 'Let me stress up front that there was no strong suggestion emerging from the campaign that Irish people are any less committed to their European identity and membership of the Union than in the past.

'Against that positive background, it is clear that the debate reflected anxieties about potential future developments and the potential future direction of the Union ... In some instances, these arose in specific sectors. For example, our farming community was and remains deeply concerned by the direction of the world trade talks. Large segments of our trade union sector were anxious about a perceived imbalance between the protection of workers' rights and market forces. Suggestions that the Lisbon Treaty would lead to European taxes, or harmonized taxes being imposed on us, were effective despite robust efforts to get the facts across.'

He also remarked perceptively that people might have come to hold a negative view of Europe as merely a 'place of treaties and protocols, directives and regulations, instead of something that makes a meaningful and beneficial impact on people's lives'.

'It is very early in our period of analysis,' he continued. 'But less explicit and less direct influences may also have been factors. Economic uncertainty, higher food prices, the credit crunch, the increases in fuel prices, on top of more expensive mortgage payments, particularly after such a long period of strong economic performance, may have contributed to frustration among the electorate.'

Cowen said that he believed it was now the collective responsibility of all EU members to work in unison in what he described as 'the spirit of solidarity which has served the Union so well for decades, to find a viable way forward'. He reminded them that the Union had found itself in 'similar situations before' and, on each occasion, had worked 'calmly, constructively and collectively' to find 'an acceptable path'.

After listening intently to Cowen's speech, the other heads of government around the table gave him a round of applause in a gesture of solidarity. In truth, the majority of those present did not envy Cowen the task of facing a packed room of irritated EU colleagues; and, while they were not enthused with the outcome, they did openly respect and admire how he conducted himself in such strenuous circumstances.

Afterwards, the EU leaders publicly gave Cowen their support by stating that Ireland should be given a few months' grace to analyse the electorate's resounding rejection of the treaty and to come up with a solution that would enable the treaty to proceed. However, privately officials from Germany, France, the Netherlands and Denmark attempted to cajole Cowen into a commitment to hold another referendum before the following summer – that is, before the European elections – and to come to the next scheduled Council meeting in October with a resolution on a second vote. There was talk about allowing Ireland to negotiate certain opt-outs – particularly in the areas of tax, abortion and neutrality – in an effort to win over the Irish electorate. Cowen, however, resisted their attempts, explaining that no sensible solution could be arrived at within such a restricted timeframe. 'I stressed that the views and concerns expressed in the campaign were varied and complex. There is no quick fix or easy solution at this stage. I underlined that we must not pre-judge how this dilemma might be resolved,' he later explained.

On his return home, Cowen read a statement to the Dáil about the European Council meeting. He said that he was pleased by how his EU colleagues had reflected on 'the views and concerns I brought to the meeting, including the need to fully respect the Irish No vote in the referendum'. However, he told the House that many members of the Council were 'perplexed' by the Irish rejection of the treaty. 'Some found it hard to understand how Ireland could reject a Treaty which they see as improving the functioning of the Union and redressing perceived difficulties of democratic accountability,' he said.

For Cowen, the Council meeting could be deemed a success, in that he had achieved what he had set out to do – namely, to buy some time, without making any commitments, in order properly to evaluate what was being described as the 'Irish problem'. Speaking today on the issue, Cowen is still uncertain about Ireland's future role within the EU:

'We're left now with a situation where Ireland has to consider how we conduct our affairs within the European context in the future. We are left in a period of uncertainty now. It's not clear what's going to happen. We have to analyse the conclusions and then try and decide what is relevant to our own internal concerns and how colleague member states can assist us in providing greater clarification around certain issues on which people remain to be persuaded. You can't really speculate beyond that, because we are only at the start of that process. We can't underestimate the political capital that has been invested in this process by other member states and we now find that our position may be the means by which they can't complete ratification of the treaty. That has its own political consequences, which are unstated or unknown at the moment.'

With France holding the presidency of the European Council, its president Nicolas Sarkozy decided to make a four-hour visit to Dublin on 21 July. He stressed that his whistle-stop visit to the Irish capital was to 'listen and talk and try to find solutions'. However, before setting foot in Ireland he antagonized the Irish electorate and many politicians by declaring in the European Parliament that 'Europe must not be condemned to inaction' and that the 'Irish problem' must be resolved in time for the next summer's European elections. On 15 July it was then reported in the French press that Sarkozy had brazenly told his own party colleagues in France that 'The Irish will have to vote again.'

The anti-Lisbon Treaty campaigners were quick to pick up on this unhelpful comment. Sinn Féin's Aengus Ó Snodaigh described Sarkozy's comments as 'insulting', while Declan Ganley of Libertas told RTÉ radio that the reported remarks 'typify the anti-democratic nature of what's going on in Brussels'. At the time of this overconfident statement by Sarkozy, Cowen was in New York for a series of meetings with members of the city's business and Irish American communities, and to plead the case of the 50,000 undocumented Irish living illegally in the US. Though there was much later speculation in the media that he was infuriated by the French president's comment, in public he played down the remarks.

'We had to acknowledge that there were many views across Europe about the problems we face after the rejection of the measure,' he told the Irish media contingent in New York.

Prior to Sarkozy's visit to Dublin, his special adviser, Henri Guaino, attempted some damage limitation. Appearing on the French television station France 2, Guaino said that Sarkozy would only 'probably', as one of many 'possible solutions', ask Cowen to conduct a second referendum on the Lisbon Treaty. Guaino also added that France now believed that the text of the treaty should be modified to deal with the Irish concerns.

There is no disputing that the rejection of the treaty was an unmitigated disaster for the newly appointed Taoiseach. Reflecting on the Lisbon Treaty, Cowen speaks about contending 'forces' in Irish society 'trying to pull us in different directions'. He continues: 'The idea that we can go back to some comfort zone where the old certainties will reassert themselves is a comforting notion. But I don't think it's one that's consistent with the times we live in. We are a less homogeneous society than thirty or forty years ago. We are a changing nation in terms of our make-up and that brings its own challenges and tensions, but it also brings great opportunities for us to redefine a country that, in our lifetime, has become one to which people come to work with us. We have come a long way from when half of my generation, or more, had to emigrate to make their way elsewhere.'

For Cowen, Ireland's full participation in the European Union – and in his view that means ratification of the Lisbon Treaty – is vital to ensure the country continues to thrive. However, asking the electorate to vote again on exactly the same treaty would seriously damage his government's credibility. His options are limited, and demanding negotiations with European colleagues no doubt lie ahead. If he is fortunate in any aspect of this difficult situation, it is in that all twenty-seven member states have an investment in finding a solution.

During his first one hundred days in office, Cowen has perforce focused primarily on two key issues: the Lisbon Treaty crisis and the economy. Less than two weeks after the disastrous outcome of the Lisbon Treaty referendum, the European Studies Research Institute warned that Ireland, over-reliant on the construction sector to boost the economy and so affected particularly badly by the global economic downturn, the credit crunch and the ensuing crash in the housing market, was slipping into recession.

Ever the pragmatist, Cowen announced in the Dáil that he was planning a package of measures to curtail government spending. A week later, the exchequer returns for the first six months of the year warned of a shortfall of €3 billion in tax revenue – a total that rose further in August when a further €766 million shortfall was projected for July. These figures meant that if Cowen's government wanted to implement its election manifesto promises, it would have to cut spending or borrow. On 8 July Cowen and his Minister for Finance, Brian Lenihan, held a press conference to announce cutbacks of €1.44 billion over a two-year period – including, significantly, a reduction of 3 per cent in the public payroll.

'Spending is still increased compared with 2007 but, through a number of initiatives, such as not implementing pay increases for Government Ministers and senior public servants, we are curbing any excess so as to keep the public finances secure,' Cowen explained. 'Importantly, reductions on planned expenditure are designed so as not to affect front-line services in health and education. I believe they represent a measured and reasonable response to current challenges and I am confident that the Irish people will see that the Government is pursuing a sensible course of action.'

Despite all such confident public statements, conditions deteriorated even further. Figures showing unemployment rising by 10,000 in July were a further warning sign of Ireland's precarious position. However, it was the collapse of the national pay deal between the social partners which marked the next real low point for Cowen's government. The 'social partnership' had been initiated back in 1987 to ensure moderation in wage increases and reduce the frequency of strikes, and the triennial national agreement based on it is perceived as a significant contributor to the Celtic Tiger economy, bringing regularity and coherence to an environment previously managed through local negotiations, with sometimes chaotic results. The latest national pay talks had begun before Cowen's appointment as Taoiseach, since when the situation had been made more difficult by the economic downturn, which had prompted employers to seek pay restraint, alongside rising food and energy prices, which had prompted the unions to seek corresponding pay rises, arguing that wage increases would encourage consumer spending and thus help the economy to recover.

Cowen kept himself briefed on every aspect of the negotiations and available at all times to anyone seeking to contribute to the discussions. When it became clear that no agreement was within immediate reach, he recognized that attempting to push through a deal would be counterproductive – a judgement with which, interestingly, negotiators on both sides have since concurred. Cowen then let it be known that he was willing to return to the issue with the partners in autumn 2008, as this book goes to press.

Cowen's handling of the negotiations to date illustrates his philosophy of always striving to see the bigger picture. He knew that he would come in for short-term criticism for using hardball tactics – but in doing so he had shown that he would not bow to pressure in sanctioning a public sector pay deal that his government simply could not afford. His decision demonstrates his belief that political decisions should be based on a considered assessment of the greater good of the country, not on individual self-interest or electoral advantage.

Indeed, there is an acute danger that such a political ideology, while admirable, could damage his popularity among the electorate. But Cowen did not enter politics to be popular, and he has already reluctantly accepted that certain sections of the media, specifically some elements of the press, have thrown their hats in the ring against him and will lambast him whenever possible. Cowen appears steadfast in refusing to permit his policy-making to be unduly influenced by the media. He certainly doesn't waste time agonizing over every critical article in every newspaper – as became evident when, on a family holiday in August 2008, he was midway through what he thought was a social conversation before he discovered that one of those in his company was a high-profile reporter from the *Sunday Independent*. An observant reader of the paper would have immediately recognized the reporter from her photo by-line. Cowen, however, says that he barely has time to absorb what he needs from the papers even without paying attention to journalists' portraits.

Cowen sees promoting the expansion of the Irish economy as his immediate priority. In July 2008, he used a business breakfast meeting at the New York Stock Exchange, which had been organized by Enterprise Ireland, as an opportunity to remind his audience that Ireland remains an attractive location for investment. The Irish economy, he said, was well positioned to overcome the 'challenging times out there'. Cowen spoke of his aim to 'strategically position' Ireland in an effort to 'weather this turbulence' so that the country would be in a position 'to take advantage of the inevitable upturn we hope will come to the global economy'.

In the meantime, however, Cowen faces the unenviable task of ensuring that Ireland does not fall into a recession akin to that the country faced in the 1980s. The circumstances are different now, with the global economy faltering as a result of various factors, including significantly higher interest rates and unprecedented rises in energy prices. But Cowen acknowledges that the source of the problem is not the major concern for people currently facing financial difficulties. He declares himself 'fully aware' of these difficulties and is adamant that his government is 'resolutely committed' to dealing effectively with the country's predicament. He understands that the Irish people want to be reassured and to feel confident about the future. 'I believe that people can take confidence from a number of factors. For example, our economy is fundamentally strong, and that will help us withstand this global pressure,' he says. For Cowen, the 'real issue' is to put in place policies that take account of the change in circumstances the country is facing now. 'It is a world that is changing at a rate far greater than we have seen before,' he says. 'We need to position ourselves correctly to capture that market of international investment.' He believes that Ireland cannot simply rely on methods that have brought success in the past, and that his government will have to bring the country to the 'next stage' by making difficult decisions to ensure its long-term economic growth.

He explains: 'We need to recognize that we have to continue to change in order not just to progress, but to maintain the standards of living that we are achieving in this country. We can be proud of that – it's not a time for self-congratulation, but it's a time for recognizing solid achievement – and it should also motivate us to recognize that it's by continually being open to change and adaptation that we can surmount the challenges that face us now; we will miss opportunities if we keep this status quo approach.

'There is no doubt that we are facing into a budgetary strategy that will tighten up things considerably, but I think people understand that and expect the government to make the changes that are necessary so that we can sustain the standard of living that we have achieved so far. There won't be easy choices, but they have to be confronted because the one thing we've learned in the past is that deferral of necessary decisions would only further complicate the situation and make it even more difficult to retrieve the lost ground that inevitably arises out of deferring those decisions. We have to do this sensibly and we have to do it mindful of the need to protect the most vulnerable in society. We have to do it in a way that is as fair as possible, while acknowledging at the same time that there is no painless way of doing it.

'In addressing that issue, we are coming off a far higher base of expenditure and resources than was the case before we had to consider these sorts of approaches in the past. Therefore, we are in a better position than in the past, and what we are trying to do is incrementally provide sustainable improvements, year on year. We need to maintain our confidence in our ability to overcome these problems and confidence in our ability to make the correct strategic choice. It's about acting now in order to advance again when times pick up. People, I think, are prepared to go with that approach because they know from the past that ignoring the realities that face us now will make it even more difficult for them and their families to progress in the future. They are prepared to take some of the hits now for better times. That's the responsible and right thing to do. People expect you to do the right thing by the country in the long term and that sometimes means making difficult choices,' he concludes.

The most important message Cowen wants to convey is that – despite media reports to the contrary – Irish economic activity remains at a record level. 'Substantial investment in education has created a dynamic labour force, which is highly skilled and flexible, and now stands at more than two million – a doubling in two decades,' Cowen outlined in a feature he penned for the *Irish Times*. 'We have invested heavily in the knowledge economy through research and development. Our low tax regime remains attractive for foreign direct investment. But the Government has also put in place welfare supports to assist those most in need and those most at risk in the downturn. We saved while times were good, recording budget surpluses in ten of the past eleven budgets. We have halved the national debt as a percentage of national income. We have made unprecedented investments in key infrastructure.'

The Ireland of 2008 is a very different place from that of the 'dark days' of the 1980s, and Cowen is determined to ensure that the country and its citizens continue to prosper. 'So, while we must not overstate the difficulties, equally we must not understate the necessity for decisive action. By making the right decisions, we can emerge from the current global difficulties and return to a stable growth rate. We must act responsibly to secure the long-term future of our economy and our people and I am determined to do just that,' he explains.

Cowen plans to ensure that 'every effort' is made to

maintain the level of employment. Unemployment is now less than half what it was in 1997, and Cowen is determined that his government will continue to secure 'high-quality jobs'. To this end he intends to introduce measures to reduce the cost of doing business in Ireland, in order to stimulate export-led growth and enhance productivity. In addition, he wants to 'explore initiatives to increase competition to enhance consumer value and dampen rising prices'. He is also determined that his government will proceed with the National Development Plan, which he describes as a vital capital investment that will have 'the greatest impact on stimulating the economy and enhancing quality of life'.

Cowen is determined to be remembered as a Taoiseach who took decisions in the long-term interest of the nation. He is not interested in short-term gains as a means to secure votes. (A good example of this was his decision to bring forward the 2008 budget to October to help tackle the problems facing the economy.) He believes that one of his tasks as leader of the government is to help 'instil and clarify' for the nation the direction Ireland needs to take to ensure the country develops. He hopes his tenure as Taoiseach will be categorized by competence, understanding and the ability to manage any difficult situation. He explains:

'What I want for Ireland is that we develop as a country with an outlook and a psychology that will provide us with sufficient self-confidence in our own ability to manage change, to adapt it to our own set of circumstances, to meet our own needs – needs that are consistent with our values of social inclusion . . .

'I want a stable country. I want a country that's together. I want a country that has an increasingly expansive view of itself. I want us to be self-confident and civic-minded. What we don't want is a society that sees itself merely as a collection of consumers – where our involvement in democratic life, as a country, is something done simply through the act of voting or not voting. We all need to be active citizens – citizens that participate and contribute to their own communities.'

During his homecoming speech as Taoiseach in May 2008, Cowen told the audience in Tullamore: 'I ask you to stick with me. I ask you to believe in me.' Among his wider audience, in particular certain sections of the media, not everyone has opted to do so, and he has already attracted a substantial amount of criticism. But it must be emphasized that within his first one hundred days in office Cowen has endured an unusual level of ill fortune – most notably, of course, the downward turn in the global economy and the country's failure to ratify the Lisbon Treaty. We should also remember that many of his predecessors in the highest office experienced difficulties in their early weeks, and yet survived. The truth is that it is too soon to judge Cowen's performance as Taoiseach. For his first three months, Cowen has been attempting to steer the economy out of the metaphorical storm and into calmer climes. It might well be a year before all the immediate problems he now confronts have been sufficiently tackled. Perhaps it is only then that we will be in a position to begin to assess his leadership.

Sources

The author acknowledges with thanks the following sources of information and quotations used in the text.

Interviews
Author's interviews with Brian Cowen, May 2007, June 2007, May 2008, June 2008, August 2008
Author's interview with John Gormley, June 2007
Author's interview with Albert Reynolds, 3 July 2008

Books
Stephen Collins, *The Power Game* (O'Brien Press, 2001), pp. 237–8, 248, 313, 319
John Downing, *Bertie Ahern* (Paperview/*Irish Independent*, 2007), p. 197
Sean Duignan, *One Spin on the Merry Go Round* (Blackwater, 1995), pp. 66, 78, 80, 83, 88, 90, 95, 112, 130
Dean Godson, *Himself Alone: David Trimble and the Ordeal of Unionism* (HarperCollins, 2004), pp. 557–8
Katie Hannon, *The Naked Politician* (Gill & Macmillan, 2004), p. 81
Gene Kerrigan and Pat Brennan, *This Great Little Nation: A–Z of Irish Controversies* (Gill & Macmillan, 1999)

Ray Mac Manais, *The Road from Ardoyne* (Brandon, 2004), pp. 316, 336

Declan McSweeney, *A Scribe in Cowen's Country* (privately published, 2008)

Ed Moloney, *Paisley* (Poolbeg, 2008), p. 406

Ted Nealon, *Tales from the Dail Bar* (Gill & Macmillan, 2008), p. 71

Jonathan Powell, *Great Hatred, Little Room* (Bodley Head, 2008), p. 188.

Other Published Sources

Prologue

Jody Corcoran, 'Pride in heart of Cowen country', *Sunday Independent*, Sunday, 11 May 2008

Lise Hand, 'Tears, laughter and song welcome a native son', *Irish Independent*, Monday, 12 May 2008

Gearoid Keegan, 'Inspiring speech marks Taoiseach's return to Tullamore', *Tullamore Tribune*, Wednesday, 14 May 2008

Chapters 1–5

Pádraig Boland, 'The Cowen we love so well', *Leinster Express & Offaly Express*, Saturday, 10 May 2008

Sean Boyne, *Sunday World*, 'Small interview with Ger Connolly', 13 April 2008

Conor Brady, 'An Irishman's Diary', *Irish Times*, Monday, 26 May 2008

Nicola Byrne, 'Keeping it in the family', *Irish Mail on Sunday*, May 2008

Gearoid Keegan, 'Inspiring speech marks Taoiseach's return to Tullamore', *Tullamore Tribune*, Wednesday, 14 May 2008

Ruadhán Mac Cormaic, 'Clara's pride in pedigree of local hero steeped in community', *Irish Times*, Thursday, 10 April 2008

Grace O'Dea, 'Fianna Fail, Clara and his family', *Leinster Express & Offaly Express*, Saturday, 10 May 2008

Gemma O'Doherty, 'Spot the next Taoiseach', *Irish Independent*, Saturday, 3 May 2008

Jason O'Toole, 'The man who would be king', interview with Brian Cowen, *Hot Press*, May 2007

Maol Muire Tynan, 'Realpolitik is telling workers what their TD does to improve their pay packets', *Irish Times*, Tuesday, 8 April 1997

'Locals delighted for Clara son made good', *Offaly Independent*, Saturday, 10 May 2008

Chapter 6

Fergal Bowers, 'Nurses win substantial deal, but casualty fallout outweighs gains', *Irish Times*, Thursday, 28 October 1999

John Bruton TD, leader of Fine Gael, address to the Fine Gael Ard Fheis in the RDS

Chris Dooley, 'Minister apologises for remark on dispute', *Irish Times*, Saturday, 16 October 1999 (Cowen apologizes for remark)

Nuala Haughey, 'Minister announces increase in annual funding for family carers', *Irish Times*, Wednesday, 20 October 1999

Dick Hogan, 'Church, State represented as Cork bids emotional farewell to former Taoiseach', *Irish Times*, Monday, 25 October 1999

Kathryn Holmquist, 'All is rosy in Cowen's garden', *Irish Times*, Monday, 22 February 1999

Renagh Holohan, 'Gloves off, fangs out', *Irish Times*, Saturday, 20 February 1999

Joe Humphreys, 'Positions harden ahead of crucial talks on NI logjam', *Irish Times*, Saturday, 26 June 1999

Roisin Ingle, ' "Nurse power" hits the city with a vengeance', *Irish Times*, Friday, 22 October 1999

Frank McNally, 'PD watchdog fails to bark despite pressing invitations', *Irish Times*, Thursday, 28 January 1999 (T Rex comment)

Frank McNally, *Irish Times*, Monday, 15 February 1999

Michael O'Regan and Marie O'Halloran, *Irish Times*, Monday, 3 May 1999 (on calls to resign)

Kevin Rafter, 'All-party consensus on abortion unlikely to be reached', *Irish Times*, Saturday, 11 September 1999

Medb Ruane, 'Irate public identifies with action by nurses', *Irish Times*, Monday, 25 October 1999

Dick Walsh, *Irish Times*, Saturday, 11 September 1999 (on abortion)

'Abortion findings: too hot to handle?' *Irish Times*, Saturday, 7 February 1998

'Cowen spurns the quick solution', *Irish Times*, Wednesday, 25 November 1998

'The tortuous route leads back to a rerun of talks on nurses' pay', *Irish Times*, Friday, 22 October 1999

'Doing their best to bring the jobs home', *Irish Times*, Saturday, 14 October 2000

Chapter 7

Harry Browne, 'Highlights of the it-will-have-to-do week', *Irish Times*, Saturday, 29 December 2001

Vincent Browne, 'Brings combativeness to bear on his brief', *Irish Times*, Saturday, 19 May 2001

Joe Carroll, 'Mandelson warns he will not wait indefinitely for movement', *Irish Times*, Friday, 17 March 2000

Brian Cowen, 'It is right for Ireland to help a friend in need', *Irish Times*, Wednesday, 26 September 2001

Paul Cullen, 'National platform demands resignation of minister', *Irish Times*, Tuesday, 12 June 2001

Darina Daly, 'Cowen in Brussels for EU emergency meeting', *Irish Times* website, Wednesday, 12 September 2001

Deaglán de Bréadún, 'Brian brings all Europe to Tullamore', *Irish Times*, Saturday, 17 April 2004

Deaglán de Bréadún, 'Interview with Brian Cowen', *Irish Times*, Thursday, 23 September 2004

Niall Donald and Deirdre O'Donovan, 'No deal done but bookies rarely wrong', *Irish Sunday Mirror*, 27 May 2007

Mark Hennessy, 'Taoiseach names Cowen as FF deputy leader', *Irish Times*, Saturday, 27 July 2002

Renagh Holohan, 'Bruising BIFFO', *Irish Times*, Saturday, 8 July 2000

Renagh Holohan, 'Pragmatism in Cowen's purity', *Irish Times*, Saturday, 21 October 2000

Renagh Holohan, 'Running for mayor', *Irish Times*, Saturday, 12 May 2001

David Horovitz, 'Israel protests bitterly over Cowen's statement', *Irish Times*, Friday, 21 May 2004

Lara Marlowe, Liam Reid and Jamie Smyth on Cowen speaking in Luxembourg, *Irish Times*, Thursday, 8 June 2006

Greg Meylan and Pádraig Collins, 'Cowen rejects Amnesty claim on Chechnya', *Irish Times* website, 30 April 2001

Gerry Moriarty and Rachel Donnelly, 'Reid appointed to Stormont after Mandelson's sudden resignation', *Irish Times*, Thursday, 25 January 2001

Clodagh Mulvey, 'Minister for Foreign Affairs signs Treaty of Nice', *Irish Times* website ('Breaking news'), Monday, 26 February 2001

Jason O'Toole, 'The man who would be king', interview with Brian Cowen, *Hot Press*, May 2007

Derek Scally, 'Reject anti-Semitism but reserve right to criticise Israel's politics – Cowen', *Irish Times*, Thursday, 29 April 2004

Patrick Smyth, '875,000 Irish jobs depend on EU ties – Cowen', *Irish Times*, Monday, 7 October 2002

Denis Staunton, 'State must seek Irish solution to problems from Nice rejection', *Irish Times*, Tuesday, 12 June 2001

Denis Staunton, 'Cowen promises to run EU with a smile', *Irish Times*, Friday, 19 December 2003

Dick Walsh, 'Security Council role the challenge of lifetime', *Irish Times*, Saturday, 14 October 2000

'Mandelson's trip to the park', *Irish Times*, Saturday, 5 February 2000

'Is the world ready for Brian Cowen?', *Irish Times*, Saturday, 16 September 2000

'China off for Cowen', *Irish Times*, Saturday, 19 May 2001

'Cowen visits Middle East', *Irish Times*, Tuesday, 11 September 2001

'Cowen at the Helm', *Irish Times*, Saturday, 22 September 2001

Chapter 8

Arthur Beesley, 'O'Donoghue backs artists' tax exemption', *Irish Times*, Wednesday, 22 June 2005

Arthur Beesley, 'Please stand up for us', *Irish Times*, Wednesday, 22 June 2005

Dermot Bolger, Open letter to Minister for Finance, *Irish Times*, Friday, 30 September 2005

Ali Bracken, 'Mature reflection: Cowen launches FitzGerald's latest book', *Irish Times*, Friday, 11 November 2005

Mark Brennock, 'Big change, little difference, say voters', *Irish Times*, Saturday, 9 October 2004

Mark Brennock, 'Cowen delivers on a day when Government needed some cheer', *Irish Times*, Thursday, 12 December 2005

Eoin Burke-Kennedy, 'Cowen rejects opposition claims on budget', *Irish Times*, Thursday, 7 December 2006

Eoin Burke-Kennedy, 'Government leaves stamp duty rates unchanged', *Irish Times*, Thursday, 7 December 2006

Marc Coleman, 'Cowen in the money with surplus revenue', *Irish Times*, Saturday, 3 December 2005

Stephen Collins, 'FF accused of "desperation" after spending plan unveiled', *Irish Times*, Monday, 26 March 2007

Stephen Collins, 'Ahern throws away the best card in FF's hand', *Irish Times*, Saturday, 31 March 2007

Brian Cowen, text of Minister for Finance Brian Cowen's budget speech, part 1, *Irish Times* website, Wednesday, 7 December 2005

Miriam Donohoe, 'Taoiseach rules out spending spree prior to election', *Irish Times*, Monday, 20 November 2006

'Drapier' column, *Irish Times*, Saturday, 4 June 2005

Shane Hegarty, 'Will artists stay for the breaks?' *Irish Times*, Saturday, 10 December 2005

Mark Hennessy, 'Cowen abandons Fianna Fáil tent at Galway races', *Irish Times*, Friday, 23 May 2008

Joe Humphreys and Frank Millar, 'Move to renege on aid promise defended', *Irish Times*, Saturday, 12 March 2005

George Jackson, 'Cowen backs Durkan during Derry visit', *Irish Times*, Tuesday, 26 April 2005

Miriam Lord, 'Nimble Biffo puts home side into knock-out stages', *Irish Times*, Thursday, 7 December 2006

Frank McNally, 'Homes scandal puts bite into a united opposition', *Irish Times* (Dáil sketch), Thursday, 2 June 2005

Michael O'Regan, 'Cowen threatens to sue if "jibes" repeated outside Dail', *Irish Times*, Thursday, 2 June 2005

Jason O'Toole, 'The man who would be king', interview with Brian Cowen, *Hot Press*, May 2007

Jason O'Toole, 'Cowen vows he won't cut back on budget deficit', *Irish Mail on Sunday*, 6 July 2008

Liam Reid, 'Aid target is "demanding", Cowen admits', *Irish Times*, Tuesday, 27 September 2005

Kathy Sheridan, 'Zest for life', *Irish Times*, Saturday, 4 February 2006

Olaf Tyaransen, 'The fifth element', *Hot Press*, September 2006

Jimmy Walsh, 'Cox calls for vote on Finance Bill', *Irish Times*, Thursday, 29 March 2007

'Dáil row breaks out over Cowen's speech length, *Irish Times*, Thursday, 8 December 2005

Chapter 9

Stephen Collins, 'Ahern names Cowen as favoured successor', *Irish Times*, Saturday, 16 June 2007

John Downes, 'Church condemns VAT change on packet of condoms', *Irish Times*, Friday, 1 February 2008

John Downes and Mark Hennessy, 'Ahern intends to be Taoiseach until 2012', *Irish Times*, Saturday, 16 June 2007

Mark Hennessy, 'Ahern's anointing of Cowen as his successor may not be a selfless act', *Irish Times*, Friday, 22 June 2007

Mark Hennessy, 'Ahern decision to favour Cowen criticized', *Irish Times*, Wednesday, 19 September 2007

Michael O'Regan, 'Cowen refuses to be drawn on tribunal', *Irish Times*, Friday, 30 November 2007

Jason O'Toole, 'The man who would be king', interview with Brian Cowen, *Hot Press*, May 2007

Jason O'Toole, 'The bearing of the Greens', interview with Trevor Sargent, *Hot Press*, May 2007

Jason O'Toole, 'It's not easy being Green', interview with John Gormley, *Hot Press*, July 2007

Jason O'Toole, 'Cowen vows he won't cut back on budget deficit', *Irish Mail on Sunday*, 6 July 2008

Liam Reid, 'Cowen says leadership has "the bottle for the battle"', *Irish Times*, Wednesday, 6 September 2006

Chapter 10

Stephen Collins, 'Cowen gives cabinet fresh look with more changes than expected', *Irish Times*, Thursday, 8 May 2008

Deaglán de Bréadún, 'Kenny questions if Cowen is up to task', *Irish Times*, Monday, 14 April 2008

Deaglán de Bréadún, 'Cowen talks of "greatness" in graveside oration', *Irish Times*, Thursday, 17 April 2008

Deaglán de Bréadún, 'I'm a very simple person, says Taoiseach', *Irish Times*, Monday, 5 May 2008

Deaglán de Bréadún, 'Kenny calls on Cowen to sack Harney in first move as Taoiseach', *Irish Times*, Tuesday, 6 May 2008

Alison Healy, 'Harney defends cabinet reshuffle', *Irish Times*, Friday, 9 May 2008

Mark Hennessy, 'Prospective candidates eye Kitt seat', *Irish Times*, Friday, 9 May 2008

Eoghan MacConnell, 'Brother hails Brian's elevation as akin to All-Ireland triumph', *Offaly Independent*, Saturday, 10 May 2008

Eoghan MacConnell, 'Offaly senator hails a great day for county', *Offaly Independent*, Saturday, 10 May 2008

Eoghan MacConnell, 'The faithful departed . . .', *Offaly Independent*, Saturday, 10 May 2008

Sarah Mcinerney and Shane Coleman, 'My agenda as Taoiseach', *Sunday Tribune*, 6 April 2008

Marie O'Halloran, 'Young people urged to vote Yes in Lisbon poll', *Irish Times*, Wednesday, 23 April 2008

Jason O'Toole, interview with Ciaran Cannon, *Hot Press*, May 2008

Interview with Cowen, *Tullamore Tribune*, Wednesday, 9 April 2008

Chapter 11

Eoin Burke-Kennedy, 'Taoiseach emphasises Irish competitiveness', *Irish Times*, Thursday, 17 July 2008

Addy Clancy, 'Man fined after Cowen's oath fails as precedent', *Irish Times*, Saturday, 7 June 2008

Stephen Collins, 'No appetite for reopening Lisbon text – Cowen', *Irish Times*, Saturday, 21 June 2008

Deaglán de Bréadán, 'Lenihan rejects FG claim Cowen is "control freak"', *Irish Times*, Monday, 26 May 2008

Deaglán de Bréadán, 'Taoiseach says FG and Labour must intensify Yes campaigns', *Irish Times*, Monday, 26 May 2008

Deaglán de Bréadán, 'Cowen to visit New York for series of business meetings', *Irish Times*, Tuesday, 15 July 2008

Mary Fitzgerald, 'Ganley describes rejection of treaty as "brilliant" decision', *Irish Times*, Monday, 16 June 2008

Mary Fitzgerald, 'Call for McCreevy removal in heated Brussels debate', *Irish Times*, Friday, 20 June 2008

Mark Hennessy, 'Cowen accuses Lisbon opponents of confusing voters', *Irish Times*, Tuesday, 13 May 2008

Mark Hennessy, 'Opposition parties slow to get fully behind Yes campaign', *Irish Times*, Tuesday, 27 May 2008

Mark Hennessy, 'Cowen's comments hinder FG's Yes effort', *Irish Times*, Wednesday, 28 May 2008

Mark Hennessy, ' "Softly-spoken, polite, even shy betimes", Cowen goes forth to drum up support', *Irish Times*, Saturday, 7 June 2008

Mark Hennessy, Harry McGee and Deaglán de Bréadún, 'FF and main opposition parties unite to push for Yes vote', *Irish Times*, Friday, 30 May 2008

Patrick Logue, Jason Michael, Éanna Ó Caollaí and Elaine Edwards, 'Result has created a "difficult situation", Cowen says', *Irish Times*, Saturday, 14 June 2008

Harry McGee, 'Cowen says he was not sniping at Labour, FG', *Irish Times*, Tuesday, 27 May 2008

Harry McGee, 'EU protects small states, says Cowen', *Irish Times*, Tuesday, 27 May 2008

Ronan McGreevy, 'Applause for Cowen as he brings the sunshine to Cavan', *Irish Times*, Saturday, 31 May 2008

Jonathan Saul and Andras Gergely, 'Now Taoiseach says sorry for four-letter outburst in the Dáil', *The Scotsman*, Friday, 23 May 2008

'EU states "should continue to ratify Lisbon" – Barroso', *Irish Times* website, Friday, 13 June 2008

'Treaty rejection a "source of disappointment", says Cowen', *Irish Times*, Saturday, 14 June 2008

Picture Acknowledgements

Election victory: Richard May, Tullamore

Group photo of the Irish cabinet, 2000: © Reuters/Corbis; Good Friday Agreement: Martin McCullough/Rex Features; BC and Jack Straw: Chris Young/PA Photos; BC and Colin Powell: © Reuters/Corbis; BC and David Trimble: Paul Faith/PA Photos

BC and Pope Paul II: AP Photo/Arturo Mari; BC and George W. Bush: Martin Cleaver/Associated Press; BC and Yasser Arafat: AFP/Getty Images; BC and Kofi Annan: AFP/Getty Images; BC, Chris Patten and Li Zhaoxing: © Paul McErlane/Reuters/ Corbis; BC and Hamid Karzai: © Reuters/Bob Strong

BC with Mary Cowen and daughters Maedhbh and Sinead: Julien Behal/PA Photos; BC and family on his victory parade: Jeff Harvey Photography; BC watching the Grand National: Richard May, Tullamore; BC, Martin McGuinness and Ian Paisley: AFP/Getty Images; BC, Bertie Ahern and Seamus Kirk: Niall Carson/PA Photos

PICTURE ACKNOWLEDGEMENTS

BC: Michael Chester; BC and Garrett Fitzgerald: Richard May, Tullamore; BC with Micheal Martin, Mary Harney and John Gormley: Niall Carson/PA Photos; BC and Gordon Brown: AFP/Getty Images; BC and Nicolas Sarkozy: Barbara Lindberg/Rex Features.

Index

BC = Brian Cowen; FF = Fianna Fáil.

abortion issue, 82–3, 84–6
Adams, Gerry, 104–5, 117, 221
Aer Lingus, 61, 62–3, 64, 66, 68
Aer Rianta, 61, 63
Afghanistan, 134
African Development Bank, 151
agriculture, 78
Ahern, Bertie: aid policy, 149, 150; BC's
    budgets, 160, 161–2, 171; BC's career,
    79, 100–1, 138, 188–90; election
    (2007), 177–83; European issues,
    83–4, 117, 119–20; FF leadership,
    77–8; financial affairs, 173–7, 181,
    192–4, 196–7, 219; financial policy
    announcement, 163–4; Fine Gael
    assault on, 89–90; Labour
    negotiations, 59; Middle East issues,
    124; Minister for Finance, 46, 51;
    Minister for Labour, 51; Northern
    Ireland issues, 104, 106, 110–11;
    Reynolds relationship, 95–6;
    resignation, 200–2, 210, 218–19;
    resignation question, 194–7, 198–200;
    Taoiseach, 79, 158, 188–90; view of
    Cahill, 63; view of Hogan, 74; wage
    issues, 91

Ahern, Dermot, 167, 189, 203, 215
aid, overseas, 149, 150–2
All-Party Oireachtas Committee on the
    Constitution, 85
Amnesty International, 114–15
Andrews, David: career, 46, 100;
    education, 14, 17; relationship with
    BC, 38; Reynolds support, 95; UN
    policy, 113
Annan, Kofi, 117, 130
Arafat, Yasser, 123, 124–6
Arcon Resources, 72–3
Ard Scoil Naomh Chiaráin, 12
Arts Council, 146
aviation, 62–5

bank strike, 52–3
Barroso, José Manuel, 229–30, 231
Bell, Paul, 110
Binchy, William, 85
Bird, Charlie, 215
Blair, Tony, 110, 150
Boland, Patrick, 11
Bonner, Kevin, 50–1
Bono, 149
Bowers, Fergal, 94
Boyle, Dan, 156, 158, 159
Brady, Conor, 15, 20, 137

Brennan, Pat, 74
Brennan, Séamus, 46, 164, 167, 186, 215
Brian P. Adams & Co., 31
British–Irish Inter-Parliamentary Body, 39
Broderick, Larry, 52–3
Brok, Elmar, 231
Brown, Gordon, 229
Browne, Harry, 134
Browne, Vincent, 101, 118
Bruton, John, 79, 86, 89, 90, 183
Bruton, Richard, 167–8
Burke, Ray, 46, 90, 100
Burton, Joan, 156–7, 158
Byrne, David, 84

Cable & Wireless, 66
Cahill, Bernie, 63
Cahill Plan, 63, 65
Campbell, Gregory, 111
Cannon, Ciaran, 207
Carers' Association, 92
Carey, Pat, 216
Carey, Tadgh, 215
Carruth, Gráinne, 193–4, 197
Cassells, Peter, 91
Cassidy, Donie, 138
Catholic Church, 136, 152, 154, 166
Chechnya, 114–15
CIE Group, 61
Cistercian College of Mount St Joseph, Roscrea, 12, 14–21, 100
Clara: BC's early life, 12–13, 14, 22; BC's family background, 7–8; BC's homecoming as Minister for Labour, 47–8; BC's homecoming as Taoiseach, 4, 7; Hillery's visit, 206; history, 11–12; response to Bruton's gibe, 90; sport, 13, 40
Clara National School, 12
Clarke, James Pius, 43
Clinton, Bill, 69, 102, 181
Collins, Gerard, 46

Collins, Stephen, 59, 228
Collins–Hughes, Eddie, 92
co–location project, 167–8
Connolly, Frank, 174
Connolly, Gerald (Ger), 9, 10–11, 45
Conroy Petroleum, 72
Corcoran, Jody, 3
Cosgrave, Liam, 41
Coughlan, Anthony, 119
Coughlan, Mary, 203, 215, 217, 224
Council of Europe, 114–15, 130
Cowen, Andrew (Father Andrew, uncle): career, 12, 14–15, 134; death, 20, 199, 204; education, 15; sports, 13
Cowen, Barry (brother), 4, 11, 12, 29, 109
Cowen, Bernard (Ber, father): character, 8; death, 1, 28–9, 32, 49; marriage, 7; political career, 5, 9–10, 21, 25–6, 29–30, 32, 50, 214; singing, 12; song about, 4–5; sons, 7–8, 14, 29; Clara swimming pool, 5, 13; work, 8–9
Cowen, Brian: awards, 208–9; character, 8, 18, 23, 205, 210; finances, 72–3; interviews, 86–7; language, 223–6; marijuana smoking, 180–2; mimicry, 18, 23; music, 12–13; public speaking, 18–19, 21–2, 75, 205; religion, 135–6, 152, 154; road accident, 115; singing, 2–3, 4–5, 48, 110; smoking, 80–1, 180–2; sport, 13, 16–17, 21, 25, 40
EARLY LIFE: birth, 8; childhood, 9–10, 12–13; schooling, 12, 14–21; university, 19–20; work in family pub, 21–3; legal career, 30–1, 33, 77–8; father's death, 1, 4, 18, 29, 33, 49, 102; marriage, 33–4
POLITICAL CAREER: Ógra Fianna Fáil involvement, 25; local politics, 25–6; political ambitions, 29–30; Offaly County Council, 32, 36–8; elected to Dáil, 1, 31–2; constituency work, 35–6; backbencher, 39–40, 41; Minister

for Labour, 46–7, 50–6; Minister for Transport, Energy and Communications, 60–1, 72; spokesperson for agriculture, 77, 78; spokesperson for health, 77; Minister for Health and Children, 79–81, 96–9; Minister for Foreign Affairs, 86, 100–2, 134, 220; deputy leadership of FF, 138; Minister for Finance, 145, 154, 166, 171–2, 180, 196, 209; budgets, 145, 158–9, 160–2, 165, 169–72; Tánaiste (deputy prime minister), 188–90; Taoiseach nomination, 203–11, 215; elected Taoiseach, 1–3, 211–15; cabinet, 215–16; priorities as Taoiseach, 236–44

Cowen, Christopher (Christy, brother), 14, 21, 29, 209
Cowen, Christopher (Christy, grandfather), 8, 214
Cowen, Maedhbh (daughter), 214, 217
Cowen, Mary (Molloy, wife), 33–4, 101–2, 135, 210, 214
Cowen, May (Weir, mother), 7, 12, 14, 110, 134, 210
Cowen, Michael (uncle), 199, 204
Cowen, Rosanna (Dowling, grandmother), 8
Cowen, Sinead (daughter), 214
Cox, Margaret, 162–3
Crisis Pregnancy Agency, 166
Culliton, Jim, 62
Culliton Report, 62
Curiel, Ran, 141

Daily Mirror, 181
Daily Telegraph, 139
Daly, Dom Kevin, 17–18, 19
de Bréadún, Deaglán, 142
de Valera, Eamon, 71, 173, 189
de Valera, Síle, 71
Democratic Left, 74
Dempsey, Noel: career, 4, 46, 95–6, 189,
203; Green negotiations, 185; Labour negotiations, 59
Department of Agriculture, 78
Department of Education, 149
Department of Finance, 145, 168, 209, 215
Department of Foreign Affairs, 86, 107, 133–4
Department of Health and Children, 79–81, 86–7, 94, 99, 100, 150
Department of Justice, 149
Department of Labour, 50–6
Department of Transport, Energy and Communications, 60–1, 69
Diana, Princess, 80
Dignam, Andrew, 8–9
Dobson, Bryan, 175
Dodds, Nigel, 111
Doherty, Sean, 44–5
Dooley, Eddie Joe, 38
Dorrian, Paudge, 225
Downing Street Declaration, 75
Drapier, 158
Drury Communications, 86
Duffy, Jim, 42
Duignan, Michael, 22
Duignan, Sean, 58, 65, 76
DUP, 108, 110, 111
Durkan, Mark, 155–6

East Timor, 127
Egan, Kieran, 10
Egan, Nicholas, 10
elections: 1969, 9; 1973, 10; 1977, 10; 1984 (by-election), 31–2, 46; 1992, 58–9; 1997, 79; 2002, 133, 136–7; 2007, 137, 173–4, 177, 182–3, 189, 192
employment, 47, 54–6, 61, 120, 238
Enterprise Ireland, 239
ESB (Electricity Supply Board), 61–2, 71
European Commission, 65
European Council, 230–5

European Parliament, 230
European Studies Research Institute, 237
European Union (EU): directives, 61–2; employment, 54–6; foreign ministers' meeting over 9/11, 127; French presidency, 235–6; Gothenburg summit, 119–20; Irish involvement, 113; Irish presidency, 138–40, 142–4; Israel relations, 141–2; Lisbon Treaty, 144, 218–23, 229–32, 235–7; Luxembourg summit, 118; Nice Treaty, 116–20

Fahey, Frank, 101
Fallon, Sean, 47
Farrell, Kevin, 47
Farrell, Pat, 96
FÁS, 51, 54, 56
Feeney, Geraldine, 210
Feery, Frank, 48
Fianna Fáil: Ard Fheis (1991), 43; Ard Fheis (1999), 87; Ard Fheis (2007), 163–4; 'Country and Western wing', 48; Cowen family links, 8, 9, 31–2; election (1997), 79; election (2007), 173–4, 177, 182–3; foundation, 8, 71; fundraising, 157; Green Party relationship, 133, 183–8; Hogan leaks, 74; Labour Party relationship, 59–60, 75–7; Laois–Offaly constituency, 9, 10, 11, 137; leadership, 37, 45, 98, 122, 138, 201–5, 218; Lisbon Treaty referendum, 222; party structure, 39; PD relationship, 42–3, 45, 57–8, 59; SDLP relationship, 156
Fine Gael: abortion issue, 85–6; aid policy, 151; Ard Fheis (1999), 89–90; budget leaks, 74; Cowen relationship, 48, 89–90, 122, 207, 223–5; election (1997), 79; election campaign (2007), 178, 179, 180; Labour Party relationship, 10, 77, 173; leadership, 151, 177; Lisbon Treaty referendum,

223, 227; objection to McDaid, 43
Finnegan, Marian, 161
Fitzgerald, Garrett, 42, 120–2
Fitzgerald, Gene, 38
Flynn, Beverly, 193
Flynn, Padraig, 90
Flynn, Philip, 67–8

GAA, 13, 25, 51, 93
Gallagher, Dermot, 68
Galway, 162–3
Galway Races, 157
Ganley, Declan, 220–1, 235
Geldof, Sir Bob, 150
Geoghegan-Quinn, Máire, 77, 83–4
Geraghty, Des, 212
Gilmartin, Tom, 90, 201
Gilmore, Eamon: Labour Party leadership, 193, 196, 208, 216; Lisbon Treaty referendum, 227–8; marijuana smoking, 182; Taoiseach nomination, 211
Giuliani, Rudolph, 131
Godson, Dean, 108
Good Friday Agreement, 106, 112, 155, 200
Goodbody family, 11
Goodman, Larry, 57
Gorman, Paddy, 38
Gormley, John: nomination of BC, 210; career, 133; FF negotiations, 184–8; Green Party leadership, 184, 195, 208; marijuana smoking, 182; UN criticisms, 133
Graham, Justin, 38
Green Party, 133, 156, 159, 184–8, 193
Guaino, Henri, 236
Guardian, 106

Hanafin, Mary, 19, 101, 167, 202, 215–16
Hannon, Katie, 138
Harney, Mary, 195, 207–8
Harris, Eoghan, 182

INDEX

Hatuel, Tali, 142
Haughey, Charles: cabinet, 44, 46; FF
    leadership, 37, 41–5; resignation, 41,
    45; scandals, 44–5, 57, 90, 174;
    taxation policy, 146, 148; Tullamore
    convention, 32; view of Ahern, 190
health service, 87–9, 96–9, 150, 167
Healy-Rae, Jackie, 193
Heffernan, Kevin, 51–2
Hennessy, Mark, 138, 158
Hennessy, Patrick, 141
Hennessy, Seamus, 16, 17
Higgins, Joe, 221
Hillery, Patrick, 42, 206–7
Hogan, Phil, 73–4
Hot Press, 81, 149, 179, 180, 208
Howlin, Brendan, 59
Hume, John, 155
Hunt, Colin, 167
Hurley, John, 198
Hyland, Liam, 11

industrial relations, 52–3, 64–8, 91–4
International Monetary Fund, 151
IRA, 75, 107, 112, 174
Irish Bank Officials Association (IBOA),
    52–3
Irish Congress of Trade Unions, 91
Irish Creamery Milk Suppliers
    Association, 228
Irish Examiner, 225
Irish Farmers Association, 228
Irish Independent, 4, 225
Irish–Portuguese Friendship Society,
    114
Irish Times, 15, 77, 82, 87, 90, 101, 107,
    113, 118, 121, 124, 129, 133, 138, 142,
    158, 174, 175, 204, 207, 218, 225, 227,
    228, 242
Israel, 123, 126–7, 139–42

John Paul II, Pope, 134–5
Juncker, Jean-Claude, 229

Kane, Alfie, 71
Katsav, Moshe, 140
Kelly, Fiona, 53
Kelly, Mary, 129
Kenny, Enda: aid issue, 151; attacks on
    FF, 216; election campaign (2007),
    177, 179, 183; Lisbon Treaty
    referendum, 226–8; no-confidence
    motion, 193; relationship with BC,
    196, 207, 223–5, 226–8; Taoiseach
    nomination, 211
Kenny, Pat, 92
Kerrigan, Gene, 74
Kiely, Rory, 163
Kitt, Tom, 203, 216
Korei, Ahmed, 140

Labour Party: Aer Lingus problems, 65;
    aid policy, 151; budget leaks, 74;
    budget speeches, 159; conference
    (1999), 83; election manifesto (2007),
    178, 179; FF relationship, 59–60,
    75–7; Fine Gael relationship, 10, 77,
    173; leadership, 60, 86, 151; Lisbon
    Treaty referendum, 223; taxation
    issues, 157; Telecom Éireann issue, 66
Labour Relations Commission, 64
Lalor, Paddy, 11
Laois–Offaly constituency: BC's
    commitment to, 102; BC's early work
    in, 25; election (2002), 137; FF
    organization, 10–11, 35–6, 137;
    support for BC, 2, 205, 209
Larkin, Celia, 193
Leinster Express, 137
Leinster Leader, 137
Lemass, Seán, 189
Lenihan, Brian, Junior, 203, 215, 219,
    226, 237
Lenihan, Brian, Senior, 32, 42, 43, 160
Lenihan, Conor, 160
Leonard, Jimmy, 38
Libertas, 220–1, 229, 235
Lindh, Anna, 118

261

Lisbon Treaty: document, 144, 219–21; EU response to Irish referendum, 230–7; protests against, 210; referendum, 201, 219, 229–30, 244; referendum 'no' campaign, 220–2, 228–9; referendum 'yes' campaign, 116, 198, 212–13, 222–3, 226–9
Live Mike, The, 48
Lodge, Gerry, 32
Long, Martin, 166
Loscher, Damian, 218
Loughnane, Seamus, 32, 38
Lowry, Michael, 71, 193
Lynch, Charlie (Father), 93
Lynch, Jack, 93
Lynch, Máirín, 93

McAleese, Mary, 95–6, 104, 214–15
MacConnell, Eoghan, 209–10
McCormack, Jason, 225–6
McCreevy, Charlie: career, 46, 91, 138, 145, 230–1; European issues, 120, 230–1; Minister of Finance, 91, 97; relationship with BC, 38–9, 97; Reynolds support, 95
McDaid, Jim, 43, 93
McDowell, Michael, 84, 111, 149
McGahern, John, 146–7
McGee, Harry, 204
McGrath, Finian, 193
McGuinness, Ken, 111
McGuinness, Martin, 111–12
McGuinness, Paul, 148–9
McKenna, Patricia, 129
Mac Manais, Ray, 95, 96
McManus, Liz, 82, 93
McNally, Frank, 90
McNeill, Hugo, 16–17
McSweeney, Declan, 47, 103, 121, 143
Maginniss, Alban, 109
Mahon, Alan, 192
Mahon Tribunal: Ahern's appearances, 173, 175–6, 190, 192–3, 196, 199, 219; FF contributions issue, 158, 176, 177;

role, 173–4
Major, John, 75, 103
Mandelson, Peter, 101, 104–6
Manning, Maurice, 130
Martin, Micheál: Minister for Education, 87; Minister for Foreign Affairs, 215, 228; Minister for Health, 86, 101, 150; Nice Treaty referendum, 121; Taoiseach question, 189, 203
Marty, Dick, 130
Meagher, Peadar, 10
Merkel, Angela, 229
Middle East, 28, 122–7, 139–42
Midland Butter and Bacon, 47
mining licences, 72–3
Mitchell, George, 122–3
Monnet, Jean, 54
Moore, Christy, 110
Moore, Count Arthur, 15
Moriarty, Dr P. J., 62
Morris Tribunal, 217
Mount St Joseph, *see* Cistercian College of Mount St Joseph
Moylan, Isolde, 125
Mubarak, Hosni, 123
Mullingar Accord, 173
Murphy, Mike, 48
Murphy, Paul, 104

National Development Plan (NDP), 168–9, 243
National Platform, The, 119
NCB stockbrokers, 175–6
Nealon, Ted, 60
New York: BC's visits, 24–5, 130–2, 235–6, 239–40; Twin Towers (9/11), 123, 130–1
Nice Treaty, 116–21, 122, 219, 222
Noonan, Michael, 79, 89
Northern Ireland: BC's policy, 155–6; BC's role in peace process, 103–4, 107–12; Mandelson's role, 101, 104–6; Paisley's role, 108–11
nurses' strike, 91–4, 97

O'Brien, Denis, 71
O'Brien, Michael, 147
O'Callaghan, Owen, 177, 201
O'Connor, Padraic, 175–6
Ó Cuív, Éamon, 116
O'Dea, Willie, 208
O'Donnell, Liz, 107
O'Donoghue, John, 138, 147
O'Donovan, John, 63
O'Donovan, Tom, 31
O'Donovan and Cowen, 31
Offaly County Council, 32, 36–8
Offaly Express, 26
Offaly Independent, 209, 214–15
Offaly Vocational Education Committee, 39
Ógra Fianna Fáil, 25
O'Keefe, Batt, 215–16
O'Malley, Desmond, 58
O'Neill, Des, 194
O'Neill, Tip, 103
O'Rourke, Mary, 45, 46, 138
O'Rourke, Seán, 189
Ó Snodaigh, Aengus, 235

Paisley, Ian, Senior, 108–11
Palestinian issue, 123–6, 140–2
Parlon, Tom, 137
Partnership 2000, 91
Pataki, George, 131
Patten Commission, 105–6
Pay-Related Social Insurance (PRSI), 163, 171–2
Peña, Federico, 69–70
Peres, Shimon, 123
Post Office strike, 52
Powell, Colin, 128, 140
Powell, Jonathan, 104–5
Power, Sean, 44
Prodi, Romano, 84, 127
Progressive Democrats (PDs): Ahern issue, 193; election (2002), 137; FF coalition partners, 42–3, 45, 57–8, 59, 84, 188; leadership, 207; in opposition, 59

Quinlan, Tim, 4
Quinn, Ruairi, 59, 62, 65–6, 86, 88

Rabbitte, Pat: aid policy, 151; memories of BC, 60; no-confidence motion, 92; taxation policy, 160–1, 165–6; view of Ahern, 164; view of BC, 167
Rapid Reaction Force (EU), 117
Reid, John, 104
Reynolds, Albert: BC's career, 41, 46–7, 60–1, 214; cabinet, 41, 46; coalition government with Labour, 59–60; election (1992), 58–9; fall of government, 57–8; FF leadership, 45, FF leadership bid, 43–4; friendship with BC's father, 28–9, 49; Northern Ireland, 75, 103–4; presidential nomination bid, 94–6; relationship with BC, 33, 49–50, 72, 214; resignation, 76; singing, 48; speech-making advice, 139; Taoiseach, 46; US relations, 68–9; view of BC, 18, 33, 46–7, 66, 190
Reynolds family, 14, 76
Roberts, Ivor, 108
Robinson, Mary, 42
Robinson, Peter and Iris, 111
RTÉ, 22, 45, 48, 53, 76, 91, 159, 162, 175, 189, 201, 215, 219, 220
RUC, 105
Russian Federation, 115
Ryan, Eamon, 184
Ryan, Eoin, 101
Ryan, Richard, 127
Ryan, Sean, 60
Ryanair, 62

St Andrews Agreement, 112
Sargent, Trevor, 183, 184, 185
Sarkozy, Nicolas, 229, 235–6
Schulz, Martin, 230–1
Schwimmer, Walter, 115
Scully, Ger, 20
Scully, Paddy, 38

SDLP, 109, 155–6
Shaath, Nabil, 140
Shannon airport, 68–70, 129, 130, 133, 186–7
Sharon, Ariel, 140
Shatter, Alan, 86
Sherry Fitzgerald, 161
Sinn Féin: BC's view of, 112–13, 155; budget speech, 159; Lisbon Treaty referendum, 221–2, 229, 235; peace talks, 104
Smith, Brendan, 215
Smyth, Brendan (Father), 75
Smyth, Dan, 16
Smyth, Michael, 16
Social Finance Foundation, 154
Spillane, Caroline, 166
Spring, Dick: education, 14, 17, 100; end of coalition, 76; Labour leadership, 59–60; Minister for Foreign Affairs, 100; Reynolds relationship, 75
Stagg, Emmet, 159
Steinmeier, Frank Walter, 231
Straw, Jack, 143
Sunday Business Post, 72
Sunday Independent, 3, 177, 189, 239
Sunday Press, 45
Sunday Tribune, 204

taxation: Ahern's finances, 196–7; artists and writers, 145–9; changes (2007), 160–2; non-residency issue, 157–8; personal rates, 61, 161, 172; shortfall in revenue, 237; stamp duty, 160, 161, 163, 164, 165–6; VAT on condoms, 166
Taylor, Mervyn, 59
TEAM Aer Lingus, 61, 63–8
Technical Group, 159
Telecom Éireann, 61, 62, 66, 71

Thuran, Archbishop, 134
Trimble, David, 107, 108
Trinity College abortion report, 82–3
Tullamore: BC's homecoming as Taoiseach, 1–4, 244; BC's legal career, 30–1, 33, 41; Bruton's attack, 90; canvassing, 33–4; electoral area, 38; EU visit, 142–3; FF convention, 32; Fitzgerald's visit, 121–2; hospital, 97; music and drama, 12; Muslim convention, 103
Tullamore Express, 54
Tullamore Tribune, 20
Twin Towers (9/11), 123–6, 130–1
Tynan, Maol Muire, 77

U2, 148–9
Ulster Unionist Party, 107
UN Millennium Summit, 149
UN Security Council: Irish chairmanship, 102, 122, 127–8, 132–4; Irish seat, 102, 113–14, 143; meetings after 9/11, 130; Resolution 1368, 129
unemployment, *see* employment
University College Dublin (UCD), 19, 21–2, 24, 181

Village magazine, 195

Wall, Micheál, 176, 193
Wallace, Danny, 77
Walsh, Dick, 107
Waterford Crystal, 52, 90
Waterford Regional Hospital, 90
Weir, Tommy (grandfather), 22
Whelan, John, 137
Whelehan, Harry, 57, 75–6
WLR, 90
Woods, Michael, 45, 101
World Bank, 151